MUSICIANS WRESTLE EVERYWHERE
Emily Dickinson & Music

Aaron Copland. "Nature, the Gentlest Mother," from *Twelve Poems of Emily Dickinson*. London; New York: Boosey & Hawkes, Inc., ©1951. Reprinted by permission of Whitman & Ransom.

MUSICIANS WRESTLE EVERYWHERE
Emily Dickinson & Music

Carlton Lowenberg

Fallen Leaf Press
Berkeley, California

Published by Fallen Leaf Press
P.O. Box 10034
Berkeley, CA 94709

Library of Congress Cataloging-in-Publication Data

Lowenberg, Carlton.
  Musicians wrestle everywhere: Emily Dickinson & music / Carlton
Lowenberg.
  p. cm. -- (Fallen Leaf reference books in music, ISSN 8755-268X;
no. 19)
  Includes indexes.
  ISBN 0-914913-20-4
  1. Dickinson, Emily, 1830-1886--Musical settings--Bibliography.
2. Dickinson, Emily, 1830-1886--Knowledge--Music.
I. Title. II. Series.
ML 134.5.D5L7   1992
  92-9923
CIP   MN

The following have generously given permission to reproduce copy-
righted works: "Heart, We Will Forget Him," from *Thirty-Four Songs
on Poems of Emily Dickinson,* by Arthur Farwell. New York: Boosey &
Hawkes, ©1983. Reprinted by permission of Boosey & Hawkes, Inc., and
Brice Farwell. "Nature, the Gentlest Mother," from *Twelve Poems of
Emily Dickinson,* by Aaron Copland. London; New York: Boosey &
Hawkes, Inc., ©1951. Reprinted by permission of Whitman & Ransom.

To Territa

List of Illustrations

Contents

VILLAGE HYMNS

FOR

SOCIAL WORSHIP.

SELECTED AND ORIGINAL.

DESIGNED AS

A SUPPLEMENT

TO THE

PSALMS AND HYMNS

OF

Dr. Watts.

BY ASAHEL NETTLETON.

And the ransomed of the Lord shall return, and come to Zion with songs and everlasting joy upon their heads . . . . *Isaiah*

STEREOTYPE EDITION.

NEW-YORK:

PUBLISHED AND SOLD BY E. SANDS,
Corner of James and Oak Streets,
AND MAHLON DAY, NO. 374 PEARL STREET
And sold by the Booksellers generally

1840.

Title page of *Village Hymns for Social Worship*, by Asahel Nettleton, textbook used at Mount Holyoke Female Seminary (New-York, E. Sands, 1840). "I shall send you Village Hymns by earliest opportunity."—Letter of Emily Dickinson to her brother Austin, March 27, 1853.

Foreword

In our attempt to understand the workings of genius, no clue can be overlooked. Even the slightest detail may turn out to be important. Nothing is irrelevant. It is worth pointing out why this is especially true of Emily Dickinson.

Born in Amherst, Massachusetts in 1830, she led a happy and outgoing life as a child and schoolgirl. She wrote the liveliest papers in composition class and was known as the wit of the school. She kept the best herbarium, wrote the best valentines, went on promenades and "sugarings-off" (in maple syrup season), became a good cook, learned to draw and to play the piano so well her father bought her a piano of her own.

As she grew out of her teens, she became increasingly secretive about the major concerns in her life. She wrote a friend, "I find I need more vail" (her spelling). All the while, apparently, she was trying her hand at another hobby practiced by young ladies at the time: writing poetry. She gave more and more time to it—and less and less to what we call the outside world. She reduced her circle of friends to a minimum and, by the time she was thirty, had all but stopped going to church. She became a virtual recluse. By the time she was fifty, she was known in Amherst as "The Myth."

She died in 1886, leaving nearly two thousand manuscript poems in her bureau drawer. The thousand or so of her letters that were collected after her death told us much but left so many vital questions unanswered that what we had was a virtual knowledge vacuum.

When three slim volumes of selections from those bureau-drawer manuscripts came out in the 1890s, the questions came pouring in. Who is this Emily Dickinson? What is the secret of her career? How could this unknown recluse who never married, never traveled, never published, have written such powerful and passionate poetry? (The handful of her poems that had found their way to the popular press during her lifetime were all anonymous and hardly counted.) Where did all the *knowledge* come from and those startling insights into human experience in almost all its phases—joy, delight, ecstasy, hope; pain, renunciation, defeat, despair? How did she come by that extraordinary "inner music" that a few discerning people began to hear in her poems—that magical feeling for just the right sound of words-in-combination that can be summed up in the frequently heard tribute, "She had an incredible *ear*"? One is reminded of the perennial question about Shakespeare: How did the country boy from Stratford write all those plays and poems?

As with Shakespeare, so with Dickinson. The vacuum invited all kinds of theory and speculation—understandable, in view of the minimal help she'd given the world—but for years public interest centered less on her poetry than on the fascinating mystery of her life.

The decade of the 1950s, which produced the first complete, well-edited *Poems* and *Letters*, did much to get critics and scholars on the proper track. And in 1960 appeared a study of particular interest in our present context: Jay Leyda's *The Years and Hours of Emily Dickinson*. Leyda made no attempt at large speculation. He advanced no overall theory. His only commentary was limited to a brief Introduction. He set out to assemble as many facts about Dickinson's life and times as a decade of research could uncover, and he put them together in chronological order, thus providing a solid basis for all future work, critical or biographical, on Dickinson.

But more than that, *Years and Hours* is an encouragement and a model for those who, like Carlton Lowenberg, choose to apply the method of the historian or bibliographer to the elusive life of our poet. Lowenberg's *Emily Dickinson's Textbooks* (1986) shows how illuminating such as study can be. Emily was an excellent student, with a tenacious memory. Here are the books that she met with during the most impressionable years of her life; there are many lively echoes of them in the poems of her maturity. How does genius get its start? Sometimes from those lowly schoolbooks the rest of us looked upon as sheer drudgery.

And how did she come by that "incredible ear"?—to which should be added at once a sense of rhythm that enabled her to make the tight, limited form of the Common Meter (the "8's and 6's" of the hymnals) a medium of great flexibility, responsive to a wide range of mood and tone. (She seldom slipped into the thump-thump of all too many hymns.) By nature she was an experimenter, both with words and in music: one of her musical talents was improvising. She soon outgrew the popular tunes of the day and followed her own devisings on the piano, often (when the family was away) at night, when, as she said, "I can improvise better...."

Perhaps one of the reasons why so many composers have been attracted by her lyrics is (beside obvious matters of feeling and mood) the challenge of her rhythms. It is not too much to suggest a carry-over from the "odd, old tunes" (as she later called them) that "madden[ed] me, with their grief and fun," to the poems she wrote later, whose "jingling cool[ed] my tramp."

All of which shows how rich a subject Emily Dickinson and Music is. It could be said that she *thought* musically. She often called her poems "hymns"; the verb "to sing" often meant "to write a poem" ("Let Emily sing for you," she wrote her bereaved cousins, "because she cannot pray.") Sometimes in her letters whole passages are written (consciously or not) in Common Meter.

One aspect of Lowenberg's research deserves special praise. He took the trouble to ask all the composers he could reach to comment on why they decided to set Dickinson to music. I found the answers extremely interesting. The Russian Chalayev, sensing Dickinson's kinship with Shostakovich, found her understanding of death and ritual "very Russian." A soprano cherished the feeling of "a woman writer" writing for "a woman singer." Another composer, looking for a text, described how one of the poems ("He fumbles at your Soul") "jumped off the page with its power." Another spoke of her "passionate spirituality and spiritual passion." For another, "her force echoes around the world and across the centuries" (a formulation that even the most ardent Dickinson reader would be hard put to improve on). It was this "force" that led Aaron Copland to set twelve of her poems and (as he wrote his friend Ernst Bacon) to "orchestrate eight of my own settings." Arthur Farwell found in her poems "new colors, new relations, exhaustless and compounded symbolism, the awe and wonder of the boundless universe."

Among other things, the data collected by Lowenberg includes records of performances all over the world—further evidence, if any is needed, of Dickinson's international stature. Shortly after the first selection of her poems appeared in 1890, a literary gentleman from Boston wrote Thomas Wentworth Higginson, who had helped with the editing: "She may become world famous, or she may never get out of New England." *Musicians Wrestle Everywhere* is further proof that his first guess was right.

Richard B. Sewall
Bethany, Connecticut

CORRECT POSITION OF THE HANDS.

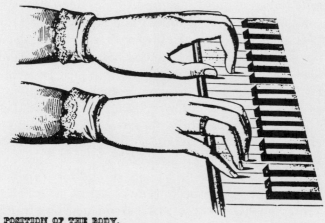

CORRECT POSITION OF THE BODY.

From Henri Bertini, *A Progressive and Complete Method for the Piano-Forte*. Boston: E. H. Wade, [n.d.]. "I have the same instruction book you have, Bertini."—Emily Dickinson, letter of August 3, 1845 to Abiah Root.

Preface

This book gathers together a variety of material documenting both the involvement of Emily Dickinson in music and the inspiration that her works and life have aroused in composers. Citing some 1,615 musical settings of her poems and letters, it suggests a unique transformation from one generation to later ones, from one medium of expression to another, in which poetry and music are joined.

With time, patience, and help from charitable persons, we have pieced together—from such intractable sources as sketchy, incomplete databases and frustratingly disordered catalogues of personal archives—a colorful portrait of the musical Emily. This portrait adds new information to previously incomplete knowledge of her study, performance, and use of music.

For our account of the musical incidents in Emily Dickinson's life, given in the Introduction, we have depended on collected works, diaries, biographies, bibliographies, and other works, by Dickinson scholars such as Willis J. Buckingham, William G. Hammond, Thomas H. Johnson, Jay Leyda, S. P. Rosenbaum, and Richard B. Sewall. Johnson's edition of *The Poems of Emily Dickinson* (1955) and *The Letters of Emily Dickinson* (1958), both published by The Belknap Press of Harvard University Press, were indispensable throughout this work. Without S. P. Rosenbaum's *A Concordance to the Poems* (1964), the tracking down of titles of the poems often would have been impossible. Mount Holyoke College Library, The Jones Library, Inc., Amherst College Library, the Harris Collection of the Brown University Library, and the libraries of Harvard and Yale Universities generously provided archival material.

Arrangement of the Book

The INTRODUCTION outlines Emily Dickinson's knowledge of and training in music, and briefly addresses the question of setting her works to music.

The main section, MUSICAL SETTINGS OF EMILY DICKINSON'S POEMS AND LETTERS, cites some 1,615 settings of 654 of her poems and letters by 276 composers. It is arranged alphabetically by composer. Under individual composers, entries are subarranged chronologically. Each entry gives the following information, as available:

- · Publisher, with place and date of publication; or whether the work is in manuscript
- · Commission
- · Date of composition
- · Medium of performance, with voice(s) listed first and then names of instruments in score order.
- · Date and place of first performance
- · Commercial recordings
- · Bibliographies of writings about the work
- · Identifying numbers for each poem and letter set, referring to Thomas H. Johnson's definitive editions of the poems and letters
- · Personal statements by the composers explaining their choice of specific selections and giving technical information about their settings and performances

Following the list of settings, a MISCELLANY section notes various types of works and performances involving Emily Dickinson and music: plays, pedagogical materials, musical arrangements and contrafacta, lectures and lecture-recitals, concerts, and readings with musical accompaniment.

A concordance, INDEX TO MUSICAL TERMS IN THE POEMS AND LETTERS, lists musical terms that appear in Emily Dickinson's works. The terms are arranged alphabetically, each identified by Johnson number ("P" for poem, "L" for letter) and provided with a contextual example.

Four APPENDIXES provide further information about music in the life of Emily Dickinson:

1. EMILY DICKINSON'S PERSONAL ALBUM OF SHEET MUSIC. This album, now housed in the Houghton Library at Harvard University, is the best direct evidence

of the kind of music that interested her. The contents are listed here in full, in the order they appear in the album. Although classical composers such as Bellini and Weber are represented, popular composers of the time—such as Valentine, Dutton, and Balfe—predominate.

2. BOOKS WITH MUSIC IN THE DICKINSON LIBRARY lists a selection of the some hundreds of books and periodicals that are documented in the Houghton Library Handlist and Daniel Lombardo's *Tales of Amherst*.

3. MUSIC PUBLICATIONS OF EMILY DICKINSON'S UNCLES, MARK HASKELL NEWMAN AND THE REVEREND ASA BULLARD. These publications were selected from the Newman company's and the Massachusetts Sabbath School Society's lists of music publications. A short description of Newman and Bullard are found in the preface to each of these lists.

4. MOUNT HOLYOKE FEMALE SEMINARY MUSIC INSTRUCTION MANUSCRIPT. Mount Holyoke College Library/Archives, Music Department Records, Series A, Folder 1. Circa 1837-1840. This manuscript is a capsule description of the teaching of vocal music at the Seminary.

The BIBLIOGRAPHY lists writings pertinent to the study of Emily Dickinson and music. The SOURCES section gives names and addresses of organizations and societies that have information about musical settings of Emily Dickinson's writings. The LIST OF COMPOSERS provides addresses, as available.

The following indexes provide access to the musical settings:

INDEX OF FIRST LINES. Arranged alphabetically by the first line of the poem (or the key line of the letter), this index lists the Johnson number of each work and the names of the composers who have set it, giving dates of composition for composers with numerous settings.

INDEX BY JOHNSON NUMBERS. Arranged numerically by Johnson numbers (first for the poems, then the letters), this index lists the names of the composers who have set each work, giving dates of composition for composers with voluminous settings.

INDEX OF COMPOSERS AND TITLES, listing all composers and arrangers of musical works in alphabetical order. Titles are given under composers' or arrangers' names.

INDEX BY PERFORMANCE MEDIUM. This index enables performers to locate works written for a specific type of voice, chorus, chamber ensemble, or other performance medium. Entries are arranged alphabetically under major categories.

Acknowledgements

I am most grateful to the following for their invaluable assistance:

Rosalie Calabrese, Executive Director, American Composers Alliance, New York City. Evelyn Davis Culbertson (Davis/Farwell Archive), Tulsa, Oklahoma. Rosemary Cullen, Curator of The Harris Collection, Brown University Library, Providence, Rhode Island. Eva Einstein, El Cerrito, California. Patricia Elliott, Beethoven Center, San Jose State University, San Jose, California. Brice Farwell, Ashland, Oregon. Lisbeth Holm, Music Library, The Swedish National Radio Company, Stockholm, Sweden. John Lancaster, Curator of Special Collections, Amherst College Library, Amherst, Massachusetts. Daniel Lombardo, Curator of Special Collections, The Jones Library, Inc., Amherst, Massachusetts. Ruth Grace Lowenberg, Lafayette, California. Frances Richard, Director, Symphonic and Concert Department, American Society of Composers, Authors, & Publishers, New York City. Eero Richmond, Director of Information Services, American Music Center, Inc., New York City. Sophie Sinkovich and Judy Tsou, Music Library, University of California at Berkeley. Elaine D. Trehub, College History and Archive Librarian, Mount Holyoke College Library.

I would also like to thank all of the composers who responded to my questions, and who commented on their relationship to the works of Emily Dickinson.

No one can know to what extent my publisher is an integral part of my book. Ann Basart is an editor of ever-perceptive expertise. But more! She is an empath of rare sensitivity from which has come a special friendship. To her I owe profound gratitude.

C. L.

Introduction

Emily Dickinson was a literary markswoman. Unmindful of the effect that her poetry was to have on people, she very privately created a special poetic world for them—not only in her native place, but eventually in Europe and Asia, the fact of which would have astounded her. Though she had no target in mind but her own personal revelation, her poems became personal revelations to thousands of readers. Her tense and poignant poetic insights, as vital now as when she wrote them, leap into and through our century. Her works have inspired hundreds of composers.

Emily Dickinson's poems, composer Alan Leichtling has said, "have been an important literary staple of the musical world. I suspect that a sizable amount of American vocal music would not exist but for her poetry."[1]

Although critic Thomas Wentworth Higginson, her editor and literary mentor, found Emily Dickinson eccentric, abnormal, even partially cracked, her wide circle of family friends saw in her little more than an increasingly shy and reclusive, well-educated, and busy woman with a dimity conviction. She said she saw New Englandly, and that was certainly true.

But there was little of dimity or of the New England compound in the far reaches of her poetry. In a 1991 interview, Julie Harris, solo performer in William Luce's one-woman play, *The Belle of Amherst*, said of Emily Dickinson, "I think because her sensitivity and sensibility were so highly tuned she would seem strange to the most ordinary of us. She heard things, saw things, felt things that most of us don't ever see or hear or feel in a lifetime. . . . She was supremely gifted. I can't even begin to imagine what her inner life was like."[2]

Only ten of Emily Dickinson's 1,775 poems were published during her lifetime.[3] After her death in 1886, her sister discovered more than a thousand poems in Emily's bureau. Emily's posthumous fame began after Mabel Loomis Todd and Thomas Wentworth Higginson issued the first collection of her poems, in 1890, and *Poems Second Series*, in 1891. Todd also edited *Poems*

Third Series, which appeared in 1896, and two volumes of Emily's letters, published in 1894.

The poems sold well and went into many printings over the years. With the publication of *The Single Hound*,[4] edited by Emily's niece Martha Dickinson Bianchi, many additional poems appeared. The growing popularity of Emily Dickinson's poetry was reflected in the increasing number of her poems that were anthologized. A definitive edition of her works was not available until the 1950s, when Thomas H. Johnson published his editions of the poems (1955)[5] and letters (edited with the assistance of Theodora Ward, 1958).[6]

Born in 1830 in Amherst, Massachusetts, Emily Dickinson lived her life in one of New England's small-town communities, many of which exist today virtually unchanged. They were the backbone of America, strong in religious disciplines, with pervasive social values and extraordinary economic productivity.[7]

The men of Emily Dickinson's immediate family were lawyers, politicians, and educators. Her grandfather, Samuel Fowler Dickinson, is remembered for his contribution to the establishment of Amherst College. Her father, Edward, served as treasurer of the College for thirty-seven years, and was also state senator and a representative to the Thirty-Third Congress (1853-1855). It was with her brother, William Austin Dickinson, that Emily shared the aesthetics of life, mostly from their books.[8] The Dickinsons maintained a large family library, and Emily's reading was eclectic.[9] Whatever she derived from her studies and reading, the visions in her poetry appear singularly personal and unique.

Shortly after the birth of her sister Lavinia, on February 29, 1833, Emily, then two years old, visited her Aunt Lavinia Norcross, who wrote to her father: "She has learned to play on the piano—she calls it 'moosic.' "[10] In February of 1838, Edward Dickinson wrote from Boston to his wife, "I send two numbers of Parley's Magazine, for which I subscribed for them—all of them. They will find them interesting." He added a note, "My Dear little Children—I send you some of Parleys Magazine—They have some interesting stories for you to read. I want to have you remember some of them to tell me when I get home."[11] For nine months of 1838, each issue contained a song with music by Lowell Mason.[12]

Emily's schools, Amherst Academy (1840-1847) and Mount Holyoke Female Seminary in South Hadley (1847-1848), offered as good a curriculum as any in rural New England. As the list of textbooks used in these acade-

mies testifies,[13] Emily was exposed to a diversity of sciences, particularly botany, as well as to rhetoric, history, languages, religion, and music. Some of her
textbooks and the Hampshire County textbooks in her family's library
(such as Denison Olmsted's *A Compendium of Natural Philosophy* and Lowell
Mason's *Carmina Sacra*) contained references to the theory and philosophy of
music.[14] (See Appendix 2.)

In a letter of August 3, 1845, Emily wrote to her friend Abiah Root, "I am
taking [piano] lessons this term, of Aunt Selby who is spending the summer
with us. . . . I have the same Instruction book you have, Bertini."[15] From this
initial training, evidently a good one with a disciplined daily practice, she
quickly became a competent pianist.

How much musical training Emily had at Amherst Academy is not known.
She may have received her first church music instruction from William O.
Gorham, an assistant to the principal, Rev. Nahum Gale (1837-1841), who
taught sacred music. The unnamed lady of "distinguished talents and repu-
tation" who taught instrumental music during 1841–1843 may have aug-
mented Emily's early wish to play the piano.[16]

Judge William Gardiner Hammond, while a sophomore at Amherst College, recorded in his diary details of Emily's graduation exhibition, August
10, 1847. "To serve as music," he wrote,

> the place of a band was most beautifully and to my mind most appropri-
> ately filled by a choir of young girls and several youths, led by John M.
> Emerson; they sang most beautifully, and I thought the music far better
> adapted to a literary exhibition than the loud notes of martial music.[17]

When Emily enrolled in Mount Holyoke Female Seminary in the autumn
of 1847, she had had a solid musical background: a summer of learning to play
the piano, two years of faithful piano practice, singing lessons, some instruction in sacred music, weekly exposure to church music, and performances for
her family. The seminary's founder, Mary Lyon, continued an early interest in
vocal music in her new school. Miss Lyon had said in an 1832 letter to her
Ipswich Seminary colleague Zilpah Polly Grant,

> Ever since vocal music was introduced into our Seminary, I have had an
> increasing sense of its great practical importance. I have sometimes felt that
> I would have given six months of my time could I have enjoyed the
> privileges for learning vocal music that some of our pupils enjoy.[18]

Music and music education were important in South Hadley's academic and social life. The frequency of study and practice of music at Mount Holyoke Female Seminary is detailed in a contemporary manuscript (1840) (Appendix 4), and in the unique *Journal/Letters* written by the teachers for the seminary's missionary women overseas or serving in America.[19] Thomas Hastings, a notable music teacher and compiler of music books, visited in August, 1843, as the *Journal* records. Many of Hastings's books were published by Mark Haskell Newman, Emily's uncle. (See Appendix 3.) The *Journal* notes: "We sung Hymn 381, Vill[age] Hymns [Nettleton's]. We closed with singing Hymn 409, 'Beware of Peter's word.'" At a service devoted to Miss Fisk, "Music was interspersed through the whole the choir struck up & sung 'How beautiful upon the mountains.'"

In the *Journal* entries for the period of Emily's enrollment, 1847-1848, we read the following:

> Meeting was closed by singing "From Greenland's Icy Mountains"....The singing was also commenced today. I am taking general care of the two choirs. One of these sings at 9 A.M., the other at 3 3/4 P.M. They sing three days a week. All who can sing belong to one of these....We sung "Grace is a charming sound"....This morning we had devotions at 8 1/2, sung the 586 hymn [Nettleton's], "Through sorrows night & dangers path."

> [At the Holyoke Hotel,] they are seated on the rock overlooking Northampton, just now they sung "When up the Mountain Climbing," then "The Silver Moon," and now "Love not."

Traveling groups of singers occasionally gave concerts in South Hadley village. Miss Lyon refused to cancel evening study hours for one public performance but arranged the next morning's schedule so the Hutchinson family could give an hour's private concert in Seminary Hall.[20]

William Gardiner Hammond, in his diary entry for August 4, 1847, wrote about a visit to the seminary to witness a part of the examinations there : a class in Virgil, the first four books of Euclid, then a class in botany. No less important than these subjects was an examination in music: "Then music from the piano, and singing: very fair.... Then more music, and the performance closed."[21]

The tradition of hymn writing was close to Mary Lyon's heart; some of her most notable associations were with the composers Lowell Mason, Phoebe Hinsdale Brown, and Abby Hyde. (Many of Phoebe Brown's hymns, including

"I Love to Steal Awhile Away," were written in Monson, close to South Hadley.) Four of Abby Hyde's hymns were included in Mary Lyon's favorite hymnal, Asahel Nettleton's *Village Hymns*,[22] used both by Emily and her brother Austin. Nettleton included nine of Hyde's hymns in his 1824 edition of the hymnal, and thirty-four more in the revised and enlarged edition of 1851, each carrying the signature "Hyde."[23]

Henry Wadsworth Longfellow's *Kavanagh, A Tale*, which had been a favorite of the young Dickinsons, gives a vivid picture of the church music of the time. Newly installed as Fairmeadow's preacher, Kavanagh

> desired that the organist should relinquish the old and pernicious habit of preluding with triumphal marches, and running his fingers at random over the keys of his instrument, playing scraps of secular music very slowly to make them sacred, and substitute instead some of the beautiful symphonies of Pergolesi, Palestrina, and Sebastian Bach. He held that sacred melodies were becoming to sacred themes; and did not wish, that, in his church, as in some of the French Canadian churches, the holy profession of religion should be sung to the air of "When one is dead 'tis for a long time"—the commandments, aspirations for heaven, and the necessity of thinking of one's salvation, to "The Follies of Spain," "Louisa was Sleeping in a Grove," or a grand "March of the French Cavalry."[24]

Another colorful account of mid-nineteenth century American music appeared in *Dream Life* by Ik Marvell (Donald G. Mitchell), published in December, 1851. Austin gave his sister a copy of the book in early 1852, and in a letter of February 1852 (Johnson: 75), she told him that she enjoyed it and "liked particularly its exquisite language though it was not so good as *Reveries of a Bachelor*." She would have read this bit of nostalgia in *Dream Life*:

> The singing has a charm for you. There is a long, thin-faced, flax-haired man, who carries a tuning fork in his waistcoat pocket, and who leads the choir. His position is in the very front rank of gallery benches, facing the desk; and by the time the old clergyman has read two verses of the psalm, the country chorister turns around to his little group of aids—consisting of the blacksmith, a carroty-headed school-master, two women in snuff-colored silks, and a girl in pink bonnet—to announce the tune. This being done in an authoritative manner, he lifts his long music book, glances again at his little company, clears his throat by a powerful "ahem," followed by a powerful use of a bandanna pocket-handkerchief, draws out his tun-

ing fork, and waits for the parson to close his reading. He now reviews once more his company, throws a reproving glance at the young woman in the pink hat, who at that moment is biting off a stout bunch of fennel, lifts his music book, thumps upon the rail with his fork, listens keenly, gives a slight "ahem," falls into the cadence, swells into a strong crescendo, catches at the first word of the line, as if he were afraid it might get away, turns to his company, lifts his music book with spirit, and gives it a powerful slap with the disengaged hand, and with a majestic toss of the head, soars away, with half the women below straggling on in his wake, into some such brave old melody as "Litchfield."[25]

Three of the music books containing the song "Litchfield" were used at the Mount Holyoke Female Seminary. Lowell Mason, professor in the Boston Academy of Music, both edited *Carmina Sacra*[26] and composed the music for "Litchfield."

Aside from church hymns, Emily's taste in music was predominantly secular. In her letters, she casually mentioned a few songs with which she was familiar: "Oh! Susannah," "Last Rose of Summer," "Auld Lang Syne," "My Country, 'Tis of Thee," "Home, Sweet Home." Of classical composers, her personal album contains arrangements of nine waltzes attributed to Beethoven, Bellini's "Grand March" from *Norma*, one Weber waltz, and a polka by Offenbach. Popular music was represented by "Yankee Doodle," "Coolidge Quickstep," "Baden Baden Polka," "The Jolly Raftsman," and "Speed the Plough."[27] She mentioned only Mozart in her poems.[28]

After her formal education ended, Emily's references to music over the next thirty-eight years were casual and passim, with the notable exception of Jenny Lind's concert at Northampton, July 3, 1851, and the performance of the Germania Serenade Band at the Spring Exhibition at Amherst College, April 19, 1853, about which she said, "I never heard [such] sounds before."[29]

Jenny Lind's audience came from a wide area and represented the aristocracy of central Massachusetts. The setting of the concert was Jonathan Edwards's Congregational Church. Jenny's sponsors had created a stage for her in front of the pulpit, with an improvised dressing room built in a corner behind it. Jenny was now arranging her own concerts and, as usual, had little trouble in obtaining permission to stage her concert in a church building.[30] Emily Dickinson, who attended, was not overly impressed with Jenny Lind's singing.

> How we all loved Jennie Lind, but not accustomed oft to her manner of
> singing didn't fancy that so well as we did her. No doubt it was very fine
> —but take some notes from her "Echo," the Bird sounds from the "Bird
> Song" and some of her curious trills, and I'd rather have a Yankee.[31]

The *Hampshire Gazette* of July 8, 1851, in a review of the concert, wrote:

> Then came Jenny....In the first song, "I Know That My Redeemer
> Liveth," she did not seem to get that hold upon the audience which was
> anticipated. But "Casta Diva" was received with great applause....The
> "Bird Song"—a wild bird-like melody, that nobody but Jenny could
> sing—was loudly encored, as was also "Home, Sweet Home"....The
> Scotch melody, "Coming thro' the Rye," and the "Echo Song" closed the
> programme.[32]

(An interesting footnote to this concert: Jenny Lind was so struck by the
beauty of the Connecticut River Valley countryside that after her marriage to Otto Goldschmidt, her accompanist, in Boston, February 5, 1852,
the couple moved to Northampton for a three-month honeymoon.
They accepted the loan of a house at Round Hill, the former site of the Cogs-
well and Bancroft school for boys. On May 6th they emerged from the seclu-
sion of their marriage and gave their first concert as wife and husband at the
Young Men's Institute in Northampton.[33])

In her diary, Mabel Loomis Todd noted:

> I used to sing to Emily frequently, in the long, lonely drawing-room. But
> she never came in to listen—only sat outside in the darksome hall, on the
> stairs. But she heard every note. When I had finished she always sent me
> in a glass of wine on a silver salver, and with it either a piece of cake or
> a rose, and a poem—the latter usually impromptu, evidently written on
> the spot. [34]

Clara Newman Turner, Emily's cousin, child of Mark Haskell and Mary
Dickinson Newman, wrote that Emily

> was very fond of music, and at one time played not a little on the piano....
> She had learned it ["The Devil"] on an old-fashioned piano two octaves
> shorter than the modern Chickering which then stood in her home parlor,
> and always before seating herself to play, she covered these superfluous

octaves, that the keyboard might accord with her education....I had the pleasure of playing for her.[35]

Martha Dickinson Bianchi recalled,

In those earlier days Aunt Emily often came over.... She played brilliantly upon the piano, and travestied the descriptive pieces popular at that period with as much skill as wit. One improvisation which she called the "Devil" was, by tradition, unparalleled.[36]

In a letter to Martha Dickinson Bianchi (October 8, 1917), Kate Scott Anthon remembered those "blissful evenings at Austin's when Emily was often at the piano playing weird & beautiful melodies, all from her own inspiration." Millicent Todd Bingham was willing to conclude that "whether or not Emily Dickinson was really musical is hard to say."[37] But Emily's devotion to music and the place music held in her life and writing suggest that she was.

The musicality—or lack of musicality—of Emily Dickinson's poetry has been the subject of critical discussion. J. P. Dabney asserted, in his *The Musical Basis of Verse* (1901), that rhymes having imperfect cadence

are just as tonally satisfying to the ear as [those having] perfect cadence because, although they have not the sense of absolute finality of the tonic, or true rhyme, they produce upon the ear the same tonal impression.

He went on to observe,

Of course it requires much nicety of ear to distinguish between tones which are correlated and those which are not. A conspicuous absence of this discriminatory faculty is observable in the odd, flashing, often wonderfully prismatic, bits of verse—bits, rather than coherent verses —of the late Emily Dickinson where are frequent such startling tonal combinations as denied, smiled; book, think; all, soul; own, young.[38]

Dickinson scholar Grace Perkinson suggests that

Her work is not of the lyrical sort such as Jonson or Burns. The relationship is more like that between mathematics and music—the ordered or structured abstraction that gives us the sense of having tapped into something universal.[39]

Some critics have questioned whether Emily Dickinson's poems can be successfully set to music. They claim that the music gets in the way of the surprise that is essential to full appreciation; that the poems move too quickly from the saying to the concept; that the words are too tight for expanded melodies. Critic Will Crutchfield has said that Dickinson's poems

> both invite and resist song. Many burn with intensity, but brought into the outward, open utterance of public singing, they seem to want the privacy of the quiet page. Or perhaps it is just that they have not yet found a composer equal to the subtle range of their thought.[40]

On the other hand, some commentators think that music can intensify the texts. Evelyn Davis Culbertson found that Arthur Farwell's thirty-nine Dickinson songs, for example, "...do more than wed music to text. In each song he catches the spirit of her poem and then deftly amplifies and embellishes the meaning with a new excitement and understanding."[41] Joseph Jones, who has adapted old hymn tunes as settings of Dickinson's poetry, has written:

> When we add music to verse, we see the poet's achievement in a new perspective. His piece is singable, we discover, perhaps to our surprise— and once we have overcome the novelty of the situation it seems natural and right that it be sung....But granting that the use of music is more pleasing than not, we are ready to explore the qualities in a poem that neither silent reading nor reading aloud will quite bring out. We now hear the poem in a different context, literally as never before. Most important of all, perhaps, we have undertaken for ourselves the role of performer —a role moreover in which we act simultaneously as performer and audience. Not only have we given the poem a new dress; we have placed ourselves in a new and more responsible relation to it.[42]

Composer George Perle writes, in regard to his *Thirteen Dickinson Songs*:

> Out of all the possible ways of reading and interpreting a poem, the musical setting fixes just one, and it must do so in the most spontaneous and authentic way, without seeming to encroach upon the prerogatives of the poet and the listener. Not only must it seem right, and seem so at once without seeming coercive and demanding, but it must go beyond this and elucidate the words—otherwise why bother to put music to them at all?[43]

Introduction

To date, more than 275 composers have written music to over 650 poems and letters of Emily Dickinson. The first composer known to have set a Dickinson poem to music was Etta Parker, whose "Have You Got a Brook in Your Little Heart?" appeared in 1896. In the following year Clarence Dickinson set six poems, and what had been a trickle of Dickinson settings throughout the 1920s became a stream in the 1930s and 1940s, as such distinguished composers as Arthur Farwell, Adolf Weiss, Ernst Bacon, Elliott Carter, Vivian Fine, Wallingford Riegger, Ned Rorem, and Aaron Copland added to the collection. The stream became a flood after 1950, with Roy Harris, Vincent Persichetti, Alec Wilder, Ulysses Kay, John Harbison, George Perle, John Adams, Leon Kirchner, and many others composing Dickinson settings.

Although most of these works are for solo voice and piano, the settings range from choral music to operas, from Hunter Johnson's 1940 ballet for Martha Graham, *Letter to the World*, to purely instrumental compositions inspired by Emily Dickinson's poetry or life. Some composers have returned to Dickinson's works repeatedly—among them Ernst Bacon, Gloria Coates, Robert Convery, Arthur Farwell, Richard Hoyt, Ken Langer, and Leo Smit, who continues to add to his great cycle of seventy-one settings that he began in 1989. And some poems are favorites: twenty-nine composers have set "I'm Nobody! Who are you?", twenty-eight "Wild Nights, Wild Nights!", twenty-one "I Taste a Liquor Never Brewed." By their selections, and their comments on why they made these selections, the composers have documented their wide interest in what and how Emily Dickinson wrote about her "flood subjects"—nature, life, death, and immortality.

Sources

1. Alan Leichtling. Letter to Carlton Lowenberg, December 22, 1990.

2. Georgiana Strickland. "Thunderstruck! A Conversation with Julie Harris." *Emily Dickinson International Society Bulletin*, 3/1 (May/June 1991): 1-2, 11.

3. Karen Dandurand. *Legacy* 1 (spring 1984).

4. Emily Dickinson. *The Single Hound: Poems of a Lifetime. With an Introduction by Her Niece Martha Dickinson Bianchi.* Boston: Little, Brown, 1914.

5. *The Poems of Emily Dickinson.* Ed. by Thomas H. Johnson. Cambridge, MA: The Belknap Press of Harvard University Press, 1955. 3 vols.

6. *The Letters of Emily Dickinson*. Ed. by Thomas H. Johnson. Assoc. ed., Theodora Ward. Cambridge, MA: The Belknap Press of Harvard University Press, 1958. 3 vols.

7. United States. Census Office. 7th Census, 1853. *Statistical View of the United States....Being a Compendium of the Seventh Census....*By J. D. B. De Bow. Washington, D.C.: Robert Armstrong, 1853, pp. 58-60. Reprint: New York, Gordon & Breach, 1970.

8. Jack L. Capps. *Emily Dickinson's Reading, 1836-1886.* Cambridge, MA: Harvard University Press, 1966.

9. *Handlist of Books Found in the Home of Emily Dickinson at Amherst, Massachusetts, Spring, 1950.* Cambridge, MA: Houghton Library, 1951.

10. *The Letters of Emily Dickinson*, ed. Johnson and Ward. Letter 11, p. 33.

11. Jay Leyda. *The Years and Hours of Emily Dickinson.* New Haven: Yale University Press, 1960, I:44-45. Reprinted Hamden, CT: Archon Books, 1970.

12. *Parley's Magazine*. Ed. by Samuel Griswold Goodrich. New York: Charles S. Francis & Co., 1838. Works by Lowell Mason: "Resolutions," "Nancy Ray," "The Wintry Blast is Ended," "The Thunder Storm," "We Sing the Praise of Water" (Poetry by John Pierpont), "The Beautiful May," "The Moon," "Happy Valley," "Parting Song at Vacation" (Ipswich Female Seminary, September 1838.)

13. Carlton Lowenberg. *Emily Dickinson's Textbooks*. Lafayette, CA: Carlton Lowenberg, 1986.

14. Carlton Lowenberg. "Hampshire County Textbooks, 1812-1850." Manuscript, 1988.

15. *The Letters of Emily Dickinson*, ed. Johnson and Ward. Letter 7, p. 16.

16. Frederick Tuckerman. *Amherst Academy: A New England School of the Past, 1814-1861.* Amherst, MA.: Trustees, 1929, pp. 98, 99, 100, 104, 112.

17. Hammond, William Gardiner. *Remembrance of Amherst: An Undergraduate's Diary, 1846-1848.* New York: Columbia University Press, 1946, p. 168. Musical Interludes were: "Hark! The Hollow Woods," "Over the Mountain Wave," "The Brave Old Oak," "The Sun's Gay Beam," "Away! Away! Away!"

18. Edward Hitchcock. *The Power of Christian Benevolence Illustrated in the Life and Labor of Mary Lyon.* Northampton: Hopkins, Bridgman, 1851, pp. 81-82.

19. *Mount Holyoke Journal/Letters, 1843-1891.* Mount Holyoke College Library/Archives. Emily Dickinson's teachers: Sept. 1846-April 1848, Susan L. Tolman. Nov. 23-27, 1847, Rebecca Fiske. May 1848, Harriet Johnson. May 12-Aug. 3, 1848, Rebecca Fiske. July 14, 1848, Mary C. Whitman. July 29, 1848, Susan L. Tolman. Aug. 29-Oct. 17, 1848, Mary C. Whitman. Oct. 17, 1848, Mary Lyon.

20. Philip D. Jordan. *Singin' Yankees*. Minneapolis: University of Minnesota Press, 1946.

21. Hammond. *Remembrance of Amherst*, p. 162.

22. Lowenberg. *Emily Dickinson's Textbooks*, pp. 77-78.

23. John Julian. *A Dictionary of Hymnology*. New York: Scribners; London: John Murray, 1892, p. 546.

24. Henry Wadsworth Longfellow. *Kavanagh*. Boston: Ticknor, Reed, and Fields, 1849, pp. 103-104.

25. Ik Marvel [pseud. of Donald G. Mitchell]. *Dream Life: A Fable of the Seasons*. New York: Charles Scribner, 1851, p. 96.

26. Boston: J. H. Wilkins & R. B. Carter, 1841.

27. Houghton Library, Harvard University. Music: a bound volume of miscellaneous sheet music, without title page, with Emily Dickinson's autograph [?] on flyleaf.

28. "Better than music! For I, who heard it," *The Poems of Emily Dickinson*, ed. Johnson, Poem 503, p. 386.

29. *The Letters of Emily Dickinson*, ed. Johnson and Ward. Letter 118, p. 245-246.

30. W. Porter Ware and Thaddeus C. Lockard, Jr. *P. T. Barnum Presents Jenny Lind*. Baton Rouge: Louisiana State University Press, 1980, p. 104.

31. *The Letters of Emily Dickinson*, ed. Johnson and Ward. Letter 46, p. 121.

32. Leyda. *The Years and Hours of Emily Dickinson*, I: 205.

33. Ware and Lockard. *P. T. Barnum Presents Jenny Lind*, p. 126.

34. Richard B. Sewall. *The Life of Emily Dickinson*. New York: Farrar, Straus and Giroux, 1974, I:218.

35. Clara Newman Turner, "My Personal Acquaintance With Emily Dickinson," In Sewall, *The Life of Emily Dickinson*, p. 272.

36. Dickinson. *The Single Hound*, p. xi.

37. Millicent Todd Bingham. *Emily Dickinson's Home: Letters of Edward Dickinson and His Family*. New York: Harper, 1955, p. 153. Reprinted New York: Dover, 1967.

38. J. P. Dabney. *The Musical Basis of Verse*. London: Longmans, Green, 1901, pp. 106-107.

39. Grace Perkinson. Letter to Carlton Lowenberg, February 26, 1991.

40. Will Crutchfield. [Review of a 92nd Street YMCA concert.] *New York Times*, December 12, 1987.

41. Evelyn Davis Culbertson. "Arthur Farwell and Emily Dickinson." Unpublished manuscript, 1989.

42. Joseph Jones. Preface to *Poems and Hymn-Tunes as Songs: Metrical Partners*. Guilford, CT: Jeffrey Norton Publishers, 1991.

43. George Perle, program notes to recording, Composers Recordings, Inc. CRI SD 403, quoted by Marshall Bialowsky in *Notes* 45 (June 1989) 862.

Musical Settings of Emily Dickinson's Poems and Letters

This list is arranged alphabetically by composer, subarranged first chronologically and then by title of composition. Individual entries give, as available: publication data; information on commissions, date of composition, performance medium, first performance, and recordings; the identifying Johnson numbers for each poem and letter set by the composer; bibliographies of writings about the work; and comments by the composer. Johnson numbers refer to Thomas H. Johnson's editions of *The Poems of Emily Dickinson* (1955) and *The Letters of Emily Dickinson* (1958), both published by The Belknap Press of Harvard University Press. Unless otherwise specified, quotations are from letters addressed to Carlton Lowenberg.

Adams, John. Harmonium, for Mixed Chorus and Orchestra. New York: Associated Music Publishers, 1981.
Commissioned by the San Francisco Symphony, Edo de Waart, music director.
Composed: 1981.
Setting: SATB chorus, orchestra.
Duration: 35:00.
Johnson: 249, 712.
First performance: San Francisco Symphony Orchestra and Chorus, Edo de Waart, conductor; January 4, 1984.
Recording: ICM 1277 821465-1 (LC 2516), San Francisco, January 1984. Program notes by John Adams, 1984.
Adams contributed this music for two dances in the ballet, *Rowing in Eden*, for the Royal Danish Ballet. First performance: the Royal Theatre of Copenhagen (the Old Stage), January 10, 1987. The music was not performed live. Warren Spears had choreographed his ballet to a recording, which was played during the performance. [Information from the Library of the Royal Theatre of Copenhagen, and a letter of August 30, 1991, from Pastor Niels Kjaer, Emily Dickinson Center, Denmark.]
Reviewed in *Dickinson Studies* 65 (1988) 27.
Also includes text by John Donne.

Adams, Robert Train. It Will be Summer Eventually [manuscript].
Commissioned by Oure Pleasure, Ltd., Attleboro, MA, Robert Train Adams, music director.
Composed: 1988.
Setting: SATB chorus (342, 549, 712); SATB chorus, soprano solo (449); TBarB, (919); SSATBarB, two choruses STBar/SAB (250); SSA (1483); SATB, optional tenor solo (1690).
Duration: 18:00.
Johnson: 250, 342, 449, 549, 712, 919, 1483, 1690.
Location: composer.
Recording: Amherst, MA., The Jones Library, Inc.
"Although the movements may be performed individually, the work is intended to be performed as a whole and employs musical procedures that encourage unity as well as relying on

textual relationships. The final movement, for example, features the return of the material heard earlier as well as the more obvious return of the men who did not sing in 'The Robin is a Gabriel.'

"The brief interludes after movements 2, 3, 5 and 6 strengthen the unity both in music and text: 'It will be summer—eventually' (interlude 1); 'If I can stop one Heart from breaking, It will be Summer' (interlude 2); 'It will be summer—eventually' (interlude 3); 'And yet—It will be summer' (interlude 4, which follows directly the line 'and yet Feels shorter than the Day I first surmised the Horses' Heads Were toward Eternity').

"The poems were chosen to present both the coming of spring and the poet's interest in immortality (the return of spring seems to be a metaphor for the ongoing, never-ending quality of life)."—letters of April 11 and April 25, 1989.

Adler, Samuel. In Nature's Ebb and Flow. New York: Southern Music Publishing, 1968.
Composed: 1959.
Setting: 2 sopranos, 2 contraltos.
Johnson: 757.
"The 'Mountains Grow Unnoticed' is [the fourth] movement out of the suite of five movements called 'In Nature's Ebb and Flow.' I set some Dickinson songs early in my life, but they no longer exist. However, I do plan to use her poetry more in the future. I am a great admirer of it."—letter of April 24, 1989.

Annicchiarico, Michael. Four Dickinson Songs [manuscript].
Composed: 1986.
Setting: soprano, flute, piano.
Johnson: 254, 472, 512, 953.
Location: composer.
"These pieces spoke very powerfully to me. The song cycle in particular passes through a range of emotions from the darkness of 'Loss' to the brightness of 'Hope.'"—letter of September 10, 1989.

Annicchiarico, Michael. I Shall Keep Singing [manuscript].
Composed: 1986.
Setting: SATB chorus a cappella.
Johnson: 250.
Location: composer.

Appleton, Jon H. Three American Songs [manuscript].
Composed: 1965. Orchestral version 1966.
Setting: tenor, piano; tenor, orchestra.
Johnson: 1419.
Location: composer.
First performance: Ernest Murphy, tenor; Jon Appleton, piano. Eugene, Oregon, July, 1965.

Backer, Bill. See "Miscellany" section. Gould, John A., arr. I Like to See It Lap the Miles.

Ernst Bacon

"When Emily Dickinson died in 1886, she must have had a faint glimmer of hope that some day someone would discover her poems, and that she might earn a position of importance in American literature. What she could not have dreamed in her wildest imaginings was that her work would eventually draw three American composers of the twentieth century, all Pulitzer Prize winners, back from the world of instrumental music into the vocal area by virtue of their settings of her poems, and that a fourth composer, also a Pulitzer winner, would base much of his life's work on her lyrics, only to be unjustly ignored by the fashion-ridden American musical public and critics.... [Of these composers—Copland, Perle, Kirchner, and Bacon—] Ernst Bacon...has by far the largest and in many ways the best Dickinson catalogue...but continues to be largely ignored as he lacks influential advocates in our centers of musical power. However, when the final reckoning is made, it would not surprise me to learn that his work had been placed at the top of the list."—Marshall Bialosky, *Notes* 45 (June 1989): 861-863.

"The poetry of Emily Dickinson has long seemed to me one of the great achievements of womankind. Her style of lyricism lends itself more perhaps than any other poetry of this country to musical setting, for it gives lyric expression to philosophical human thought without the latter being too apparent."—letter from Ernst Bacon to Marian Anderson, February 10, 1939.

"Your absorption with Emily Dickinson delights me. It happens that I, of all composers, was one of the first to discover this unique poet as early as the late twenties, whereupon I must have written at least 30 songs in a short time."—letter from Ernst Bacon, February 21, 1986.

The dates of many of Ernst Bacon's compositions are approximate. The Bacon archives are presently being assembled from a variety of sources, mainly those in the possession of Mrs. Ellen Bacon and Ms. Madi Bacon.

Bacon, Ernst. Fifty Songs. Limited 1st ed. Georgetown, CA: Dragon's Teeth Press, 1974.
Composed: ca. 1926-28.
Setting: voice, piano.
Johnson: 4, 149, 189, 211, 217, 288, 311, 456, 482, 695, 761, 1079, 1138, 1523, 1540, 1575, 1695, 1740.
"Ernst Bacon: a contemporary tribute," by Paul Horgan, p. iii-iv. "Compositions (partial list) by Ernst Bacon," p. 128-129.

Bacon, Ernst. Quiet Airs. Syracuse, NY: Syracuse University Press; Mercury Music, 1952.
Composed: ca. 1927.
Setting: high voice, piano.
Johnson: 211, 536, 1510.

Bacon, Ernst. A Word [manuscript].
Composed: ca. 1930s-40s.
Setting: voice, piano.
Johnson: 1212.

Bacon, Ernst. At The Gate [manuscript].
Composed: ca. 1930s-40s.
Setting: voice, piano.
Johnson: 150.

Bacon, Ernst. Few Get Enough [manuscript].
Composed: ca. 1930s-40s.
Setting: voice, piano.
Johnson: 1596.
The Dickinson line is "Few, yet enough."

Bacon, Ernst. Morning Is The Place For Dew [manuscript].
Composed: ca. 1930s-40s.
Setting: voice, piano.
Johnson: 197.

AARON COPLAND

1538 L. WASHINGTON STREET   PEEKSKILL, N. Y. 10566

May 10, 1979

Dear Ernst:

It was nice to hear from you
after so long a time. Naturally I
was interested to know that you had
also produced a number of songs
based on the poems of dear Emily.
(I wonder if you know that I orchestrated 8 of my own settings of 12
of her poems.)

I hope our paths cross in the
not-too-distant future.

All my best to you...

Aaron

Aaron Copland. Letter to Ernst Bacon, May 10, 1979. Collection of
Carlton Lowenberg. Reprinted by permission of Whitman & Ransom.

Bacon, Ernst. She Dwelt So Close—Past
   Surmise [manuscript].
   Composed: ca. 1930s-40s.
   Setting: voice, piano.
   Johnson: 1702.

Bacon, Ernst. Snowfall [manuscript].
   Composed: ca. 1930s-40s.
   Setting: voice, piano.
   Johnson: 311.

Bacon, Ernst. The Banks of The Yellow
   Sea [manuscript].
   Composed: ca. 1930s-40s.
   Setting: voice, piano.
   Johnson: 266.

Bacon, Ernst. The Train [manuscript].
   Composed: ca. 1930s-40s.
   Setting: voice, piano.
   Johnson: 585.

Bacon, Ernst. There Came a Day [manu-
   script].
   Composed: ca. 1930s-40s.
   Setting: soprano and contralto duet, piano.
   Johnson: 322.

Bacon, Ernst. Tributaries: Songs. Lim-
   ited ed. Berkeley, CA: The Musical
   Offering, 1978.
   Composed: ca. 1930s-40s.
   Setting: voice, piano.
   Johnson: 26, 57, 135, 211, 266, 311, 390,
   695, 1079, 1332, 1540, 1575, 1755.
   Also settings of Whitman, Shakespeare,
   Housman, Teasdale, Burns, and others.
   Edition limited to 200 copies.

Bacon, Ernst. We Never Know [manu-
   script].
   Composed: ca. 1930s-40s.
   Setting: voice, piano.
   Johnson: 1523.

Bacon, Ernst. Yellow [manuscript].
   Composed: ca. 1930s-40s.
   Setting: voice, piano.
   Johnson: 1045.

Bacon, Ernst. Songs From Emily
   Dickinson. San Francisco, CA: Ernst
   Bacon, 1932.
   Composed: ca. 1931.
   Setting: voice, piano.
   Johnson: 149, 162, 217, 249, 288, 333,
   390, 536, 695, 761, 1008. 1065, 1079.

Bacon, Ernst. The Bells [manuscript].
   Composed: ca. 1931.
   Setting: SATB chorus, piano or organ.
   Johnson: 24.

Bacon, Ernst. The Grass. New York:
   Associated Music Publishers, 1944.
   Composed: ca. 1931.
   Setting: soprano or mezzo-soprano, piano.
   Johnson: 333.

Bacon, Ernst. The Postponeless Crea-
   ture [manuscript].
   Composed: ca. 1931.
   Setting: SATB chorus, piano.
   Johnson: 390.

Bacon, Ernst. Songs of Eternity
   [manuscript].
   Composed: ca. 1932.
   Setting: baritone or contralto, harp,
   percussion, string orchestra.
   Johnson: 390, 695, 1079.
   First performance: San Francisco Federal
   Orchestra, Ernst Bacon, conductor,
   1936.

Bacon, Ernst. As Well as Jesus [manu-
   script].
   Composed: ca. 1935.
   Setting: voice, piano.
   Johnson: 456.

Bacon, Ernst. No Dew upon the Grass.
Bryn Mawr, PA: Merion Music, 1942.
Composed: ca. 1935.
Setting: contralto or bass, piano.
Johnson: 692.

Bacon, Ernst. So Set Its Sun in Thee
[manuscript].
Composed: ca. 1935.
Setting: voice, piano.
Johnson: 808.

Bacon, Ernst. And This of All My Hopes
[manuscript].
Composed: ca. 1936.
Setting: voice, piano.
Johnson: 913.

Bacon, Ernst. My River [manuscript].
Composed: ca. 1936.
Setting: medium voice, horn, celesta, percussion, string orchestra.
Johnson: 162.
First performance: San Francisco Federal Orchestra, Ernst Bacon, conductor, 1936.

Bacon, Ernst. Five Poems Set to Music.
New York: G. Schirmer, 1944.
Composed: ca. 1936-44.
Setting: soprano or high voice, piano.
Johnson: 26, 91, 192, 913, 1755.

Bacon, Ernst. The Arctic Flower [manuscript].
Composed: ca. 1938.
Setting: voice, piano.
Johnson: 180.

Bacon, Ernst. Nature. Ten Songs for Chorus of Women's Voices, Soprano and Alto Soli, and Piano.
Boston: E.C. Schirmer, 1971.
Composed: ca. 1938-64.
Setting: SATB chorus, soprano and contralto soloists, piano.

Johnson: 180, 258, 322, 695, 790, 975, 1104, 1138, 1332, 1593.
First performance: Festival of Twentieth-Century American Music, Brevard, NC: Music Center, 1964-65.
Dedicated to Paul Horgan.

Bacon, Ernst. Is There Such a Thing as "Day"? New York: Associated Music Publishers, 1944.
Composed: ca. 1940.
Setting: soprano, piano.
Johnson: 101.

Bacon, Ernst. O Friend. New York: Associated Music Publishers, 1946.
Composed: ca. 1940.
Setting: medium voice, piano.
Johnson: 729.
In Poems (1890) "Sir" is rendered "O friend," which Bacon used as his title.

Bacon, Ernst. Solitude [manuscript].
Composed: ca. 1940-50.
Setting: voice, piano.
Johnson: 1695.

Bacon Ernst. Six Songs. New York: New Music Society, 1942. (New Music 15, No. 2)
Composed: ca. 1942.
Setting: contralto or baritone, piano.
Johnson: 266, 692; also works by Carl Sandburg and Walt Whitman.

Bacon, Ernst. From Emily's Diary. [Secular cantata.] New York: G. Schirmer, 1947.
Composed: ca. 1944.
Setting: 4-part chorus of women's voices and small orchestra (horn, piano, string orchestra), with incidental soprano and contralto soloists.
Johnson: 32, 106, 113, 162, 390, 401, 489, 657, 794, 823, 964.

First performance: St. Cecilia Society, New York, December 13, 1944.

Bacon, Ernst. **Velvet People.** New York: Carl Fischer, 1948.
Composed: ca. 1945.
Setting: medium or low voice, piano.
Johnson: 138.

Bacon, Ernst. **Angels in the Early Morning** [manuscript].
Composed: ca. 1965.
Setting: voice, piano.
Johnson: 94.

Bacon, Ernst. **The Last Invocation. A Requiem** [manuscript].
Composed: ca. 1968-70.
Setting: SATB chorus, percussion, piano, string orchestra.
Johnson: 482, 813, 1147, 1187, 1402.

Bacon, Ernst. **The Bat** [manuscript].
Composed: ca. 1970-80.
Setting: voice, piano.
Johnson: 1575.

Bacon, Ernst. **Summer's Lapse** [manuscript].
Composed: ca. 1970-80.
Setting: voice, piano.
Johnson: 1540.

BACON – SELECTED RECORDINGS

The Art Song in America. Durham, NC: Duke University Press, 1965. DWRM 7501, DWR 7506. John Kennedy Hanks, tenor; Ruth Friedberg, piano.
Johnson: 26, 913, 1080

Bacon, Ernst. *Four Songs to Emily Dickinson.* Eleanor Steber, soprano. New York: Strand Records, [n.d.].
Johnson: 26, 91, 1755.

Bacon, Ernst. *Songs From Emily Dickinson.* Helen Boatwright, soprano; Ernst Bacon, piano. Wellesley, Mass.: Cambridge Records, 1967. Cambridge CRM 1707. 1967.
Johnson: 4, 26, 57, 91, 101, 149, 189, 211, 217, 288, 311, 333, 456, 695, 729, 761, 1079, 1138, 1212, 1540, 1740, 1755.

Carolyn Heafner, Soprano, Sings Songs by Amy Beach, Jack Beeson, Hugo Weisgall, Lee Hoiby, and Ernst Bacon. (This same recording also has the title, *Carolyn Heafner Sings American Songs.*) Composers Recordings CRI SD 462, 1981.
Johnson: 57, 83, 192, 266, 288, 1510, 1657.

BACON – REFERENCES

"Amherst, Massachusetts; Home of Emily Dickinson." Item 4, page 19 of *Spirits and Places.* Organ Solo by Ernst Bacon. Bicentennial Cycle Honoring American Personages and Geography of the Native Soil, Published in Honor of America's 200th Birthday. Cincinnati: World Library Publications, 1975.
Emily Dickinson quote under Amherst title is Johnson, 1206.

Ernst Bacon. [Orinda, CA: Ernst Bacon, ca. 1974] 23 pp.
An incomplete list of Bacon's works, compiled by the composer. Gives name, description, and instrumentation of compositions. Discography, pp. 19-20.

Ernst Bacon: a Life in Music. (Videotape prepared by Channel KTEH TV, San Jose, CA; broadcast on San Jose's Channel 54, 9:30 p.m., June 28, 1984.) Reviewed by Terrence O'Flaherty in the *San Francisco Chronicle*, June 29, 1984.

Discussion, in part, of Emily Dickinson's place in Ernst Bacon's compositions. Bacon said, "They just ravished me, these poems—they were so economical."

Nassau Community College. [Playbill] "The Committee on the Emily Dickinson Festival in Association with the Department of Theatre Presents the Premiere Production of 'Come Slowly, Eden,' a Portrait of Emily Dickinson by Norman Rosten. Songs by Ernst Bacon and Philip Springer. May 3 through May 15, 1966."
Johnson: 211.

St. Edmunds, John. "The Songs of Ernst Bacon." "Ernst Bacon. Poetry in Search of Music." *Sewanee Review* (October 1941).
Reprint: Sewanee, TN: University of Tennessee Press, 1941.

Swift, Page. "Ernst Bacon: The Man and His Songs." D.M.A. Dissertation, Indiana University, 1982.
Detailed discussion of Bacon's songs generally, and his settings of Emily Dickinson's poems specifically.

Baksa, Robert. Seven Songs to Poems of Emily Dickinson. Opus 38. New York: Composers Library Editions, 1977.
Composed: 1963-66.
Setting: soprano or mezzo-soprano, piano.
Johnson: 115, 278, 288, 303, 435, 449, 540.
First performance: Carolyn Reyer, mezzo-soprano; James Benner, piano. Carnegie Recital Hall, May, 1967.

"Though published together, [these do] not constitute a cycle, since the voice requirement varies from song to song.

"I often get letters from around the country from people who are requesting permission to include the songs in their dissertations. [These songs] can comfortably be done by most female voices."—letter of July 3, 1989.

Baksa, Robert. More Songs to Poems of Emily Dickinson. Opus 40. New York: Composers Library Editions, 1978.
Commissioned by Carolyn Reyer, 1967.
Composed: 1967.
Setting: soprano or mezzo-soprano, piano.
Johnson: 12, 41, 192, 258, 347, 533, 704.
First performance: Carolyn Reyer, mezzo-soprano; James Benner, piano. Carnegie Recital Hall, May, 1986.

"As with 'Seven Songs,' 'More Songs' should not be considered as a cycle .... It's hard for me to make comments about these songs so long after they were written. Some I like and some I am displeased with, but I find that the public doesn't always agree with my present judgments about the individual songs. So I prefer to keep my counsel and simply express my gratitude that performers still find them of interest and continue to perform them.

"Also I must chide you for your complaint about your energies freezing over by winter. Unless I am mistaken, no one living in sunny California can legally claim to be in such a condition. P.S. Will you please send me Emily's recipe for black cake? [Johnson: Letter 835a.]"—letter of January 9, 1990.

Barber, Samuel. Let Down the Bars, Oh Death, Op. 82. New York: Carl Schirmer, 1942.

Composed: 1936.

Setting: SATB chorus a cappella.

Johnson: 1065.

Bibliography: Jean Louise Kreiling. "The Songs of Samuel Barber: A Study in Literary Taste and Text-Setting." Ph.D. Dissertation, Department of Music, University of North Carolina, 1986.

"I am especially interested in Barber's attitude toward his song texts—the literary tastes and influences which guided his selection of texts, and the principles which governed his musical settings of them. I have studied both published and unpublished songs, as well as some sketches and correspondence."—letter of September 6, 1984, Jean Louise Kreiling to Roland Leich.

"The late Samuel Barber did just one ED setting chorally (sung at his burial ceremony): 'Let Down the Bars, O Death!' (1936). In 1948, he sent me a postcard warning: 'Be careful not to turn into ED yourself—do you go around dressed in white already?'"—letter of May 29, 1990 from Roland Leich.

Barkin, Elaine. Two Emily Dickinson Choruses. Hillsdale, NY: Mobart Music, 1978. Ship Bottom, NJ: Association for the Promotion of New Music, 1982, 1986.

Composed: 1976.

Setting: SATB chorus.

Duration: 5:00

Johnson: 204, 471.

Recording: *New England Conservatory Chorus Sings Contemporary Music.* Composers Recordings CRI SD 482, 1982. Conductor: Lorna Cooke de Varon.

Barkin, Elaine. The Supple Suitor: a Song Cycle. Ship Bottom, NJ: Association for the Promotion of New Music, 1979-86.

Composed: 1978-79.

Setting: mezzo-soprano, flute/alto flute/piccolo, oboe, harpsichord/piano, vibraphone/orchestral bells, violoncello.

Duration: 24:00

Johnson: 54, 749, 935, 1026, 1047, 1149, 1445, 1588, 1605, 1633, 1692, 1742.

"Emily Dickinson's manifold attitudes and concerns about dying, death, and loss emerge in the texts. She is distressed, resigned, sorrowful, ingenuous, witty, and ironical. Although unwelcome, death is a part of life. I sought to compose musical voices for each of Dickinson's and felicitously to entwine hers and my own."—letter of July 5, 1991.

Bartlett, Floy Little. I Shall Not Live in Vain. Boston: Arthur P. Schmidt, 1915.

Composed: 1915.

Setting: voice, piano.

Johnson: 919.

Reprinted in his *Selected Songs*. Boston: Schmidt, 1932.

Bartow, Jim. An American Poet's Songbook [manuscript].

Commissioned: New York State Council on the Arts, 1970.

Composed: 1970-73.

Setting: voice, trumpet, guitar, contrabass.

Johnson: 47, 101, 568.

Duration: 8:43.

Recording: Blues Blood BB132, 1975.

These settings were composed and sung in cooperation with the Harlem Blues

Consort. Includes settings to poems by Paul L. Dunbar, Robert Frost, and others. The Dickinson settings are titled "Will There Really Be a Morning?" (101), "E.D.'s Blues" (47), "We Learned" (568).

"I have also set 'Read, sweet, how other strove' [260], 'To fight aloud' [126], and 'I taste a liquor' [214]." —letter of December 1991.

Beale, James. Three Songs for Soprano with Violin and Viola. Opus 33. New York: American Composers Edition, 1965.

Setting: soprano, violin, viola.

Johnson: 266.

Dickinson setting is the second of three songs. Other texts are by Robert Herrick and William Morris.

Beaty, Dan. Seven Songs on Six Poems of Emily Dickinson. Nacogdoches, TX: MUSECOMP Press, 1972-1984.

Composed: 1972 (revised 1981).

Setting: soprano, oboe.

Johnson: 47, 585, 587, 621, 1078, 1212 (2).

Beaty, Dan. Four Songs. Nacogdoches, TX: MUSECOMP Press, 1983.

Composed: 1983.

Setting: soprano, flute, and oboe.

Johnson: 162, 228, 249, 1619.

Beaty, Dan. A Habit of a Laureate. An Etude. Nacogdoches, TX: MUSE-COMP Press, 1984.

Composed: 1984.

Setting: voice, chimes, 4 snare drums.

Johnson: 785.

"The composition was inspired by both the poem and a bit of delving into the Fibonacci sequence. The poem is not intended to be read but is printed on the title page. The poetry of Emily Dickinson is, beyond its beauty of symbol and meaning, perfectly musical in sound and rhythmic syllabization. The poems' compactness and singular subjects are, along with the above traits, models of the lyrical foundation on which any good and effective song must be based."—letter of June 21, 1989.

Beckler, Stanworth. Five Poems of Dickinson. Opus 56. Stockton, CA.: Stanworth Beckler, 1961.

Composed: 1961.

Setting: tenor, flute, bassoon, piano, violin.

Johnson: 136, 254, 328, 374, 605.

First performance: Anastasios Vrenios. Conservatory, University of the Pacific, Stockton, CA, 1961.

"My opus 56 was written for, and premiered here by, Anastasios Vrenios, who also participated at about the same time in the premiere of my second opera, 'Outcasts of Poker Flat.' As for 'Cricket' [see Opus 75], I had not realized that she had treated the subject in eleven other poems. You can see from my work that I am in agreement with your assessment of the Dickinson poems. I wish I had the time to set more of them."—letters of April 8 and April 18, 1989.

Beckler, Stanworth. Four Short Poems of Emily Dickinson. Stockton, CA: Stanworth Beckler, 1969.

Composed: 1969.

Setting: soprano, piano.

Johnson: 135, 345, 1747, 1755.

"I'm starting a new piece which will include 12 poems by Dickinson as part of a set of probably 22 poems (others by Amy Lowell and Sylvia Plath). The whole set will be my Opus 102, No. 3, and will be called 'Trio.'"

Beckler, Stanworth. Man & Divers Bestiall Companyons. Opus 75. No. 4, "The Cricket." Stockton, CA: Stanworth Beckler, 1969.
Composed: 1969.
Setting: SATB chorus, piano, harpsichord.
Johnson: 1276.

Belet, Brian. Five Songs [manuscript].
Composed: 1982.
Setting: lyric coloratura soprano, flute, percussion, piano, viola.
Johnson: 449.
Location: composer.
First performance: Concert conducted by the composer, Arizona State University, May, 1982.
"The second song is a setting for Emily Dickinson's 'I died for Beauty.' With two 11th- and 8th-century Japanese poems, William Blake's 'A Poison Tree,' and Mark Strand's 'Seeing Things Whole.' The first two poems [Blake and Dickinson] deal with death, although in different ways. I have not fully analyzed why these two poems fit together in my song set—I do know that they both affected me very deeply; and perhaps that is enough of a connection for them to reside in the same song set. The Blake and Dickinson poems are always grouped together in performances."—letters of November 7 and December 26, 1989.

Belkin, Alan. Four Emily Dickinson Songs [manuscript].
Composed: 1981-82.
Setting: mezzo-soprano, piano; or mezzo-soprano, orchestra.
Johnson: 585, 700, 712, 732.
Location: composer.
First performance: Ilya Speranza, soprano; Jorge Mester, conductor. Contemporary Music Festival, January 23, 1983.

"I chose Emily Dickinson's poems because they have strong, sharp images (the language is simple and direct, and therefore easy to set to music), and because of their emotional truth and force."—letter of June, 1990.

Benjamin, Thomas. Night Songs. Chapel Hill, NC: Hinshaw Music, 1981.
Commissioned: Sigma Alpha Iota Music Sorority.
Composed: 1981.
Setting: SSA women's chorus, woodwind quintet.
Johnson: 1104.
" 'Night Songs' won the Mars Hill Choral Competition in 1978."—letter of April 16, 1989.

Benoliel, Bernard. Eternity-Junctions, opus 1 [manuscript].
Composed: 1968.
Setting: SATB chorus.
Johnson: 30, 162, 465, 622, 664.
Location: composer.
First performance: BBC Singers broadcast, Odaline de la Marinez, conductor. October 27, 1990.
Reviewed by Calum McDonald in *Tempo* 142 (September, 1982).
"The work consists of five different types of chorale. Their texture is largely homophonic, alternating gaunt unison passages with seven-voice parallel motion in chords of stacked thirds. Counterpoint is austerely used, almost entirely canonic; the voices move for the most part in small intervals, within the compass of an octave."—letter and notes of July 25, 1989.

Berger, Jean. Three Poems by Emily Dickinson. New York: Broude Brothers, 1973.
Composed: 1973.

Setting: SATB chorus, piano.
Johnson: 386, 1459, 1755.
"This work was originally written for solo voice and piano. The quality of the poems seemed to make the more anonymous medium of the chamber chorus more appropriate."—letter of July 1989.

Bergh, Arthur. The Grass. New York: Robbins Music, 1954.
Setting: SA chorus, piano.
Johnson: 333.

Berkowitz, Leonard. Four Songs on Poems of Emily Dickinson. New York: Associated Music Publishers, 1968.
Setting: SATB chorus.
Johnson: 254, 288, 1052, 1134.

Bialosky, Marshall. Three Mysteries of Emily Dickinson. Palos Verdes Peninsula, CA: New York: Seesaw Music Corp., 1979.
Composed: 1978 (revised 1979).
Setting: mezzo-soprano, English horn.
Johnson: 101, 581, 701.

Bialosky, Marshall. The Far Theatricals of Day. Palos Verdes Peninsula, CA: Sanjo Music, 1983.
Composed: 1981-83.
Setting: mezzo-soprano, flute, oboe, clarinet.
Johnson: 152, 888, 931, 950, 1050, 1107, 1120, 1134.
First performance: California State University, Dominguez Hills, October 15, 1983.
"'The Far Theatricals of Day' is a cycle of eight songs that take the listener through an Emily Dickinson day from sunrise through noon to sunset and

evening. There are frequent musical connections between the songs in the form of cadences, quotations, or harmonic progressions. Although [the cycle is] almost totally diatonic in sound, many serial procedures from twelve-tone music are used throughout."—letter of March 29, 1989.

Bialosky, Marshall. Three Short Songs for Voice Alone. Palos Verdes Peninsula, CA: Sanjo Music, 1988.
Composed: 1980s (early).
Setting: voice.
Johnson: 254, 1078, 1206.

Bialosky, Marshall. Birds, Bees, and Butterflies. Palos Verdes Peninsula, CA: Sanjo Music, 1988.
Composed: 1988.
Setting: soprano, flute, oboe, clarinet, bassoon, horn, harp.
Johnson: 89, 214, 324, 500, 533, 682, 861, 864, 896, 1035, 1246, 1339, 1405, 1761.
First performance: California State University, Dominguez Hills, October 29, 1988.
"'Birds, Bees, and Butterflies,' a true song cycle, is divided in the manner of a sonnet; eight songs, then an instrumental interlude, then the final six. The first four are about birds, the second four are about bees, the next three about butterflies, and the final three are mixed referring to more than one of the three 'stars.' Each of the little creatures has its own motif, which is heard many times throughout the cycle. The instrumental interlude acts as a kind of 'summary' of the songs heard thus far and a herald of the songs to come."—letter of May 3, 1989.

Bialosky, Marshall. Four Dickinson Songs about Birds. Palos Verdes Peninsula, CA: Sanjo Music Co., 1990.
Composed: 1990.
Setting: voice.
Johnson: 1084, 1542, 1570, 1585.

Bialosky, Marshall. Four Songs of Emily Dickinson for Voice Alone. Palos Verdes Peninsula, CA: Sanjo Music Co., 1990.
Composed: 1990.
Setting: voice.
Johnson: 367, 423, 501, 1556.

Bielawa, Herbert. A Dickinson Album, for Choir, Piano, Guitar, Troubadour, and Tape [manuscript].
Commissioned: California Association of Professional Teachers of Music, 1972.
Composed: 1973.
Setting: SATB chorus, troubadour, piano, guitar, electronic tape.
Johnson: 126, 258, 435, 556, 1082.
Location: composer.
"The stitching together of the settings is done by the troubadour who, accompanied on his guitar, sings sections of the poem 'Emily Dickinson' by the contemporary poet James Schevill. These Dickinson poems all express states of madness, irrationality, despair, hypocracy, contamination of patriotism, brutality, futility, and humanity's insensitivity to itself, which have progressively become so characteristic of our time. Dickinson was responding to the Civil War of her own time, but the issues are shockingly universal and timeless."—from program notes, 1973.

Bielawa, Herbert. The Snake and Other Creatures [manuscript].
Composed: 1987.
Setting: soprano or tenor, piano.

Johnson: 526, 916, 986, 1275, 1356, 1379.
Location: composer.
"This song cycle includes the Snake, the Bee, the Frog, the Oriole, the Spider, the Rat. I tried for years, unsuccessfully, to set her poems; now I can't seem to get away from them. Powerful stuff! It would be interesting to give a whole concert of music on her texts."
—letters of April 6, April 12, and April 19, 1989.

Binkerd, Gordon. Four Songs for High Soprano. New York: Boosey & Hawkes, 1976.
Setting: high soprano, piano.
Johnson: 737. With poems by J. Garrigue and others.

Binkerd, Gordon. Her Silver Will: Poems by Emily Dickinson. New York: Boosey & Hawkes, 1976.
Composed: 1976.
Setting: high soprano, piano.
Johnson: 737.

Binkerd, Gordon. "Hope" is the Thing with Feathers. New York: Boosey & Hawkes, [n.d.].
Setting: SSAA chorus.
Johnson: 254.

Bird, Hubert C. A Gift of Self [manuscript].
Composed: 1975.
Setting: mezzo-soprano or contralto.
Johnson: 208, 903.
Location: composer.

Bird, Hubert C. The Distant Trumpet [manuscript].
Composed: 1975.
Setting: mezzo-soprano or contralto.
Johnson: 67, 1147.
Location: composer.

Blank, Allan. Four Poems by Emily Dickinson. New York: American Composers Edition, 1974.
Composed: 1974.
Setting: soprano, flute, clarinet.
Johnson: 108, 668, 1287, 1510.
Recording: Scarborough Chamber Players, Centaur Records, CRC 1016.
"The choice of these four poems was dictated by a variety of formal balances. These balances include such things as the specificity of the imagery, generalities, and what I conceive as both the speed and conciseness of the unfolding language. Additionally, part of my original objective was to set two movements with one instrument each. The interaction of these conditions must have been just right for me to carry through this project."—letters of February 24 and April 24, 1989.

Blank, Allan. Coalitions. New York: American Composers Edition, 1975.
Composed: 1975.
Setting: soprano, 2 clarinets, trombone, 2 percussionists, piano.
Johnson: 1354.

Bliss, Milton. There Came a Wind Like a Bugle. Evanston, IL: Summy-Birchard, [n.d.].
Setting: SSA chorus.
Johnson: 1593.

Boatwright, Howard. Three Love Songs [manuscript].
Composed: 1971.
Setting: soprano, piano.
Johnson: 26, 211, 506.
Location: composer.
First performance: Helen Boatwright, soprano; Frederick Marvin, piano. Frederick Marvin Studio, Syracuse, NY, September 12, 1971.

"'Three Love Songs' will eventually be published by my own company, Walnut Grove Press, Fayetteville, NY."—letter of March 18, 1991.

Boatwright, Howard. Three Songs of Eternity [manuscript].
Composed: 1971.
Setting: soprano, clarinet.
Johnson: 4, 237, 712.
First performance: Helen Boatwright, soprano; Ralph D'Mello, clarinet. Everson Museum of Art, Syracuse, NY, January 21, 1973.

Bottenberg, Wolfgang. Four Emily Dickinson-Songs [manuscript].
Composed: 1961-62.
Setting: high voice, piano.
Johnson: 182, 214, 333, 701.
Location: Canadian Music Centre, Toronto, Canada.
First Performance: College-Conservatory of Music, Cincinnati, OH, May 10, 1962.
"When I still lived in Germany, I saw a performance of the music theatre work, 'A Day in the Life of Emily Dickinson,' which impressed me deeply. Consequently, soon after my emigration to North America, I familiarized myself with her poetry, and chose her for my first song-compositions.
"The style of the settings is extended tonality; the overall impression is rhapsodic and intensely emotional."
—letter of May, 1991.

Bottje, Will Gay. Wayward Pilgrim: A Musical Biography of Emily Dickinson. New York: American Composers Edition, 1962.
Composed: 1962.

Setting: soprano solo, chamber choir (12-16 voices), chamber orchestra.
Duration: 48:00.
Johnson, Poems: 228, 290, 326, 365, 448, 627, 632, 657, 664, 668, 677, 712, 721, 883, 1085, 1170, 1179, 1222, 1331, 1354, 1417, 1463, 1540, 1544.
Johnson, Letters: 261, 265, 268, 271, 298, 330, 342a, 354, 364, 381, 389, 471, 498, 519, 520, 524, 555, 586, 735, 781, 860.
Location: Southern Illinois University Library, Carbondale, Illinois.
First performance: Southern University Orchestra and Choir, January 12, 1964.
"The poems numbered above are either fully or partially scored; the letters are partially scored. The intent of the composition is to merge poetic ideas with ideas in the letters to form a five-part unit cycle.

"It is difficult to say much about my attraction to Dickinson...her terseness, perhaps the unconventional turn of phrase, the universality of her themes."—letters of February 24 and July 15, 1989.

Bottje, Will Gay. Five Songs from "Wayward Pilgrim." New York: American Composers Edition, 1963.
Composed: 1963.
Setting: voice, bass instruments (unspecified).
Johnson Letters: 261, 268, 298, 342a, 381.

Bourgeois, Louis. Nunc Dimittis. See "Miscellany" section. Jones, Joseph (arr.) A Garland for Emily.

Bourland, Roger. Dickinson Madrigals, Book I. For Women's Voices, Unaccompanied. Boston: Ione Press, 1987. (Sole selling agent, E.C. Schirmer, Boston.)
Composed: 1980.
Setting: (386, 429) SSA chorus; (446) 3 voices not to be divided according to voice range; (1099, 1362) SSAA chorus.
Johnson: 386, 429, 446, 1099, 1362.

Bourland, Roger. Dickinson Madrigals, Book II. Boston: Ione Press, 1989. (Sole selling agent, E.C. Schirmer, Boston.)
Composed: 1983.
Setting: (129, 249, 593) SSAA chorus; (285, 483) SSA chorus.
Johnson: 129, 249, 285, 483, 593.

Bourland, Roger. A Slash of Blue. [Boston]: Ione Press, 1984. (Sole selling agent, E.C. Schirmer, Boston.)
Composed: 1984.
Setting: mezzo-soprano, harp, viola.
Johnson: 204, 445, 469, 629, 858.

Bourland, Roger. Dickinson Madrigals, Book III. Boston: Ione Press, 1986. (Sole selling agent, E.C. Schirmer, Boston.)
Composed: 1985-86.
Setting: SATB chorus.
Johnson: 619, 824, 1418, 1775.
"The music for the three books of 'Dickinson Madrigals' really arises from the Sacred Harp tradition as well as bits and pieces of my own musical background: the Byrds, David Crosby, Joni Mitchell, folk music, and, of course, the '60s. The settings tend to be syllabic so that the listener can understand the words better. Another aspect that attracted me was the sexual and spiritual tension in Emily Dickinson's poetry that I may

be projecting, but more likely empathising with."—letter of March 9, 1990.

Boyle, George F. The Silent Brook. New York: Galaxy Music, 1937.
Composed: 1937.
Setting: voice, piano.
Johnson: 1200.

Boziwick, George. Beyond the Last Thought [manuscript].
Composed: 1982.
Setting: soprano, oboe, bassoon, marimba.
Johnson: 130.
First performance: Hunter College, New York City, 1982. Debra Gomez, soprano; George Boziwick, oboe; John Adler, bassoon; Janice Goldberg, marimba.
Recording: To be recorded June, 1992, by Opus One.
Also includes settings of Isabella Gardner, "Knowing"; Wallace Stevens: "Of Mere Being," "The Snow Man," "Another Weeping Woman."

Brown, Allyson. Songs from Emily, for Two-part Treble Voices. Delaware Water Gap, PA: Shawnee Press, 1975.
Composed: 1974.
Setting: SA chorus, piano.
Johnson: 12, 108, 318, 1510.
"I began only with the setting of 'The Morns' [12], which had been in an anthology we'd studied in high school. A tune for those words just evolved in my head, I think, and I would sing it in the echoing stairwells in my school. It was a few years later that I wrote it down, but with a notion that kept the rhythmic freedom I'd always used in singing it. The other three settings, with more standard rhythmic notation, were added at the suggestion of my publisher. In every case, Dickinson's

spare poetry lent itself naturally to a musical setting. I had not projected any additional settings, but your prompting made me think of her work again and realize the likelihood of doing more."—letter of November 27, 1989.

Brown, Francis James. Seven: A Cycle of Seven Emily Dickinson Poems on Poetry, Love, Nature, Beauty and Death. New York: American Composers Edition, 1984.
Duration: 20:00.
Composed: 1984.
Setting: soprano or contralto, piano; or voice, chamber orchestra.
Johnson: 250, 431, 456, 510, 917, 1333, 1474. Poems 250, 431, 456, 510, 1333, are set as songs. Poems 917, 1474, are set for speaker with accompaniment.
"The cycle has been performed with great success with a 14-piece chamber orchestra and voice in Boston and in Europe, my wife singing and I at the piano. One version is for contralto, another for soprano. Emily Dickinson is one of the most remarkable American poets and grossly misunderstood. She knew she had the gift for writing poetry, and shut out the world to create it. But it is not that rare a phenomenon. Other great artists were recognized, as she was, after their deaths. They lived mostly for what they could create."—letter of August 16, 1989 from Cyclades, Greece.

Burgon, Geoffrey. Revelations. London: Chester Music; New York: Edition W. Hansen/Chester Music, 1985. [Accompaniment arranged for piano.]
Composed: 1985.
Setting: SATB chorus, orchestra; soprano, tenor, bass soloists.

Johnson: 721
Also includes poems by Walt Whitman, W. B. Yeats, and David Jones.

Butler, Martin. Three Emily Dickinson Songs. Oxford: Oxford University Press, 1987.
Setting: soprano, clarinet, piano.
Duration: 9:00
Johnson: 1540, 1593, 1755.

Butterworth, Neil. Letter to the World. London: Chiltern Music, 1983.
Setting: baritone, piano.
Johnson: 441.

Callaway, Anne. Besides This May: A Cycle of Five Songs. New York: American Composers Edition, 1977.
Composed: 1977.
Setting: soprano, flute, piano.
Johnson: 31, 808, 966, 977, 1259.
"I read in Emily Dickinson's poetry the immediacy in both spiritual passion and passionate spirituality which in many poems is linked with a deep love of the natural world around her. I chose poems that avoided a regular meter in favor of some that were more asymmetric. They seemed to lend themselves to the more freely constructed rhythms of the music of my own century. In my song cycle, the flute becomes an upward extension of the voice—its spirit, perhaps; the piano is the harmonic-rhythmic binder of both instruments. I was genuinely moved by her poetry to write this song cycle. Doing so was a way of expressing my reading of this poetry through the medium of music."—letters of February 24 and May 4, 1989.

Carlsen, Philip. I Heard a Fly Buzz When I Died. New York: American Composers Edition, 1988.
Composed: 1988.
Setting: SATB a cappella.
Johnson: 465.
First performance: Clearwater Consort, Farmington, ME, November 8, 1988.
"This may be the poem that sparked my reborn appreciation of Dickinson's work. She is a genius at putting a handful of ordinary words together in such a startling way that they take on an extraordinary meaning. In this poem, for example, 'I could not see to see.' What a challenge for the composer to find a musical setting that matches the mystery and power of such a line!"
—letter of February 7, 1990.

Carlsen, Philip. I'm Nobody! New York: American Composers Edition, 1989.
Composed: 1989.
Setting: SATB a cappella.
Johnson: 288.
First performance: Clearwater Consort, Farmington, ME, January 26, 1989.
"This uses the version of the poem with the words 'They'd banish us', rather than, as in Johnson, 'They'd advertise.' The setting is jazzy, and plays up the humor of the poem. At the end, for example, the chorus drearily sings the word 'public' again and again with frog-like voices."—letter of February 7, 1990.

Carlsen, Philip. Evening's Sabres. New York: American Composers Edition, 1990.
Commissioned: American Composers Alliance, Town Hall Commissioning Award, 1989.
Composed: 1990.
Setting: marimba quartet.

Johnson: 1127.

First performance: Manhattan Marimba Quartet, Town Hall, New York City, March 6, 1990.

"This is purely an instrumental composition, but I chose a poetic title because of my great admiration for Dickinson. Also, I had in mind the 'evening' sound of the marimba and the visual impact of its rich dark wood and golden resonators gleaming under the slashing mallets of black-clad musicians."—letter of February 7, 1990.

Carter, Elliott. Heart Not So Heavy As Mine. New York: Arrow Music Press, 1938. New York: Associated Music Publishers, 1939.

Composed: 1938.

Setting: SATB chorus.

Johnson: 83.

Recording: Choral Masters Series GSS 103.

Carter, Elliott. Musicians Wrestle Everywhere. New York: Music Press, 1948.

Composed: 1945.

Setting: SSATB chorus a cappella, or with string orchestra.

Johnson: 157.

Recording: Choral Masters Series GSS 103.

Revised ed.: Bryn Mawr, PA: Mercury Music; Theodore Presser, sole rep., 1982.

Castiglioni, Niccolò. Dickinson-Lieder. Milano: Ricordi, 1978.

Composed: 1977.

Setting: soprano, piano; or soprano, small orchestra.

Johnson: 19, 94, 189, 465, 1212, 1755.

"I found the poetry of Emily Dickinson very very modern. She wasn't the poet of a great poem, like Dante, or Ariosto or Edmund Spenser. She was the poet of the small proportion, like a painter with his miniatures. But such an essentiality remains in Dickinson's poetry, never cold: her lyricism is very warm and in such a way Dickinson had something in common with a composer like Webern or a painter like the Italian Segantini."—letter of October 2, 1989.

Chalayev, Shirvani. Circumference Between [manuscript].

Composed: 1974.

Setting: contralto, piano; also voice and chamber orchestra.

Johnson: 126, 389, 465, 511, 1078, 1084, 1732, 1736, 1746, 1756.

Location: composer.

"I took these poems from *American Poetry of the Nineteenth Century*, which contained poems of Longfellow, Whitman, and Emily Dickinson, translated by Ivan Lehachev and Vera Markov. A long time ago an American citizen who once worked in the American Consulate in Moscow heard my composition. He said it was the most tragic interpretation of Emily Dickinson's poems. He even thought of producing the work in America, but because of the relations between our countries, he could only send me copies of the original poems. I told him about my idea of writing two more compositions in English and in my Laskom language. So far this idea has not become a reality.

"Why did I turn to these poems? To begin with, I came across the very last poem: 'The Bustle in a House' [1078], whose meaning coincided with the philosophy of our people, wherein the understanding of death and ritual is put above the understanding of life. I was taken by all of Emily Dickinson's poems, and I began to worship her. With pride I can say that after I wrote my composition, her poems became very popular among our musicians, and critics acknowledged her. This composition is one of my best. We sang it a lot. (It is written for my wife, Nina Grigorenko, a contralto.)

"Your countryman told me that back home her poetry is considered lyrical, but I see in it drama and tragedy. And so the entire composition is about death. When D[imitry] Shostakovich died, I dedicated it to him (even though it was written earlier). I was surprised by Shostakovich's stubbornness and by his consistent referral to the theme of death in his compositions. The topic of death is very close to our conception of the world. Emily Dickinson writes about this. Shostakovich thought a lot about death in his final years. I don't know if he was afraid of death or just simply, as an artist, trying to define his relationship to that topic."—letter in Russian, April 24, 1990, translated by Sophie Sinkovich.

Chauls, Robert. Of Great Men and Death [manuscript].
Commissioned: Emily Dickinson International Society, 1991.
Composed: 1991. [See comment below.]
Setting: tenor, piano.
Johnson: 1065, 1445.
Location: composer.
First performance: William Wallis, tenor. Los Angeles Valley College, April 11, 1991.

"The cycle was commissioned to be sung at the Emily Dickinson International Society's Conference to be held in October, 1992, so it will probably be several months before I finish the work. According to most of my information, ED songs have been set to be sung by women. I am trying to aim for the setting of the more 'manly' poems, although I am well aware that this is a highly subjective judgment."—letter of April 3, 1991.

Ciarlantini, Paola. Duds of Emeralds: cinque liriche di Emily Dickinson, per voce femminile. Ancona, Berben: 1985.
Setting: soprano, unaccompanied.
Johnson: 219, 249, 813, 1434, 1728.

Clarke, Henry Leland. Emily Dickinson Canons. New York: American Composers Edition, 1971.
Composed: 1933; revised 1965.
Setting: medium voice with violoncello or violin or viola.
Johnson: 516, 753, 757, 1092.

Clarke, Henry Leland. I Died for Beauty. New York: American Composers Edition, 1963.
Composed: 1963.
Setting: medium voice, piano.
Johnson: 449.

Clarke, Henry Leland. Autumn. New York: American Composers Edition, 1979.
Composed: 1979.
Setting: medium voice, piano.
Johnson: 12.

Gloria Coates. "In Falling Timbers Buried." Autograph manuscript, 1984–85. Reprinted by permission of the composer.

Gloria Coates

"I have always felt a close link between my thoughts and those of Emily Dickinson. I am not sure why that is. In high school I was a 'Transcendentalist-of-sorts,' searching for the meaning of life and death in the Emersonian sense. I also feel Dickinson's isolation as an artist—a creative artist is isolated through necessity—and this isolation intensifies even more the serious encountering of life's meaning which is finally expressed in art by the artist. Emily Dickinson's love of nature and closeness to the smallest insect and bright sunset—these are also a major part of my world which I express in sounds rather than words. I strive for simplicity, compactness of idea and form, and directness, qualities I find in Emily Dickinson's poetry.

"Perhaps this is why she is such a great artist, because so many people can relate to her thoughts as I do. There is a universality in her ideas which transcends time and place, yet an intimacy of expression so that one feels he knows the 'little wren' quite well and can marvel and delight in her company. In spite of this personal expression, hers is a force so mighty that it echoes around the world and across the centuries. Emily Dickinson is truly one of the world's greatest poets.

"...as for radio recordings, European countries, especially Germany and England, have a different system from ours here in the United States. Radio stations produce taped recordings which they own and broadcast. They usually hold them much longer than those which are in print commercially. To have a work selected for radio recording in Europe is an honor in much the same way that a recording grant and acceptance are very special in the United States. It is also most unusual for one work to be recorded by more than one radio station in a country, which has happened with my ED cycle. They were produced by the West German Radio in Cologne, Radio Bremen and Sender Freies Berlin, each by different artists. Hopefully, many stations in the United States will follow the European lead in this tradition, but that would necessitate more government subsidy.

"The Cologne Radio—West Deutscher Rundfunk—invited me to program and announce a series of broadcasts on contemporary music. I not only used their archives but also those of other German radio stations to find music. The American recordings from CRI, Northeastern, and several other companies could be played on German radio only with special permission from the companies. Needless to say, I was able to bring numerous American composers to attention in Germany with these broadcasts.

"In 1976 I sent several manuscripts and tapes to the BBC in London addressed to Dr. Hans Keller. He wrote to me before going over the music to tell me to have little expectation for a BBC recording because he was obliged to give preference to works composed by British and Commonwealth members. However, after going over the music, he accepted my ED cycles for production."—letter of August 9, 1990.

Coates, Gloria. I'm Nobody [manuscript].
Commissioned: Sylvia Anderson and
Matthias Kuntzsch.
Composed: 1965.
Setting: voice, piano.
Duration: 2:00.
Johnson: 288
Location: composer.
First performance: Sylvia Anderson,
mezzo-soprano; Matthias Kuntzsch,
piano. Amerika Haus, Munich, January
29, 1973.
"The Anderson-Kuntzsch concert was a
commission for those 5 songs [see
Coates's 'I Held a Jewel,' 'I've Seen a
Dying Eye,' 'They Dropped Like
Flakes,' 'Wild Nights, Wild Nights!']
—so I really completed them as a
cycle. Matthias Kuntzsch is a conduc-
tor and Sylvia Anderson, his wife, is an
American-born opera singer."—letter
of June 9, 1990.

Coates, Gloria. To Be Somebody
[manuscript].
Composed: 1965 [with percussion, 1989].
Setting: voice, piano; or voice, percussion,
piano.
Duration: 2:00.
Johnson: 288.
Location: composer.
First performance: Christina Ascher,
mezzo-soprano; Roger Epple, con-
ductor. Ensemble Modern, Gasteig
Munich, December 14, 1989.

Coates, Gloria. I Held a Jewel [manu-
script].
Commissioned: Sylvia Anderson and
Matthias Kuntzsch.
Composed: 1966.
Setting: voice, piano.
Duration: 2:30.
Johnson: 245.
Location: composer.

First performance: Sylvia Anderson,
mezzo-soprano; Matthias Kuntzsch,
piano. Amerika Haus, Munich, January
29, 1973.

Coates, Gloria. In Search of Something
[manuscript].
Composed: 1966, 1972 [orchestrated,
1989].
Setting: voice, percussion, piano.
Duration: 3:00.
Johnson: 547.
Location: composer.
First performance: Christina Ascher,
mezzo-soprano; Roger Epple, con-
ductor. Ensemble Modern, Gasteig
Munich, December 14, 1989.

Coates, Gloria. I've Seen a Dying Eye
[manuscript].
Commissioned: Sylvia Anderson and
Matthias Kuntzsch.
Composed: 1966; 1972.
Setting: voice, piano.
Duration: 2:00.
Johnson: 547.
Location: composer.
First performance: Sylvia Anderson,
mezzo-soprano; Matthias Kuntzsch,
piano. Amerika Haus, Munich, January
29, 1973.

Coates, Gloria. They Dropped Like Flakes
[manuscript].
Commissioned: Sylvia Anderson and
Matthias Kuntzsch.
Composed: 1966; 1972.
Setting: voice, piano.
Duration: 2:00.
Johnson: 409.
Location: composer.
First performance: Sylvia Anderson,
mezzo-soprano; Matthias Kuntzsch,
piano. Amerika Haus, Munich, 1973,
in memory of Pasquale Porcelli.

Also see comment on her "In Falling Timbers Buried."

Coates, Gloria. Fünf Stücke für vier Bläser / Five Pieces for Four Wind Players; Abstractions of Poems by Emily Dickinson for Woodwind Quartet. Munich: Ahn & Simrock-Crescendo, 1981.

Commissioned for the 25th anniversary of the Centre de Musique Contemporaine et de Première Auditions de Genève, 1976.

Composed: 1967 [revised 1975].

Setting: flute/piccolo, oboe/English horn, clarinet/bass clarinet, bassoon.

Duration: 12:30.

Johnson: 250, 315, 937, 949, 1720.

First performance: Southwest German Radio Quintet. Centre de Musique Contemporaine, January 27, 1976.

Recording: Swiss Romande Radio and Southwest German Radio, Baden-Baden, 1976. Lontano for BBC, London, 1983.

Rights bought back from publisher by the composer, 1984.

Coates, Gloria. To the Civil War Dead [manuscript].

Composed: 1971-72 [orchestrated, 1989].

Setting: voice, chamber orchestra.

Duration: 3:30.

Johnson 409.

Location: composer.

First performance: Christina Ascher, mezzo-soprano; Roger Epple, conductor. Ensemble Modern, Gasteig Munich, December 14, 1989.

Coates, Gloria. Were I with Thee [manuscript].

Composed: 1971-72 [orchestrated, 1989].

Setting: voice, percussion, piano.

Duration: 4:00.

Johnson: 249.

Location: composer.

First performance: Christina Ascher, mezzo-soprano; Nicole Winter, piano. Roger Epple, conductor. Ensemble Modern, Gasteig Munich, December 14, 1989.

Coates, Gloria. Wild Nights, Wild Nights! [manuscript].

Commissioned: Sylvia Anderson and Matthias Kuntzsch.

Composed: 1971-72.

Setting: voice, piano.

Duration: 2:00.

Johnson: 249.

Location: composer.

First performance: Sylvia Anderson, mezzo-soprano; Matthias Kuntzsch, piano. Amerika Haus, Munich, January 29, 1973.

Coates, Gloria. A Formal Feeling [manuscript].

Composed: 1975.

Setting: voice, xylophone, timpani, percussion, organ.

Duration: 3:00.

Johnson: 341.

Location: composer.

First performance: Gloria Coates, mezzo-soprano and tape. Amerika Haus, Munich, June 16, 1976.

Coates, Gloria. The Tune without the Words [manuscript].

Composed: 1975.

Setting: voice, glockenspiel, (2) percussion, timpani.

Duration: 3:00.

Johnson: 254.

Location: composer.

First performance: Gloria Coates, soprano; Alexandra Coates, percussion. Amerika Haus, Munich, June 16, 1976.

Coates, Gloria. If I Can Stop One Heart
[manuscript].
Composed: 1978.
Setting: voice and piano; voice and chamber orchestra.
Duration: 2:30.
Johnson: 919.
Location: composer.
First performance: Sylvia Graeschke, soprano; Elzbieta Sternlicht, piano. Amerika Gedankbibliothek Concert Hall, West Berlin, 1981.

Coates, Gloria. Mine by The Right
[manuscript].
Composed: 1978.
Setting: voice, piano.
Duration: 2:00.
Johnson: 528.
Location: composer.
First performance: Sylvia Groeschke, soprano; Elzbieta Sternlicht, piano. West Berlin, Amerika-Gedank-bibliothek, November 24, 1981.

Coates, Gloria. The Sign in the Scarlet Prison [manuscript].
Composed: 1978 [orchestrated, 1989].
Setting: voice, chamber orchestra.
Duration: 3:00.
Johnson: 525.
Location: composer.
First performance: Christina Ascher, mezzo-soprano; Roger Epple, conductor. Ensemble Modern, Gasteig Munich, December 14, 1989.

Coates, Gloria. A Word Is Dead [manuscript].
Composed: 1979 [orchestrated, 1989].
Setting: voice, piano.
Duration: 2:00.
Johnson: 1212.
Location: composer.

First performance: Sylvia Groeschke, soprano; Amerika-Gedankbibliothek, November 24, 1981.
" 'A Word Is Dead' is based on clusters, resonances and the overtone and undertone series. I orchestrated the song at the Millay Colony last October."
—letter of June 9, 1990.

Coates, Gloria. An Amethyst Remembrance [manuscript].
Composed: 1979; orchestrated, 1989.
Setting: voice, percussion, piano.
Duration: 3:00.
Johnson: 245.
Location: composer.
First performance: Christina Ascher, mezzo-soprano; Nicole Winter, piano. Andreas Schumacher, percussion. Roger Epple, conductor. Ensemble Modern, Gasteig Munich, December 14, 1989.

Coates, Gloria. Bind Me, I Still Can Sing
[manuscript].
Composed: 1979.
Setting: voice, piano.
Duration: 2:00.
Johnson: 1005.
Location: composer.
First performance: Sylvia Groeschke, soprano; Amerika-Gedankbibliothek, November 24, 1981.

Coates, Gloria. Chanting to Paradise
[manuscript].
Composed: 1979 [orchestrated, 1989].
Setting: voice, chamber orchestra.
Duration: 2:00.
Johnson: 1005.
Location: composer.
First performnace: Christina Ascher, mezzo-soprano; Roger Epple, conductor. Ensemble Modern, Gasteig Munich, December 14, 1989.

Coates, Gloria. It Just Begins To Live
[manuscript].
Composed: 1979 [orchestrated, 1989].
Setting: voice, percussion, piano.
Duration: 2:00.
Johnson: 1212.
Location: composer.
First performance: Christina Ascher,
mezzo-soprano; Roger Epple, con-
ductor. Ensemble Modern, Gasteig
Munich, December 14, 1989.

**Coates, Gloria. Now I Lay Thee Down
To Sleep** [manuscript].
Composed: 1979.
Setting: voice, piano.
Duration: 2:00.
Johnson: 1539.
Location: composer.
First performance: Sylvia Groeschke,
soprano; Elzbieta Sternlicht, piano.
West Berlin, Amerika-Gedank-
bibliothek, 1981.
"In memory of Jane Reich (Aunt Jane)."

Coates, Gloria. Thy Dust To Keep [manu-
script].
Composed: 1979 [orchestrated, 1989].
Setting: voice, chamber orchestra.
Duration: 2:00.
Johnson: 1539.
Location: composer.
First performance: Christina Ascher,
mezzo-soprano; Roger Epple, con-
ductor. Ensemble Modern, Gasteig
Munich, December 14, 1989.

Coates, Gloria. Go the Great Way
[manuscript].
Composed: 1982.
Setting: voice, timpani, (2) percussion,
organ.
Duration: 3:00.
Johnson: 1638.
Location: composer.

First performance: Allison Welles, sopra-
no; Margaret Schlicht, organ, tape.
Stifts Church-Faurndau, Göppingen,
West Germany, June 25, 1988.

Coates, Gloria. The Place Called Morning
[manuscript].
Composed: 1982 [orchestrated, 1989].
Setting: voice, chamber orchestra.
Duration: 4:00.
Johnson: 101.
Location: composer.
First performance: Christina Ascher,
mezzo-soprano; Roger Epple, con-
ductor. Ensemble Modern, Gasteig
Munich, December 14, 1989.

**Coates, Gloria. Will There Really Be a
Morning?** [manuscript].
Composed: 1982; 1984.
Setting: voice, piano.
Duration: 2:00.
Johnson: 101.
Location: composer.
First performance: Patricia Stiles, mezzo-
soprano; Nicole Winter, piano. Erlöser-
church Concert Hall, Munich, June
30, 1985.
"I wrote the melody of 'Will There Real-
ly Be a Morning' at the MacDowell
Colony in 1982. Two years later I read
a poem of E.D. and realized it was
the identical rhythm and fit exactly
to that melody. A very odd coinci-
dence!"—letter of June 9, 1990.

Coates, Gloria. In Falling Timbers Buried
[manuscript].
Commissioned: Cornelia Kallisch.
Composed: 1984-85.
Setting: voice, piano.
Duration: 3:00.
Johnson: 614.
Location: composer.

First performance: Cornelia Kallisch, mezzo-soprano; Siglind Brun, piano. Drama State Theatre, Pretoria, South Africa, September 7, 1985.

"The setting was written in memory of my father. 'In Falling Timbers Buried' was a commission from Cornelia Kallisch for her tour of South Africa. She had used 'They Dropped Like Flakes' in Pretoria and Rio de Janeiro voice contests and won 1st place in both—so wanted a cycle for the rest of the Dickinson songs for her tour of South Africa—with Moussorgsky, Ravel, and Dvorak. All twelve were recorded by Sender Freies Berlin Radio, 1985."
—letter of June 9, 1990.

Coates, Gloria. There Breathed a Man [manuscript].
Composed: 1984-85. Version with chamber orchestra, 1989.
Setting: voice, piano; voice, chamber orchestra.
Duration: 3:00.
Johnson: 614.
Location: composer.
First performance: Christina Ascher, mezzo-soprano; Roger Epple, conductor. Ensemble Modern, Gasteig Munich, December 14, 1989.
"These Twelve Songs are often sung as a cycle (voice, piano). Someone sugges-

ted the title 'Songs of a Little Pilgrim' —but I'm not sure! These twelve are: "Will There Really Be a Morning" [101]; "I Held A Jewel" [245]; "Wild Nights—Wild Nights!" [249]; "I'm Nobody!" [288]; "They Dropped Like Flakes" [409]; "Mine By The Right" [528]; "I've Seen a Dying Eye" [547]; "In Falling Timbers Buried" [614]; "If I Can Stop One Heart" [919]; "Bind Me, I Still Can Sing" [1005]; "A Word Is Dead" [1212]; "Now I Lay Thee Down To Sleep" [1539]. They are all recorded by Berlin Radio."
—letter of August 17, 1990.

"I might rename the cycle 'Songs of a Little Pilgrim.' In fact, I'm rather certain I'll do it."—card of September 27, 1990.

Commuck, Thomas. See "Miscellany" section: Jones, Joseph, arr. Twenty Songs by Emily Dickinson, Set to Tunes by Thomas Commuck (1845).

Constantinides, Dinos. I Never Saw A Moor. New York: Seesaw Music, 1984.
Composed: 1984.
Setting: SATB chorus, piano or organ.
Johnson: 1052.

Robert Convery

"I have set more poems of Emily Dickinson and William Blake than of any other poets. In addition to having a metaphysical bent, they write concisely, compactly, and lyrically, and lean toward the use of words which are monosyllabic and which convey musical word sounds.

"A sophisticated theatricality and simplicity are achieved in these songs. With regard to the integrity of a poem, words are never repeated in the musical solo setting, a limitation I have adhered to."—letter of December 9, 1990.

Convery, Robert. A Thought Went up My Mind Today [manuscript].
Composed: 1976.
Setting: high voice, piano.
Johnson: 701.
Location: composer.
First performance: Jenny Kelly, soprano. Westminster Choir College, 1977.

Convery, Robert. I Hide Myself within My Flower [manuscript].
Composed: 1977.
Setting: high voice, piano.
Johnson: 903.
Location: composer.
First performance: Jenny Kelly, soprano. Westminster Choir College, 1977.

Convery, Robert. If Recollecting Were Forgetting [manuscript].
Composed: 1977.
Setting: high voice, piano.
Johnson: 33.
Location: composer.
First performance: Jenny Kelly, soprano. Westminster Choir College, 1977.

Convery, Robert. The Butterfly upon the Sky [manuscript].
Composed: 1977.
Setting: high voice, piano.
Johnson: 1521.
Location: composer.
First performance: Jenny Kelly, soprano. Westminster Choir College, 1977.

Convery, Robert. It's All I Have To Bring Today [manuscript].
Composed: 1978.
Setting: high voice, piano.
Johnson: 26.
Location: composer.
First performance: Patricia Saunders, soprano. Westminster Choir College, 1978.

Convery, Robert. Within That Little Hive [manuscript].
Composed: 1978.
Setting: high voice, piano.
Johnson: 1607.
Location: composer.

Convery, Robert. Elysium Is As Far [manuscript].
Composed: 1979.
Setting: high voice, piano.
Johnson: 1760.
Location: composer.
First performance: Mitzie Naff, soprano. Westminster Choir College, 1979.

Convery, Robert. I Have No Life But This [manuscript].
Composed: 1979.
Setting: high voice, piano.
Johnson: 1398.
Location: composer.
First performance: Mitzie Naff, soprano. Westminster Choir College, 1979.

Convery, Robert. My Season's Furthest Flower [manuscript].
Composed: 1979.
Setting: medium voice, piano.
Johnson: 1019.
Location: composer.
First performance: Beverly Johnson, mezzo-soprano. Westminster Choir College, 1979.

Convery, Robert. Partake As Doth The Bee [manuscript].
Composed: 1979.
Setting: medium voice, piano.
Johnson: 994.
Location: composer.
First performance: Beverly Johnson, mezzo-soprano. Westminster Choir College, 1979.

Convery, Robert. They Might Not Need
Me [manuscript].
Composed: 1979.
Setting: high voice, piano.
Johnson: 1391.
Location: composer.
First performance: Mitzie Naff, soprano.
Westminster Choir College, 1979.

Convery, Robert. To Make a Prairie
[manuscript].
Composed: 1979.
Setting: high voice, piano.
Johnson: 1755.
Location: composer.
First performance: Mitzie Naff, soprano.
Westminster Choir College, 1979.

Convery, Robert. What I Can Do, I Will
[manuscript].
Composed: 1979.
Setting: medium voice, piano.
Johnson: 361.
Location: composer.
First performance: Beverly Johnson,
mezzo-soprano. Westminster Choir
College, 1979.

Convery, Robert. Come Slowly, Eden!
[manuscript].
Composed: 1980.
Setting: medium voice.
Johnson: 211.
Location: composer.

Convery, Robert. Heart, We Will Forget
Him [manuscript].
Composed: 1980.
Setting: medium voice, piano.
Johnson: 47.
Location: composer.

Convery, Robert. An Amethyst Re-
membrance. A Song Cycle On
Ten Poems by Emily Dickinson
[manuscript].
Composed: 1982.
Setting: high voice, piano.
Johnson: 19, 111, 245, 341, 434, 536,
659, 1275, 1343, 1377.
Location: composer.
First performance: Judith Pannill, soprano.
The Curtis Institute of Music, 1983.

Convery, Robert. Love's Stricken
"Why" [manuscript].
Composed: 1983.
Setting: medium voice, piano.
Johnson: 1368.
Location: composer.

Convery, Robert. Like Rain It Sounded
[manuscript].
Composed: 1990.
Setting: high voice, piano.
Johnson: 1235.
Location: composer.
"The preceding songs were written with
primary musical consideration given
to the vocal line for musical as well as
literary comprehensibility—that is, a
good tune that does not obscure the
natural inflections of the words.
Therefore the vocal lines were written
first and the piano accompaniments
were derived respectively from the
vocal lines.

Cook, Roger. See "Miscellany" section:
Gould, John A. (arranger). I Like to
See It Lap the Miles.

Aaron Copland

"I began orchestrating the Dickinson songs in 1958.... Only eight of the twelve were suitable.... I didn't finish the orchestration until 1970, just in time for the songs to be premiered for a seventieth birthday concert at the Metropolitan Museum of Art in New York City by the Juilliard Orchestra, Michael Tilson Thomas conducting, Gwendolyn Killebrew as soloist."—Copland and Perlis, *Copland Since 1943*, p. 162.

"It was nice to hear from you after so long a time. Naturally I was interested to know that you had also produced a number of songs based on the poems of dear Emily. (I wonder if you know that I orchestrated 8 of my own settings of 12 of her poems?)" —Aaron Copland, letter of May 10, 1979 to Ernst Bacon (in the collection of Carlton Lowenberg).

Copland, Aaron. Twelve Poems of Emily Dickinson, Set to Music. London; New York: Boosey & Hawkes, Inc. 1951.

Composed: 1949-50.

Setting: high or medium voice, piano.

Johnson: 13, 47, 79, 183, 248, 280, 712, 715, 790, 1080, 1320, 1593.

First performance: Sixth Annual Festival of Contemporary American Music, Columbia University, May 18, 1950.

Selected recordings:

Columbia Records ML 5106, 1956. Martha Lipton, mezzo-soprano; Aaron Copland, piano.

London: Argo, Decca Records, 1967.

CBS Masterworks, 32 11 0017-1108, 1967. Adele Addison, soprano; Aaron Copland, piano.

CBS Masterworks M 30375, 1970.

Musical Heritage Society MHS 4975, 1984.

Copland, Aaron. Eight Poems of Emily Dickinson [arranged by the composer] for Voice and Chamber Orchestra. New York: Boosey & Hawkes, 1981. Miniature score.

Orchestrated: 1958-70.

Setting: high or medium voice, chamber orchestra: flute/piccolo, oboe, 2 clarinets, bassoon, horn, trumpet, trombone, harp, strings.

Johnson: 13, 47, 79, 712, 715, 790, 1320, 1593.

Nos. 1-2, 4-7, 11-12, arranged from his *Twelve Poems.*

First performance: Gwendolyn Killebrew, soprano; Juilliard Orchestra, conducted by Michael Tilson Thomas. Metropolitan Museum of Art, New York City, 1970.

Recording: San Francisco: Reference Recordings, 1986. RR-22CD. Marni Nixon, soprano; Pacific Symphony Orchestra, cond. by Keith Clark.

COPLAND: BIBLIOGRAPHY

Borum, Poul. "Copland's Dickinson." *Det Amerikanske, Glydendal,* 1976: 70-88, 141-143. On Copland's settings, with translation into Danish of *Twelve Poems.*

Cluck, Nancy. "Aaron Copland/Emily Dickinson." *Emily Dickinson Bulletin* 32 (1977) 141-153.

Copland, Aaron and Vivian Perlis. *Copland Since 1943*. New York: St. Martin's Press, 1989. Passim. Of special interest is the evolution of the writing and the performance of the "Dickinson Songs", pages 157-166.

Cowell, Henry. "Copland's Twelve Poems of Emily Dickinson." *The Musical Quarterly*, 36 (July, 1950) 453.

Daugherty, Robert Michael. "An Analysis of Aaron Copland's 'Twelve Poems of Emily Dickinson.'" Ph.D. Dissertation. Ohio State University, 1980.

Didriksen, Helen. "Strange Company: Aaron Copland, Emily Dickinson, and America at Mid-Century." Master's Thesis, New York University, May, 1988.

Fine, Irving. "Twelve Poems of Emily Dickinson." *Notes* 11 (December 1953) 159-160.

Flanagan, William. "American Songs: a Thin Crop." *Musical America* 72/3 (February, 1952) 23, 130. A short discussion of Copland's "Twelve Poems of Emily Dickinson."

Kolodin, Irving. "Music in My Ears: I Cannot Sing the New Songs." *Saturday Review* 33 (1950) 27.

Locke, R. P. "Aaron Copland's 'Twelve Poems of Emily Dickinson.'" B.A. Honor Thesis in Music, Harvard University, 1970. "Currently being extended by the author into a series of articles on Dickinson settings by several composers."—letter of April 12, 1990.

Mabry, Sharon. "Twelve Poems of Emily Dickinson by Aaron Copland." Ph.D. Dissertation, George Peabody College for Teachers, 1977.

McDonagh, Don. *Martha Graham: A Biography*. New York: Praeger, 1973. See pp. 146-149.

Mann, William. "Twelve Poems of Emily Dickinson." *Music Review* 14/3 (August, 1953) 249-250.

Skowronsky, Joann. *Aaron Copland: a Bio-Bibliography*. Westport, CT.: Greenwood Press, 1985.

Smith, Cecil. "League of Composers Program Celebrates Copland's Birthday." *Musical America* 70/14 (December 1, 1950) 18.

Wager, Inez. "Emily Dickinson's Poems in Musical Settings." *Dickinson Studies* 49 (June 1984) 32-37.

Willison, Ann. "Composer As Interpreter: Musical Settings of the Poems of Emily Dickinson." Seminar Paper, Department of Comparative Literature, Indiana University, 1990. Compares Copland's settings with those of Ernst Bacon, Gordon Getty, and George Perle.

Young, Douglas. "Copland's Dickinson Songs." *Tempo* 103 (1972) 33-37.

Coulthard, Jean. Five Love Songs for Baritone [manuscript].
Commissioned: Bernard Diamant.
Composed: 1955.
Setting: baritone, piano.
Duration: 10:00.
Johnson: 245, 549, 644, 903, 1080.
Location: composer.
First performance: Bernard Diamant, baritone; John Newmark, piano. Canadian Broadcast Corp. National, Montréal, 1955.

"The sensitive poignancy of her writing had appealed to me greatly, as well as the clarity of her thought. The 'Set of Five' were performed first by Mr. Diamant who had a lyric-type baritone voice. Since then they've had various performances in Canada both for baritone and medium voice, and also in England. I tried in my settings to catch the sensitivity of her moods rather than thinking too technically."—letter of February 12, 1990.

Coulthard, Jean. Songs from the Distaff Muse. Set 1 [manuscript].

Composed: 1972.

Setting: soprano and contralto soloists, violoncello.

Duration: 20:00.

Johnson: 1118.

Location: composer.

First performance: Mona Mari, soprano; Kathline Hearn, contralto; Ian Hampton, cellist. Canadian Broadcasting Corp., Vancouver, 1974.

"I wrote these sets of Duets during the early seventies for the well-known duettists Mona Mari and Kathline Hearn. In the first set Ian Hampton was the cellist. All the musicians are well-known Canadians."—letter of May, 1991.

Croft, William. St. Anne. See "Miscellany" section: Gould, John A., arr. I Took My Power In My Hand.

Croft, William. St. Matthew. See "Miscellany" section: Jones, J., arr. A Garland for Emily.

Dal Porto, Mark. Five Pieces for A Cappella Choir [manuscript].

Composed: 1987.

Setting: SATB chorus.

Duration: 10:00.

Johnson: 198, 232, 668, 790, 1465.

Location: composer.

First performance: Southwest Texas State University Chorale, April 16, 1989.

"The five poems that I selected are unified in thought and content with 'nature' being their prevalent theme. Emily Dickinson's writing style is of a highly personal nature, evocative, subtle, unpretentious, and thus inspired me to create a musical setting of five of her poems dealing with the theme of 'nature.' The music is set in a highly lyrical, freely tonal, post-romantic style."—letters of November 21 and December 18, 1989.

Davis, Billy. See "Miscellany" section. Gould, John A., arr. I Like to See It Lap the Miles.

Davis, Sharon. Three Moods of Emily Dickinson. Opus 4. Los Angeles: Western International Music, 1981.

Composed: 1976.

Setting: soprano, piano, violin, violoncello.

Duration: 8:11.

Johnson: 249, 258, 288.

First performance: Los Angeles County Broadcast, February 1, 1976.

Recording: WIM Records WIMR 23. Delcina Stevenson, soprano; Sharon Davis, piano; Clayton Haslop, violin; Douglas Davis, cello.

"My prime reason for choosing Emily Dickinson's work for this composition was the need of a direct channel of expression from a woman writer to a woman singer. I chose these particular poems because of their contrasting character and stark change of mood overall—hence the title; these 'moods' may indeed represent the poet's alteregos."—letter of August 13, 1989.

Dawson, Sarah. Divinity Dwells Under Seal. A Five-Part Song Cycle [manuscript].
Composed: 1991.
Setting: soprano, chamber orchestra.
Johnson: 404, 516, 517, 662, 1099.
Duration: 18:00.
First performance: Tracy Bidleman, soprano; Bay Area Women's Philharmonic, Nan Washburn, director. Mills College, Oakland, CA, November 21, 1991.

DeFilippi, Amedeo. Once a Child [manuscript].
Composed: 1950s.
Setting: SSA chorus, piano.
Johnson: 166, 375, 600, 1185.
Location: New York Public Library.

Diaconoff, Ted. Songs of Transition and Passage [manuscript].
Commissioned: Peggy Eggers for her Master's Degree recital, Southern Illinois University, December, 1986.
Composed: 1986.
Setting: soprano, string quartet.
Johnson: 249, 279, 288, 1052, 1065, 1732.
Location: composer.
First performance: Southern Illinois University, December, 1986.
"As a composer I respond to the intensity of Emily Dickinson's poetry. I react musically to her communication of inward states of the mind and soul. She frequently uses imagery of journey or passage, and to me this suggests musical development. Often when I read her poetry, musical ideas come to mind with little effort on my part."—letter of May 9, 1990.

Diaconoff, Ted. Two Poems of Death [manuscript].
Composed: 1991.
Setting: soprano, piano, viola.

Duration: 4:30.
Johnson: 258, 1078.
Location: composer.

Dickinson, Clarence. Six Songs Addressed to Mrs. Proctor Smith. Chicago: Samuel Merwin, 1897.
Composed: 1897.
Setting: high voice or mezzo-soprano, piano.
Johnson: 136, 192, 208, 214, 794, 1761.
Reprint, as *Six Emily Dickinson Songs, for High Voice*: Huntsville, TX: Recital Publications, [198-].

Dickinson, Peter. Winter Afternoons. Sevenoaks, Kent: Novello, 1974.
Setting: 2 countertenors, tenor, 2 baritones, bass, bassoon.
Johnson: 98, 258, 524.
Recordings:
EMI EMD 5521, The King's Singers.
Moss Music Group MMG-1142, 1975. The King's Singers.
Aves INT 161.513, 1975.

Diemer, Emma Lou. Three Poems of Emily Dickinson [manuscript].
Composed: 1983.
Setting: voice, electronic tape.
Johnson: 24, 1593, 1672.
Location: composer.
First performance: (of No. 1672) Contemporary Music Festival, University of California at Santa Barbara, 1983.
"I have not written art songs using her poetry (though I have used many other poets' works, and am a great admirer of her work), but did use three poems as inspiration for a set of electronic pieces called 'Three Poems of Emily Dickinson' (for tape). These were done in 1983 in quad[raphonic sound], using synthesizer and computer. The middle

movement was used on one of the Contemporary Music Festivals at Cal Arts and the whole set elsewhere. I, like so many others, have been struck by the uniqueness of her poetry: its conciseness and depth, and the imagery that invites musical interpretation."
—letters of January 3 and February 7, 1990.

Diemer, Emma Lou. There Is a Morn By Us Unseen [manuscript].
Composed: 1991.
Setting: SATB chorus, orchestra; SATB chorus, piano.
Johnson: 24.
Location: composer.

Dinerstein, Norman. Four Settings for Soprano and String Quartet, on Texts of Emily Dickinson. New York: Independent Music Publishers, [196-?].
Setting: soprano, string quartet.
Duration: 13:00
Johnson: 449, 465, 1078, 1624.

Dougherty, Celius. Beauty Is Not Caused. New York: Associated Music Publishers, 1948.
Composed: 1948.
Setting: mezzo-soprano, piano.
Johnson: 516.
Dedicated to Eva Gauthier.

Dougherty, Celius. New England Pastoral. New York: Boosey & Hawkes, 1949.
Composed: 1949.
Setting: medium voice, piano.
Johnson: 413.
Setting: medium voice, piano.
Also published in his *Three Songs*. New York: Boosey & Hawkes, 1949.

Dowd, John A. Two Songs of Death, on Poems of Emily Dickinson. New York: Joseph Patelson Music House, 1964.
Composed: 1964.
Setting: soprano or mezzo-soprano, piano.
Johnson: 363, 1078.
First performance: Anna May Crowder, soprano; John A. Dowd, piano. Seeger Hall, Milligan College.
"[I chose] Emily Dickinson because I felt an affinity for her poetry. Also, the meaning of both poems expresses something that represents a personal tragedy in [my] own life. Technically, the poetry expresses a very highly charged emotion in the most economical way. In music this is possible, to express in a style that is neo-romantic, almost folk-like, and yet avoids overstatement."—letter of February 27, 1990.

Duke, John Woods. Six Poems by Emily Dickinson. San Antonio, TX: Southern Music Publishing, 1978.
Composed: 1978.
Setting: mezzo-soprano, piano.
Johnson: 35, 47, 198, 425, 1035, 1065.
Recording: Cambridge CRS 2776.

Duke, John Woods. Four Poems by Emily Dickinson. San Antonio, TX: Southern Music Publishing, 1979.
Composed: 1975.
Setting: mezzo-soprano, piano.
Johnson: 99, 136, 208, 214.
Recording: Cambridge CRS 2776.

Eckert, Michael. Sea-Changes. New York: American Composers Edition, 1977.
Composed: 1977.

Setting: mezzo-soprano, chamber ensemble (twelve instruments).
Johnson: 76.

Eckert, Michael. Three Poems of Emily Dickinson. American Composers Edition, 1981.
Composed: 1980–81.
Setting: soprano, chamber ensemble.
Johnson: 115, 665, 949.

Escher, Rudolf. Songs of Love and Eternity. Amsterdam: Donemus, 1956.
Composed: 1956.
Setting: SATB chorus, or SA soloists and chamber choir.
Johnson: 47, 130, 214, 249, 436, 1755.
First performance: Netherlands Chamber Choir, Hans van den Hombergh, conductor. Program notes by Roland de Beer, 1980.
Recording: Ciel, air et vents. Amsterdam: Composer's Voice CU 8104, 1980.

Arthur Farwell

"Arthur Farwell composed 116 works in various genres. Included in this prolific output were 124 art songs. Of the art songs, thirty-nine were composed for forty Emily Dickinson poems. No other poets' works were so favored. Her short almost staccato lines fell readily into melodic phrases, her vivid descriptive words stimulated a harmonic response, and her underlying metrics were easily captured in musical rhythms.

"Farwell thought Dickinson's daring use of unusual expressions was not only fascinating but very important. '[She reveals] to us in new colors and new relations the beauty of the visible universe, and then, by this exhaustless and compounded symbolism, [brings] us home to the awe and wonder of the boundless universe, which our spiritual selves inhabit.'

"Farwell set music to several of Dickinson's poems which tell a brief story. 'Unto me?' [964] is an example. He develops the dialogue between Jesus and a sinner. A warm serene melodic line in a high tessitura carries Jesus' offer of His salvation. The humble sinner's weak and hesitant response is emphasized by short melodic phrases mostly in minor seconds, always sung on lower pitches, punctuated by frequent rests. As each [character] responds with his individual pitch lines and style, both seem better delineated in music than in words.

"Farwell had much humor. He enjoyed Dickinson's poking fun at tradition and her delight in tasteful satire. Consider his setting of 'I'm Nobody! Who Are You?' He notes Dickinson's conversational approach by setting sprightly short musical phrases in very simple style. 'How dreary—to be—Somebody!' is set in short phrases, sounds which are similar to a bored 'ho-hum' sigh in the piano. 'How public—like a Frog' draws a croaking figure in the bass accompaniment all the way to an added two-measure close.

"Most interesting is Farwell's treatment of 'Tie the Strings to my Life, My Lord.' A galloping piano accompaniment sparkles with happy anticipation for the journey into life after death. He builds an exciting musical climax for 'Then—I am ready to go!' The music affirms the poet's belief in life after death. His setting for 'Presentiment is that long Shadow on the Lawn' projects musically the poet's broader view of a daily occurrence. The piano opens the song with an ominous slow soft tread of solo octaves in the bass which climb chromatically. Treble clef chords continue to rise similarly until the voice enters. The voice sings without piano in somber recitative style on a repeated G. This phrase begins slowly on sixteenth notes and stretches out rhythmically to a half note, creating musically a long shadow on the lawn.

"'Suns go down' is pictured by an octave drop in the voice and imitated in the piano, which adds accented dropped sixths in a short interlude to emphasize the rhythm and words of the text. The foreboding mood continues with notes repeated on F in the voice, and another octave drop on 'Darkness' to a low B. [Farwell] uses a suspended chord on 'is about' before allowing the melody to 'pass' to a resolved C-minor chord. Then he adds a very soft A-flat-seventh chord in the treble clef which suggests that the matter of 'Presentiment' isn't settled after all."—Evelyn Davis Culbertson. "Arthur Farwell and Emily Dickinson." Manuscript, April, 1989.

"From the list of all the music Dad wrote over half a century, he once told me late in his life that his work with Emily Dickinson's poems possibly came nearest of the whole life work to expressing the music and spirit of his main statement to the world. I paraphrase—but he found a tremendous communication of spirit in her voice." —letter from Brice Farwell, December 6, 1988.

Farwell, Arthur. Sea of Sunset. Opus 26. New York: G. Schirmer, 1926, 1928.
Composed: 1907.
Setting: medium voice, piano.
Johnson: 266.
Farwell's first setting of an Emily Dickinson poem. See Brice Farwell. *A Guide to the Music of Arthur Farwell*, 10:37.

Farwell, Arthur. Two Poems by Emily Dickinson. Opus 66. New York: G. Schirmer, 1926.
No. 1, "I Shall Know Why." No. 2, "Resurgam."
Composed: 1923.
Setting: mezzo-soprano, piano.
Johnson: 174, 193.
See B. Farwell, *Guide*, 15:92.

Farwell, Arthur. Three Emily Dickinson Poems. Opus 73. New York: G. Schirmer, 1928.
No. 1, "Summer Shower." No. 2, "Mine." No. 3, "The Sea of Sunset. "
Composed: 1926.
Setting: high or medium voice, piano.
Johnson: 266, 528, 794.
See B. Farwell, *Guide*, 16:99.

Farwell, Arthur. Four Emily Dickinson Songs. Opus 101 [manuscript].
Composed: 1936.
Setting: voice, piano.
Johnson: 217, 425, 695, 964.
Location: Evelyn D. Culbertson, Arthur Farwell Archive, 7106 E. 53d Place, Tulsa, OK 74145.
See B. Farwell, *Guide*, 19:134.

Arthur Farwell. "Heart, We Will Forget Him," from *Thirty-Four Songs on Poems of Emily Dickinson*. New York: Boosey & Hawkes, ©1983. Reprinted by permission of Boosey & Hawkes, Inc. and Brice Farwell.

Farwell, Arthur. Twelve Emily Dickinson Songs. Opus 105 [manuscript].
Composed: 1938-41.
Setting: voice, piano.
Johnson: 64, 214, 216, 318, 324, 573, 758, 764, 916, 1052, 1224, 1627.
Location: Culbertson, Farwell Archive.
See B. Farwell, *Guide*, 19-20:137.

Farwell, Arthur. Four Emily Dickinson Songs. Opus 107 [manuscript].
Composed: 1941-44.
Setting: voice, piano.
Johnson: 4, 194, 228, 279.
Location: Culbertson, Farwell Archive.
See B. Farwell, *Guide*, 20:144.

Farwell, Arthur. Ten Emily Dickinson Songs. Opus 108 [manuscript].
Composed: 1944.
Setting: voice, piano.
Johnson: 19, 47, 61, 81, 288, 413, 665, 829, 1210, 1685.
Location: Culbertson, Farwell Archive.
First performance: Opus 108, Nos. 1, 4, 8. Senior Recital by Winifred Black. State University of New York at Buffalo. April 5, 1974.
See B. Farwell, *Guide*, 20:147.

Farwell, Arthur. These Saw Vision. Opus 105, No. 4. New York: Galaxy Music, 1944.
Composed: 1941.
Setting: voice, piano.
Johnson: 758.
See B. Farwell, *Guide*, 20:137. Dickinson line is "These—saw Visions."

Farwell, Arthur. Three Emily Dickinson Songs. Opus 112 [manuscript].
Composed: 1949.
Setting: voice, piano.
Johnson: 198, 249, 333.
Location: Culbertson, Farwell Archive.
See B. Farwell, *Guide*, 22:159.

Farwell, Arthur. I Had No Time To Hate [manuscript].
Composed: 1949.
Setting: voice, piano.
Johnson: 478.
Location: Culbertson, Farwell Archive.
See B. Farwell, *Guide*, 23:160.

Farwell, Arthur. Thirty-Four Songs on Poems of Emily Dickinson. New York: Boosey & Hawkes, 1983.
Setting: high or medium voice, piano.
Johnson: Vol. 1: 64, 214, 216, 217, 318, 324, 425, 573, 695, 758, 764, 903, 964, 1052, 1224, 1627. Vol. 2: 4, 19, 47, 61, 81, 194, 198, 228, 249, 279, 288, 333, 413, 478, 665, 829, 1210, 1685.
Introductory note by Paul Sperry.
Vol. 1, Opus 101; vol. 2, Op. 105, 107, 108, 111.

FARWELL: PERFORMANCES

Farwell, Arthur. Opus 105, No. 2, 7, 9, 10. Opus 108, No. 2, 7. Opus 112, No. 2. Paul Sperry, tenor. Martin Katz, piano. Amherst Song Festival, Amherst College, Amherst, MA. July 29, 1975.
Johnson: 64, 216, 333, 829, 1224, 1627, 1685.
"At the time Paul Sperry first sang his recital at Amherst, Marty Kortz remarked about the piano on 'The Level Bee' [1224] that the buzzing (à la 'Flight of the Bumble Bee') differs from that in that there is no repeated pattern in the play of those notes— they go on in endless variation throughout the measures of the song. Difficult to master, but very effective in support of the vocal line.

"Some of the eight or nine poems selected were also included in 'The

Belle of Amherst,' though there is no known acquaintance between Dad and the playwright William Luce." —letter from Brice Farwell, November 11, 1989.

Farwell, Arthur. (Premiere.) Opus 101, No. 2, 3. Opus 105, No. 12. Opus 107, No. 2. Opus 108, No. 9. David Barron, baritone. Neely Bruce, piano. WQXR Broadcast, "The Listening Room." New York: April 16, 1975.
Johnson: 61, 279, 695, 764, 964.

FARWELL: BIBLIOGRAPHY

Culbertson, Evelyn Davis. "Arthur Farwell and Emily Dickinson." [manuscript]. Tulsa, OK: Culbertson, 1989.

Farwell, Arthur. "Emily Dickinson" [manuscript.] No date. 6 pp.
"The essay is a personal and idealistic expression of how Arthur Farwell felt about Emily Dickinson's poems and about her unique sensibilities. Brice Farwell suggests that his father's writing manner was carried down from the romantic era in which his style was first formed. "He certainly was not a writer for the late 20th-century reader— —browbeaten as we are by journalistic 'sound bites.'"—letter from Brice Farwell, December 30, 1989.

Farwell, Brice, ed. A Guide to the Music of Arthur Farwell and to the Microfilm Collection of His Work, Prepared by his Children. Briarcliff Manor, NY: Brice Farwell for the estate of Arthur Farwell, 1972.
Available from Brice Farwell, 290 West Nevada, Ashland, OR 97520.
Emily Dickinson: pp. 2, 10, 15, 16, 19, 20, 22, 23, 62, 116, 117, 118.

Moeller, Vernon H. "Theoretical Aspects of Arthur Farwell's Musical Settings of Poems by Emily Dickinson." M.A. Thesis, Austin, TX: University of Texas, 1979.

Faulconer, Bruce L. **Five Poems of Emily Dickinson.** Dallas, TX: Faulconer Productions, 1978.
Composed: 1976.
Setting: soprano, piano.
Johnson: 1229, 1290, 1292, 1367, 1368.
First performance: Voices of Change, Dallas, TX, February 8, 1979.

Ferris, William. **Indian Summer.** New York: Oxford University Press, 1979.
Composed: 1979.
Setting: SATB chorus, piano.
Johnson: 130.

Fine, Vivian. **The Riddle.** Shaftsbury, VT: Catamount Facsimile Editions, 1981.
Composed: 1933.
Setting: voice, piano.
Johnson: 50.

Fine, Vivian. **The Women in the Garden.** Chamber Opera. Shaftsbury, VT: Catamount Facsimile Editions, 1977.
Composed: 1977.
Setting: dramatic soprano, lyric soprano, mezzo-soprano, dark mezzo-soprano, or contralto; flute, clarinet, bassoon, percussion (2 players), piano, viola, violoncello, contrabass.
Johnson: 615, 636, 650, 1008, 1242, 1273.

Fine, Vivian. **Emily's Images.** Shaftsbury, VT: Catamount Facsimile Editions, 1987.
Composed: 1987.
Setting: flute, piano.
Johnson: 42, 76, 287, 341, 987, 1138, 1483.

Foreman, Burton V. Three Emily Dickinson Poems [manuscript].
Composed: 1990.
Setting: soprano, piano.
Johnson: 697, 739, 1740.
Location: composer.
"[No. 697] struck me for its exotic qualities, thus the sometimes somewhat abrupt harmonic changes. I have tried [in No. 739] to capture through the sostenuti the sad, dreamlike quality of helplessness on a vast sea with intermittent flickerings of hope. [No. 1740 is] a child's delightful afternoon in the woods, interrupted by the reality of life."—letter of May 26, 1990.

Fornuto, Donato D. Four Songs on Poems of Emily Dickinson. Del Ray Beach, FL: Accentuate Music, 1984.
Composed: 1980-81.
Setting: baritone, piano.
Johnson: 214, 258, 1075, 1593.
Location: composer. (Accentuate Music is out of business.)
First performance: Richard Frisch, baritone; Donato Fornuto, piano. New York Singing Teachers Association, Donnell Library Center, New York City, April 25, 1981.
Reviewed by Walter Martin in the *NATS Bulletin*, v.42/4 (March/April 1986).

Fortner, Jack. Emily Dickinson [manuscript].
Composed: 1976-82.
Setting: female voice, piano.
Johnson: 219, 824, 1624.
Location: composer.
First performance: Phyllis Perry Fortner, soprano; Sally Christian, piano. CSUF Music Recital Hall, California State University, Fresno, May 14, 1985.
"The voice and piano parts are quite independent of each other and the placement of events in the score is only an approximate representation of what should occur. Exact coordination of ensemble is rarely intended; thus it is sufficient that the performers are generally in the same part of the page throughout the three songs. There are very few dynamics written for the voice. The poetry should inspire the singer to discover the expressive dynamics for these words. Subtlety of shading is very important for the proper effect of these songs.
" 'Apparently with no Surprise,' the first of the cycle, was written for the senior recital of Shirley Grace (Miss Fresno of 1975). It was composed in the fall of 1976. The two companion songs were written much later, in the summer and fall of 1982. Shirley was a student in my fourth-semester theory class and turned in as one of the projects an extraordinary pictorial graph of Stravinsky's *Petrouchka*. I coveted the graph and she agreed to part with it if I would set a Dickinson poem for her recital. Apropos, the song contains two quotations from *Petrouchka* imbedded in its texture.
" 'The Wind began to knead the grass' and 'She sweeps with many-colored Brooms' were composed to complete a cycle of nature images and to explore more fully the initial musical material."—letters of April 4 and April 9, 1990.

Franchetti, Arnold. Aria Variata for Contralto and Orchestra on Poetry of Emily Dickinson [manuscript].
Composed: 1957.
Setting: contralto, orchestra.
Johnson: 425, 603, 1335, 1398, 1713.
Location: Newberry Library, Chicago (microfilm).

Freed, Isadore. Chartless. Boston: Carl Fischer, 1946.
Composed: 1946.
Setting: medium voice and piano.
Johnson: 1052.

Fuchs, Kenneth. And God Cannot Be Found [manuscript].
Composed: 1983.
Setting: soprano, string quartet.
Johnson: 50, 1053, 1065, 1551, 1577.
Location: composer; American Music Center.

Fuchs, Kenneth. Three Poems of Emily Dickinson [manuscript].
Composed: 1985.
Setting: medium voice, piano.
Johnson: 1065, 1141, 1680.
Location: composer.
First performance: Juilliard School of Music, November 11, 1985.
"I am attracted to Emily Dickinson's use of resonant and evocative words, which form profound observations about eternity, love, existence, nature, and death. For me, her highly distilled observations and striking metaphors are immediately transcribable into the abstract language of music."—letter of July 13, 1989.

Galante, Carlo.
"Perhaps you are interested to know that there is a young composer in Italy who has done music upon the poems of Emily Dickinson."—letter of October 2, 1989 from Niccolò Castiglioni. [I have not been able to get a response from Carlo Galante—C.L.]

Gardiner, William. "Dedham." See "Miscellany" section. Jones, Joseph (arr.) A Garland for Emily.

Gettel, William. I Taste a Liquor Never Brewed. New York: Carl Fischer, [n.d.].
Johnson: 214.

Getty, Gordon P. The White Election: A Song Cycle for Soprano and Piano on 32 Poems of Emily Dickinson. Bryn Mawr, PA: Rork Music, 1986.
Composed: 1982; revised, June 1983.
Setting: soprano, piano.
Duration: ca. 1 hour.
Johnson: 23, 24, 44, 99, 144, 205, 214, 303, 322, 410, 510, 574, 584, 585, 588, 589, 596, 640, 850 (major), 850 (minor), 861, 1104, 1147, 1172, 1410, 1549, 1593, 1600, 1603, 1654, 1664, 1743.
Location: composer; The Jones Library, Amherst.
First performance: Martha Ellison, soprano; Wendy Glaubitz, piano. Library of Congress, Washington, D.C., April 22, 1982.
Recording: Chatsworth, CA: Delos International, 1988. C/CD 3057.
Part 1: "The Pensive Spring." Part 2, "So We Must Meet Apart." Part 3, "Almost Peace." Part 4, "My Feet Slip Nearer."
Variant title: *The White Election: A Cycle of 32 Songs for Soprano and Piano, Set to Poems of Emily Dickinson.* (Revised 6/83).

Gibas, Barbara. Five Poems by Emily Dickinson [manuscript].
Commissioned: First Universalist Church of Minneapolis, 1985-86.

Composed: 1985-86.

Setting: SATB a cappella, or SATB, piano.

Johnson: 10, 41, 157, 1116, 1147.

Location: composer.

First performance: First Universalist Church of Minneapolis, February, 1986.

"I love both Emily Dickinson's sentiments and elegant use of words, so she was a natural choice for me when the Universalist Church commissioned me to write some choral works using poetry of my choice.

"'Who robbed' and 'My Wheel' were to be very simple settings that a small choir without a great deal of musical background could learn in an hour's rehearsal. 'Who robbed' is the simpler setting—an Adagio with a certain amount of unison singing which periodically breaks into four-part harmony. Dissonances are created when two voices are an octave apart and one voice then moves up or down a step.

"'My Wheel' is an Allegretto with a few syncopations—though these are mostly in the piano part. For the most part, the soprano and alto lines are identical, likewise with the tenor and bass, although 4-part harmonies appear at cadences.

"'Another Loneliness' is an Adagio with F-minor tonality, except the 5th tone of the scale is frequently a C flat, giving an even more melancholy quality to the piece. With the words 'whoso it befalls is richer than can be divulged' comes movement toward major tonality, but the piece winds down again to F minor. With the three top voices singing an F, the bass sings 'numeral' on E flat, G flat, E flat.

"'After a hundred years' begins with each succeeding voice coming in a little later until the full choir is singing.

Fourths play an important part both harmonically and melodically. 'Musicians' has a Phrygian quality, being predominantly in D Minor but with an E flat for the second scale tone. There are frequent changes of meter, including 5/8 and 7/8 as well as 3/4 and 4/4."
—letter of March 19, 1990.

Gibson, Paul F. He Fumbles at Your Spirit [manuscript]. Composed: 1988.

Setting: SATB a cappella.

Johnson: 315.

Location: composer.

First performance: New York Singers Collective, St. Anthony of Padua Church, New York, May 7, 1989.

"A private recording (Dominic MacAller, conductor, Mount Saint Mary's College, Los Angeles, November 16, 1988) was the original impetus for my setting. A singer friend loaned me a copy of Dickinson's collected poems when I began looking for a text. This text, 'He fumbles at your Spirit,' jumped off the page with its power. I couldn't not set it.

"Before setting a text, I usually spend a lot of time with it, often memorizing it so I have it with me constantly. At some point, I mistakenly altered one word, which I didn't catch until the recording session. I decided to leave it as I composed it, because of the vowel sound that came right at the musical climax of the piece. Therefore E.D.'s line 'Your breath has time to straighten, your brain to bubble cool' has become in my setting, 'Your breath has time to straighten, your mind to bubble cool.' I hope purists will forgive me, especially when they hear my short piece."—letter of January, 1990.

Gerald Ginsburg

"I love to set Dickinson because her poetry is the richest possible in imagery to spur the imagination of a composer and singer. She has written on every topic and her lines are pure music. Unfortunately, many singers fail to make the attempt to understand her riches. They tend to be very literal and so not grasp her unique way of expression. They will get bogged down on a line like 'Soundless as dots—on a Disc of Snow.' What can I say to them? Many young singers today lack a knowledge of poetry as a result of poor education in our schools. They can all respond, however, to a poem like 'Ample Make This Bed,' especially when I tell them it was included in the movie (and book) 'Sophie's Choice.'"—letter of December 18, 1989.

Ginsburg, Gerald. Colors; Three Poems by Emily Dickinson [manuscript].
Composed: 1974.
Setting: soprano and piano (Nos. 1 and 2); soprano, mezzo-soprano, and piano (No. 3).
Johnson: 219, 1045, 1556.
Location: composer.
First performance: Berenice Bramson, soprano; with Rose Taylor, mezzo-soprano, in No. 3. Carnegie Recital Hall, New York, February 13, 1974.
"'Colors' is a cycle made up of poems by various poets (W. C. Williams, Elinor Wylie, Millay, Richard Wilbur, Wilfred Owen, and Dickinson). There are eight songs in the cycle. Nos. 1, 2, and 8 are by Dickinson. The songs are divided between soprano and mezzo-soprano with three duets. As the title implies, each poem deals with a different color."—letter of December 30, 1989.

Ginsburg, Gerald. He Touched Me. Good Morning, Midnight. Two Poems by Emily Dickinson [manuscript].
Composed: 1977.
Setting: mezzo-soprano, piano.
Johnson: 425, 506.
Location: composer.
First performance: Rose Taylor, mezzo-soprano. Alice Tully Hall, New York City, January 10, 1977.

Ginsburg, Gerald. I Cannot Live with You [manuscript].
Composed: 1977.
Setting: soprano, piano.
Johnson: 640.
Location: composer.
First performance: Mary Beth Peil, soprano. Alice Tully Hall, New York City, January 10, 1977.

Ginsburg, Gerald. To Make a Prairie. The Moon. Two Poems by Emily Dickinson [manuscript].
Composed: 1977.
Setting: children's chorus a cappella (No. 1); children's chorus, piano (No. 2).
Johnson: 737, 1755.
Location: composer.
First performance: Alice Tully Hall, New York City, January 10, 1977.

Ginsburg, Gerald. Ample Make This Bed [manuscript].
Composed: 1984.
Setting: high voice, piano.
Johnson: 829.
Location: composer.

"No official premiere, but one of my most frequently performed songs."
—letter of December 18, 1989.

Ginsburg, Gerald. Will There Really Be a Morning? [manuscript].
Composed: 1984.
Setting: soprano, piano.
Johnson: 101.
Location: composer.
"No official premiere, but often performed."—letter of December 18, 1989.

Ginsburg, Gerald. An Amethyst Remembrance. Three Poems by Emily Dickinson [manuscript].
Composed: 1986.
Setting: mezzo-soprano, piano.
Johnson: 216, 219, 245.
Location: composer.
"I have set No. 219 ('She Sweeps') twice in totally different settings. So, 219 in 'An Amethyst Remembrance' was also composed in 1986 (along with 216 and 245)."—letter of December 30, 1989.
"Referring again to 'Alabaster Chambers' [216], I was so in awe of this great poem that for a long time I was afraid to set it, until I realized one day that it's just a New England hymn, the kind of music Dickinson knew so well. After that, the setting came easily."
—letter of December 18, 1989.

Ginsburg, Gerald. All I Have To Bring. A Cycle for Soprano and Piano [Manuscript].
Composed: 1991.
Setting: soprano, piano.
Johnson: 18, 26, 214, 216, 219, 1052.
Location: composer.

Glazer, C. G. "Azmon." See "Miscellany" section. Jones, Joseph (arr.) A Garland for Emily.

Glickman, Sylvia. After Great Pain, a Formal Feeling Comes. Bryn Mawr, PA: Hildegard Publishing, 1970.
Composed: 1970.
Setting: soprano, piano.
Johnson: 341.
See note under "From Cocoon Forth," below. Reprinted in Glickman's *Emily Dickinson Songs*, Bryn Mawr, PA: Hildegard Publishing, 1991.

Glickman, Sylvia. Black Cake. Bryn Mawr, PA: Hildegard Publishing, 1970.
Composed: 1970.
Setting: soprano, piano.
Johnson Letters: 835, 835a.

Glickman, Sylvia. It Will Be Summer—Eventually. Bryn Mawr, PA: Hildegard Publishing, 1970.
Composed: 1970.
Setting: soprano, piano.
Johnson: 342.
See note under "From Cocoon Forth," below. Reprinted in Glickman's *Emily Dickinson Songs*, Bryn Mawr, PA: Hildegard Publishing, 1991.

Glickman, Sylvia. From Cocoon Forth a Butterfly. Bryn Mawr, PA: Hildegard Publishing, 1989.
Composed: 1989.
Setting: soprano, piano.
Johnson: 354.
"[Nos. 341 and 342] were premiered in Philadelphia in the late '70s and have been sung elsewhere on the East coast, on the West coast, and in London at the Guild Hall. 'Black Cake' was premiered at Haverford College, PA, also in the late '70s. [No. 354] will be premiered this season in Philadelphia, along with repeat performances of the others."—letter of July 18, 1989.

Reprinted in Glickman's *Emily Dickinson Songs*, Bryn Mawr, PA: Hildegard Publishing, 1991.

Glickman, Sylvia. Emily Dickinson Songs. Bryn Mawr, PA: Hildegard Publishing, 1991.
Johnson: 341, 342, 354.
See her "It Will Be Summer," "After Great Pain," and "From Cocoon Forth," above.

Gold, Ernest. Songs of Love and Parting. New York: G. Schirmer, 1963.
Commissioned (second version): Orchestra Society of La Jolla, California.
Composed: 1961-62.
Setting: high or medium voice, piano. Second version arranged for high voice and chamber orchestra.
Duration: 20:44
Johnson: 739, 1732.
Recording: Marni Nixon, soprano. Vienna Volksoper Orchestra; Ernest Gold, director. Crystal Records, Crystal S501, 1974.
"In 'Songs of Love and Parting' I attempted to express the basic human experience of finding love and losing the loved one. In order to peel away all but the archetypal essence of that universal experience I chose texts of diversity. I wanted to stress the universal humanity of the ubiquitous experience. It is immaterial if the work is sung by a woman or a man. The cycle has been widely performed here and in Europe."—letter of June 30, 1989.
The two settings were also published separately by Schirmer. Reprinted in *20th-Century Art Songs*. New York: G. Schirmer, 1967.

Golub, Peter. Three Songs. New York: American Composers Edition, 1977.
Setting: soprano, flute, harp.
Johnson: 249.

Gould, John A. See under "Miscellany."

Grantham, Donald. Seven Choral Settings of Poems by Emily Dickinson. Boston: E. C. Schirmer, 1983.
Composed: 1983.
Setting: SATB chorus.
Johnson: 125, 217, 441, 670, 1138, 1275, 1330.
Recording: University of Texas Chamber Singers, conducted by Morris J. Beachy. Composers Recordings, Inc. CRI SD 458, 1983.

Green, Ray. Three Choral Songs. New York: American Music Edition, 1954.
Composed: 1954.
Setting: SSA chorus.
Johnson: 533, 1211, 1591.

Green, Ray. Concluded Lives. New York: American Music Edition, 1962.
Composed: 1962.
Setting: medium or low voice, piano.
Johnson: 735.

Greenaway, Roger. See "Miscellany" section: Gould, John A. (arranger). I Like to See It Lap the Miles.

Grier, Lita. I Cannot Live with You [manuscript].
Composed: 1961.
Setting: soprano, piano.
Johnson: 640.
Location: composer.

Grier, Lita. I Taste a Liquor Never Brewed [manuscript].
Composed: 1961.
Setting: soprano, piano.
Johnson: 214.

Location: composer.
"I felt drawn to the poems of Emily Dickinson for simplicity and power—and, of course, because I identified with those I chose to set to music."—letter of October 10, 1989.

Guzman i Antich, Josep Lluis. Dos poemas d'Emily Dickinson. Madrid: Fundacion Juan March, 1984.
Composed: 1983.
Setting: mezzo-soprano, flute, clarinet, bassoon, horn, piano, 2 violins, viola, violoncello, contrabass.
Johnson: 1065.
Location: New York Public Library.
Spanish words translated from the English by Maria Manent.

Hageman, Richard. Charity. New York: G. Schirmer, 1921.
Composed: 1921.
Setting: high voice, piano.
Johnson: 919.
Arranged in March, 1973, by Dorothy Rudd Moore for soprano and contralto duet or SA chorus, piano.
"...an arrangement for soprano and alto...of the well-known song by Richard Hageman. In other words, I arranged the voices only. It can also be performed by female chorus. The first performance was in the spring of 1973."—letter from D.R. Moore, May 3, 1989.

Hall, Juliana. In Reverence. Song Cycle of 5 Songs for Soprano and Piano on Poems of Emily Dickinson [manuscript].
Composed: 1986
Setting: soprano, piano.
Johnson: 61, 437, 946, 1672, 1743.
Duration: 8:00

First performance: Karen Burlingame, soprano; Juliana Hall, piano. Sprague Memorial Hall, Yale University, New Haven, CT, October 20, 1986.

Hall, Juliana. Night Dances. Song Cycle of 7 Songs for Soprano and Piano [manuscript].
Commissioned: Schubert Club of St. Paul, MN, for soprano Dawn Upshaw, Debut Series, 1987.
Composed: 1987.
Setting: soprano, piano.
Johnson: 1104, 1138.
Duration: 17:00.
First performance: Dawn Upshaw, soprano; Margo Garrett, piano. McKnight Theatre, St. Paul, MN, December 8, 1987.
Includes settings of poems by Emily Brontë (2), Elizabeth Bishop, Edna St. Vincent Millay, and Sylvia Plath.

Hall, Juliana. Syllables of Velvet, Sentences of Plush. Song Cycle of 7 Songs for Soprano and Piano on the Letters of Emily Dickinson [manuscript].
Commissioned: John Simon Guggenheim Foundation Fellowship, 1989.
Composed: 1989.
Setting: soprano, piano.
Johnson: Letters 56, 78, 105, 260, 270, 454, 1014.
Duration: 13:00.
First performance: Jayne West, soprano; Karen Sauer, piano. Houghton Memorial Chapel, Wellesley College, Wellesley, MA, March 10, 1991.
Letter No. 270 is a variant of Poem No. 334.

Hammond, Harold E. A Book, a Rose, a Prairie. Chicago: C. F. Summy, 1920.
Composed: 1920.

Setting: voice, piano.
Johnson: 19, 1263, 1755.

Harbison, John. Elegiac Songs. New York:
G. Schirmer, 1974.
Commissioned: Fromm Music Foundation
for Jan DeGaetani.
Composed: 1974.
Setting: mezzo-soprano, chamber or-
chestra.
Duration: 20:00.
Johnson: 457, 491, 882, 913, 1026, 1125,
1503, 1625, 1700.
First performance: Jan DeGaetani, mezzo
soprano; Arthur Weisberg, conductor.
Contemporary Chamber Players,
Carnegie Recital Hall, New York,
January, 1975.
"The incompleteness of some of these
poems, allowing music to step for-
ward and enlarge upon them, their
directness and force, their strange and
inimitable language—all these factors
were important in the setting. A thread
of dramatic narrative runs through all
of her work, and this cycle makes this
explicit."—letter of June, 1990.

**Harman, David A. Three Songs on
the Poems of Emily Dickinson.
Songs of Death** [manuscript].
Composed: 1984.
Duration: 8:00.
Johnson: 99, 654, 1711.
Location: composer.
First performance: Marie-Danielle Parent,
soprano; Catherine Courvoisier, piano.
Composer's Concert Society Series,
La Chapelle, l'Université de Montréal,
Montréal, Québec, Canada, December
6, 1984.
Recording: Margaret Palmer, soprano.
Louis-Philippe Pelletier, piano.
Musique Actuelles, Montréal, Québec,

Canadian Broadcasting Corporation,
1985.
" 'Three Songs on the Poems of Emily
Dickinson' is a miniature song-cycle.
Each poem reflects the author's interpretation of three stages of death: the
face of death; anger, cynicism and
bereavement; and finally acceptance.
The mystical style is non-tonal,
harmonic-contrapuntal, lyrical and
intense. Texture develops gradually
from very dense in the first song to
very sparse at the conclusion. The
music is highly organized through
chordal transpositions and inver-
sions of complex harmonies, these all
being derived from the vocal line."
—letter of May 27, 1990.

**Harris, Roy. Read, Sweet, How Others
Strove** [manuscript].
Commissioned: Albert Christ-Janer
(through Martha Baird Rockefeller).
Composed: 1956.
Setting: SATB chorus, organ.
Duration: 10:00.
Johnson: 260.
Location: Dr. Dan Stehman, 2915 Tennyson Place, Hermosa Beach, CA
90254.
"I do not have any information on the
first performance of this piece (a
recurring problem with a number
of Harris's smaller compositions),
although it is likely that Christ-
Janer and the Penn State choir,
which he directed during the 1950s,
may have sung it, or at least read
through it (a letter to the composer
of 4/16/56 from Christ-Janer refers to
a hymn 'sing' planned for the following day; however, I have no idea
whether this was a public performance

or a private reading)."—Dan Stehman, letter of December 10, 1990.

Hastings, Thomas. See "Miscellany" section: Jones, Joseph, arr. Twenty Songs by Emily Dickinson, Set to Tunes by Thomas Commuck (1845).

Havergal, William Henry. "Evan." See "Miscellany" section: Jones, Joseph, arr. A Garland for Emily.

Haxton, Kenneth. Life (xcvi). New York: American Composers Edition, 1949.
Composed: 1949.
Setting: high voice, piano.
Johnson: 1732.

Haxton, Kenneth. Love (xxxiii). New York: American Composers Edition, 1949.
Composed: 1949.
Setting: high voice, piano.
Johnson: 245.

Haxton, Kenneth. Tell All the Truth. New York: American Composers Edition, 1974.
Composed: 1974.
Setting: high voice, piano.
Johnson: 1129.

Haxton, Kenneth. Four American Women Poets. New York: American Composers Edition, 1984.
Composed: 1984.
Setting: high voice, piano.
Johnson: 280.
Also poems by Phyllis Wheatley, Adelaide Crapsey, and Carol Brent.

Haxton, Kenneth. Time and Eternity (cxvii). New York: American Composers Edition, 1989.
Composed: 1989.
Setting: high voice, piano.
Johnson: 1272.

"The poems I chose for setting to music all meet certain criteria that I consider essential for good vocal texts. The words must be easy to comprehend when sung; the sense of the text must be easily understood, simple but not simplistic; there should be effective imagery; the sounds in the verse should be easy to vocalize—a preponderance of open vowel sounds; the structure of the verses must be interesting but not complex; and above all, the poetry must have a narrative drive or communicate strong emotion—preferably both.

"Surprisingly few poets meet these criteria. Emily Dickinson is a poet whose work is perfect for musical treatment. Others are William Blake, William Butler Yeats, Stephen Crane, Adelaide Crapsey, and James Stephens."—letter of June 20, 1989.

Heilner, Irwin. Poem. New York: American Composers Edition, 1972.
Composed: 1972.
Setting: medium voice, piano.
Johnson: 248.

Heiss, John. Songs of Nature. New York: Boosey & Hawkes, 1978.
Composed: 1978.
Setting: mezzo-soprano, flute, clarinet, piano, violin, violoncello.
Johnson: 182, 1510.
Recording: *New American Music for Chamber Ensemble.* D'Anna Fortunato, mezzo-soprano; Musica Viva, conducted by Richard Pittman. Nonesuch H71351, 1978.
Texts by Emily Dickinson, W.C. Bryant, H.W. Longfellow, H.D. Thoreau.
"I'll have to set more (I keep intending to). Her poetry is constant in its enchantment."—note of April 13, 1989.

Hemberg, Eskil. Love Fancies, for Baritone, Obbligato Bassoon, and Strings. 1980; revised 1983 [manuscript].
Composed: 1969-75.
Setting: baritone, obbligato bassoon, strings.
Johnson: 162.
First performance: Howard Sprout, baritone; Carl-Johan Nordin, bassoon. The Royal Swedish Chamber Orchestra, Mats Liljefors, conductor.
Recording: Phono Suecia PS 17, stereo digital.
"'The Outlet' [162] is a very simple setting in 6/8 with a six-bar-pattern accompaniment as a perpetuum mobile played Allegro."—letter of February 28, 1990.

Hemberg, Eskil. Three Love Songs. Opus 38 [manuscript].
Composed: 1974-75.
Setting: baritone, piano.
Johnson: 162.
Location: composer.
First performance: Erik Saeden, baritone; Thomas Schuback, piano. Swedish Radio P 2 "Composer of the week," 1977.
Recording: Swedish National Radio Co., Stockholm, Sweden.
Poems by Emily Dickinson, Robert Graves, Edwin Arlington Robinson.
"In 1980 I did an orchestrated version of this song cycle intended to be used as ballet music. On this occasion I also added a fourth song [by T. S. Eliot] and retitled the work. In 1983 a second version was put together because of copyright problems with the estate of the late T. S. Eliot."—letter of February 28, 1990.

Hennagin, Michael. Three Emily Dickinson Songs. Fort Lauderdale, FL: Walton Music Corporation, 1971. Selling agent: Chapel Hill, NC: Hinshaw Music, 1976.
Composed: 1971.
Setting: SA, piano; or soprano and contralto soloists, piano.
Duration: 13:35.
Johnson: 47, 79, 715.
First performance: Beverly McLarry, soprano; Shirley Moore, mezzo-soprano; Paul Moore, piano. University of Oklahoma, 1971.
The setting of No. 715 was also published separately under the title "The World Feels Dusty," 1971.

Hennagin, Michael. A Time of Turning [manuscript].
Composed: 1973.
Setting: soprano, flute, oboe, clarinet, bassoon, harp, percussion, piano.
Johnson:189, 549, 583.
Location: composer.
First performance: Kathleen Harris, soprano; Edward Gates, piano. Michael Hennagin, conductor. University of Oklahoma, 1973.

Herberich, Elizabeth. Four Poems of Emily Dickinson [manuscript].
Composed: 1990.
Setting: (No. 333) mezzo-soprano, piano. (Nos. 1151, 1287, 1312) soprano or mezzo-soprano, piano.
Johnson: 333, 1151, 1287, 1312.
Location: composer.
First performance: No. 333: Kate Judd, mezzo-soprano; John McDonald, piano. Pickman Concert Hall, Cambridge, Massachusetts, January 25, 1990. Nos. 1151, 1287, 1312: Martha Peabody, soprano; John McDonald,

piano. Pickman Concert Hall, June 25, 1990.

"At first I was not moved by, nor did I even like, the poems of Emily Dickinson. But I was asked by Martha Peabody, who specializes in the performance of Dickinson songs, to consider setting some of her poems. After I read them all, I came to appreciate the simplicity and power of her varied expressions of universal truths through the imagery of her concise language. The four settings were composed to reflect those same qualities in partnership, not in competition, with her messages." —letter of February 22, 1991.

Herman, Carol. Emily Dickinson: Four Poems for Soprano Voice & Bass Viola da Gamba. Albany, CA: PRB Productions, 1991.

Composed: 1986-91.

Setting: soprano, bass viola da gamba.

Johnson: 249, 288, 315, 656.

First performance: at conference, "Emily Dickinson: A Celebration for Readers," Pomona College, 1986.

"Emily Dickinson's poems have long appealed to students, scholars, and ordinary lovers of poetry. I am fortunate to have, as friend and advisor, an Associate Professor of English at Pomona College, Dr. Cristanne Miller, who is an authority on Dickinson (*Emily Dickinson: A Poet's Grammar*, 1987). As she says, Dickinson's poems are as enigmatic as their reclusive and constantly posing author. They combine brilliant metaphors with unconventional grammar and syntax, and an unusual punctuation filled with dashes, all of which demand that each of us wrestle with a personal interpretation.

"What better poetry for a musician; many composers are fascinated. Because all of us who play and love the viola da gamba have long admired its vocal qualities, it seems the perfect instrument to combine with voice. But, more importantly, because the viol is so capable of nuance and color, it also seems the perfect instrument for poems brimming with both. I hope you find the music fits the poems, and that you recognize my use of that familiar musical tool, word painting. Before writing a single note, I read Dickinson out loud, experimenting with rhythms, trying to get a sense of how the words fall, and emphasizing those that seem especially important. In this way, I interpreted the poetry for myself, and if you sing and play this music, you must interpret it for yourself. However, I do recommend that both singer and player read the poems aloud before putting the music together. The consequent learning, experimenting, and decision-making should prove enjoyable."—Composer's note to the score.

Hess, Robert E. Our Little Kinsman [manuscript].

Composed: 1961.

Setting: SSA chorus, piano.

Johnson: 885.

Location: American Music Center.

Hess, Robert E. Two Butterflies [manuscript].

Composed: 1961.

Setting: high voice, piano.

Johnson: 533.

Location: American Music Center.

Hewitt, Harry. Chartless, Opus 36c [manuscript].
Composed: 1934-58.
Setting: mezzo-soprano or contralto, timpani, string orchestra.
Duration: 22:00.
Johnson: 12, 182, 280, 333, 449, 511, 520, 1052, 1104, 1224.
Location: composer.
First performance: Joyce Lundy, contralto; Carmine Campione, clarinet. Edna Brockstein, piano. Philadelphia Art Alliance, February, 1960.
"The cycle was written so long ago I can scarcely recall my motivations. Most of my earliest works are songs or song cycles. I'm also a poet and nearly all of my mature cycles have been written to my own texts. I would regard the 'Chartless' settings as earnest student or apprentice pieces."—letter of September 8, 1990.

Hilse, Walter. Nine Dickinson Songs [manuscript].
Commissioned: Rush Swayze, 1986.
Composed: 1986.
Setting: (232, 543, 1166) solo baritone or bass; (254, 277, 279, 280, 701, 1740) solo baritone or bass, piano.
Johnson: 232, 254, 277, 279, 280, 543, 701, 1166, 1740.
Location: composer.
First performance: Wilbur Pauley, bass; Walter Hilse, piano. Merkin Hall, New York City, March 12, 1987. Part of a concert of the Florilegium Chamber Choir.

Hilse, Walter. I Started Early [manuscript].
Composed: 1986.
Setting: mezzo-soprano, piano.
Johnson: 520.

First performance: Patricia Sullivan, mezzo-soprano; Elizabeth Rogers, piano. St. Michael's Episcopal Church, New York City, November 12, 1988.
"Dickinson's poetry has consistently attracted me because of its nobility, its generally introspective nature, and its spiritual depths."—letter of September 26, 1991.

Hinkle, Roy B. On God, Love, and Nature [manuscript].
Composed: 1982-86.
Setting: high voice, piano.
Johnson: 106, 130, 324, 429, 549.
Location: composer.
First performance: Alvernia College, Reading, PA, 1984.
"I achieved a first-prize award for the first three songs: 'The Moon is Distant,' 'A Service of Song,' and 'Proof' from the Composers' Competition sponsored by the Berks Art Council of Reading, Pennsylvania, in 1984. The judge for the competition, Dr. Jacob Neupauer, stated that the songs illustrated a 'sensitive marriage of words and music.' Todd Vunderink of Peer Southern Publishers commented: 'The song cycle has been written with obvious love and care for the poetry, which comes through in a straight-forward setting you have made.'"
—letter of March 29, 1990.

Hodges, Samuel. EMI in ABAland [manuscript].
Composed: 1986.
Setting: soprano, piano.
Johnson: 441, 540, 887.
Location: composer.
First performance: Deborah Lawson, soprano; Samuel Hodges, piano.

MacDowell Music Club, Louisville, KY, February 19, 1990.

"EMI in ABAland refers to EMILY Dickinson's poems (of which I chose three) in an overall ABA structure. However, each of the three songs could stand alone, but would be so short as to be almost flippant. The first song [540] forms the first A in the title. The second song [887] forms the B in the title. The third song [441] is the return to A as it has the same metric scheme as the first A. The melody of song three is an exact retrograde version of the first, in pitch only.

"Your project may turn up astounding numbers. What a beloved poet she is!"—letters of February 1 and February 9, 1990.

Hoiby, Lee. Four Dickinson Songs, for High Voice and Piano. New York: Southern Music Pub. Co.; Hamburg: Peer Musikverlag, 1988.
Commissioned: 1989
Composed: 1954, 1986-89.
Setting: soprano, piano.
Johnson: Poems 249, 923, 1593, Letter 261.
Duration: 9:15
First performance: see note under his "The Shining Place."

Hoiby, Lee. The Shining Place.
Commissioned: Cynthia Miller.
Composed: 1954
Setting: soprano, piano.
Johnson: 431.
First performance: Cynthia Miller, soprano; Lee Hoiby, piano. 1989.
"Unfortunately, songs 249, 923, 1593, and Letter 261, were published as 'Four Dickinson Songs' before [I felt] the need for a stronger opener. When the current edition is sold out it will be reprinted and retitled, with the addition of 'The Shining Place,' 431. The order of performance will then be 431, Letter 261, 923, 249, 1593.

"Some of the songs may be within reach of certain mezzos—they know who they are; but this is a common problem in describing the song literature. Again, some of the songs might appeal to male singers, but I feel the entire group is too intimate a portrayal of Emily to be suitable for a man, just as a man wouldn't perform 'The Belle of Amherst.'

"This song is intended as No. 1 of *Five Dickinson Songs*. The other four are published by Southern Music [see his *Four Dickinson Songs*, above]. The single song 'The Shining Place' and the group *Five Dickinson Songs* are available from me, d/b/a Aquarius Music Company, 71 Rock Valley, Long Eddy, NY 12760."—letter of December 13, 1990.

Højsgaard, Erik. Variations—Six Songs of Autumn [manuscript].
Composed: 1976. Revised version, 1980.
Setting: 1976 version: soprano, alto flute, violoncello. 1980 version: soprano, alto flute, harp, percussion, violoncello.
Duration: 13:00.
Johnson: 903.
Location: composer.
First performance: 1976 version: Nordiska Gruppen 77, Young Nordic Music Festival, Reykjavik, Iceland, June 21, 1977. 1980 version: Copenhagen, 1980.
Dickinson's "I hide myself within my flower" (903) is Variation IV.

Højsgaard, Erik. Fragmenter (1979).
Copenhagen: Samfundet til udgivelse
af dansk musik [Society for the Pub-
lication of Danish Music], 1985.
Commissioned: Trio Soleil.
Composed: 1979. Revised version, 1981.
Setting: soprano, guitar, violin.
Duration: 9:00.
Johnson: 758.
Location: Library of Congress.
First performance: 1979 version: Trio
Soleil, Numus-Festival, Arhus, Den-
mark, April 25, 1980. 1981 version:
Trio Soleil, Copenhagen, September
14, 1981.
Guitar part edited by Karl Petersen.
Texts by Emily Dickinson, T. S. Eliot,
Ole Sarvig, Arthur Rimbaud.
Recording: Paula Records, P-35.

**Højsgaard, Erik. Two Songs for Mixed
Choir** [manuscript].
Commissioned: Ars Nova Choir (Co-
penhagen) and Rilke Ensemble
(Gothenburg).
Composed: 1985-86.
Setting: SSAATTBB a cappella.
Johnson: 1619, 1622.
Location: composer.
First performance: [1619] Ars Nova Choir
and Rilke Ensemble, Gerlesborg,
Sweden, June 21, 1985. [1619, 1622]
Ars Nova Choir, Copenhagen,
November 29, 1988.
Recording: Danish Music Information
Centre, Copenhagen.

**Holab, William J. Absence Disembod-
ies.** [s.l.]: C.F. Peters; New York:
Henmar Press, sole selling agents,
1989.
Setting: contralto, tenor, bass soli; or
ATB chorus a cappella.
Duration: 9:00
Johnson: 860.

First performance: Composers' Concordance, CAMI Hall, New York
City, May 20, 1988.
"I have long wanted to write a complex
vocal piece that would take a short
text and set it in many different ways.
The opportunity arose when the
group Tres Voces commissioned an a
cappella piece for their ensemble
(countertenor, tenor, and bass). I
decided upon Dickinson's 'Absence
Disembodies' for a variety of reasons:
it had a curious ambiguity about it
that led to different interpretations;
the words seemed to carry a great deal
of weight and had a strong evocative
power; and I thought as there was no
one 'right' way to set it to music, many
types of settings came to mind.

"Because of this, I decided to set it
a number of different ways and to
separate each setting with an Interlude
based on one line of the poem. The
force that unifies the piece is a gradual
'disembodying' of the music and text as
the piece progresses. While the first
movement is a somewhat straight setting, the second and third movements
gradually break apart the music and
text, until in the Postlude only the
vowels of the poem are sung and the
music presents a jumbled-up version of
what we have heard before. My attempt was to mirror some of the layers
and ambiguities of the text in the
musical material for the piece."—letter
of September 20, 1989.

Holman, Derek. Laudes Creationis
[manuscript].
Composed: 1987.
Setting: oboe, harp, 3 percussionists, piano
4-hands.
Johnson: 128.
Location: composer.

Holmes, Markwood. The Birds [manuscript].
Setting: voice, piano.
Johnson: 783.
Location: composer.

Horvit, Michael. Three Songs of Elegy.
Boston: E. C. Schirmer, 1970.
Composed: 1964.
Setting: soprano, piano.
Duration: 1:52.
Johnson: 280, 829, 937.

"Though personally not a great fan of J.F.K., I was horrified at his assassination. These songs were written in 1964, in reaction to that awful event, and titled: 'Three Songs on the Death of an American President.' Considering the history of Emily Dickinson, it was most appropriate to use her poetry in this instance.

"I submitted the songs for publication to E. C. Schirmer. At that time Robert MacWilliams (now deceased) was the owner-publisher. He liked the songs, but not President Kennedy. He insisted that I change the title prior to publication, hence the subsequent title."—letter of April 10, 1989.

Horvit, Michael. Two Songs for Choir and Electronic Tape [manuscript].
Composed: 1974.
Setting: SATB chorus, 2-channel electronic tape.
Johnson: 465, 712.
Location: composer.

Howe, Mary Carlisle. Three Emily Dickinson Pieces for String Quartet [manuscript].
Composed: 1951.
Setting: string quartet [2 violins, viola, violoncello].
Johnson: 135, 1067, 1090.
Location: For information, Dorothy Indenbaum, 315 East 65th St., New York, NY 10021.
First performance: Chamber Arts Society, Catholic University of America, Emerson Myers, director. Textile Museum, Washington, D.C., July 21, 1951.
Recording: Chamber Arts Society, Catholic University of America, Emerson Myers, director. WCFM Recording Corp., LP-9, 1951

Richard Hoyt

"Emily Dickinson's poems have so much music in them that it's hard to refrain from adding a few notes in way of a frame. I am continually drawn back to her poetry."
—letter of September 2, 1990.

Hoyt, Richard. The Sky Is Low [manuscript].
Composed: 1962.
Setting: high voice, piano.
Johnson: 1075.
Location: composer.
First performance: Corinne LaPointe, soprano. New York City: 1968.

Hoyt, Richard. Departed to the Judgment [manuscript].
Composed: 1965.
Setting: high voice, piano.
Johnson: 524.
Location: composer.

Hoyt, Richard. There's a Certain Slant of Light [manuscript].
Composed: 1966.
Setting: medium voice, piano.
Johnson: 258.
Location: composer.
First performance: Louise Wagner, soprano. University of Montana, Missoula, 1974.

Hoyt, Richard. Blazing in Gold [manuscript].
Composed: 1967.
Setting: medium voice, piano.
Johnson: 228.
Location: composer.
First performance: Deborah Kieffer, mezzo-soprano. National Association of Composers Concert, New York, 1979.

Hoyt, Richard. Have You Got a Brook [manuscript].
Composed: 1967.
Setting: high voice, piano.
Johnson: 136.
Location: composer.
First performance: Deborah Kieffer, mezzo-soprano. Wilmington, Delaware, 1969.

Hoyt, Richard. An Awful Tempest [manuscript].
Composed: 1968.
Setting: medium voice, piano.
Johnson: 198.
Location: composer.
First performance: Deborah Kieffer, mezzo-soprano. National Gallery of Art, Washington, D.C., 1982.

Hoyt, Richard. I'll Tell You How the Sun Rose [manuscript].
Composed: 1971.
Setting: high voice, piano.
Johnson: 318.

Location: composer.
First performance: Gretchen McBroom, soprano. University of Montana, Missoula.

Hoyt, Richard. Threesome [manuscript].
Composed: 1971.
Setting: medium voice, piano.
Johnson: 189, 1212, 1377.
Location: composer.

Hoyt, Richard. Two Butterflies Went Out at Noon [manuscript].
Composed: 1973.
Setting: soprano, piano.
Johnson: 533.
Location: composer.
First performance: Deborah Kieffer, mezzo-soprano. National Association of Composers Concert, New York, 1979.

Hoyt, Richard. Some Keep the Sabbath [manuscript].
Composed: 1975.
Setting: medium voice, piano.
Johnson: 324.
Location: composer.
First performance: Eva de La O, soprano. Composers' Showcase of the New York Singing Teachers' Association, New York, 1980.

Hoyt, Richard. Will There Really Be a "Morning?" [manuscript].
Composed: 1975.
Setting: high voice, piano.
Johnson: 101.
Location: composer.
First performance: Ingrid Sobolewska, soprano. New York, 1977.

Hoyt, Richard. I Know Lives [manuscript].
Composed: 1977.
Setting: medium voice, piano.

Johnson: 372.

Location: composer.

First performance: Deborah Kieffer, mezzo-soprano. National Association of Composers Concert, New York, 1979.

Hoyt, Richard. Seven Songs [manuscript].

Composed: 1980-1985.

Setting: medium voice, piano.

Johnson: 371, 516, 585, 661, 1532, 1654, 1764.

Location: composer.

First performance: Deborah Kieffer, mezzo-soprano. Carnegie Recital Hall, March 3, 1986.

"Six of the Seven Songs were written especially for the hundredth anniversary of Miss Dickinson's death. Only 'I Like to See' is earlier."—letter of December 7, 1989.

Hoyt, Richard. The Sun and Fog [manuscript].

Composed: 1980.

Setting: high voice, piano.

Johnson: 1190.

Location: composer.

Hoyt, Richard. The Wind Tapped Like a Tired Man [manuscript].

Composed: 1981.

Setting: medium voice, piano.

Johnson: 436.

Location: composer.

Hoyt, Richard. Said the Year [manuscript].

Composed: 1983.

Setting: high voice, piano.

Johnson: 386, 1250, 1271.

Location: composer.

First performance: Helen Stephenson, soprano. Annapolis, MD, 1988.

Hoyt, Richard. I Many Times Thought Peace Had Come [manuscript].

Composed: 1984.

Setting: medium voice, piano.

Johnson: 739.

Location: composer.

Hoyt, Richard. The Mountain Sat upon the Plain [manuscript].

Composed: 1985.

Setting: medium voice, piano.

Johnson: 975.

Location: composer.

Hoyt, Richard. The Wind Didn't Come from the Orchard Today [manuscript].

Composed: 1985.

Setting: medium voice, piano.

Johnson: 316.

Location: composer.

Hoyt, Richard. Some Iotas for Soprano [manuscript].

Composed: 1987.

Setting: soprano, piano.

Johnson: 1448, 1583, 1763.

Location: composer.

First performance: Helen Stephenson, soprano. Annapolis, MD, 1988.

Hoyt, Richard. The Most Triumphant Bird [manuscript].

Composed: 1989.

Setting: medium voice, piano.

Johnson: 1265.

Location: composer.

Hoyt, Richard. The Robin is the One [manuscript].

Composed: 1989.

Setting: medium voice, piano.

Johnson: 828.

Location: composer.

Hundley, Richard. Will There Really Be a Morning? [manuscript].
Composed: 1988.
Setting: soprano or tenor, piano.
Johnson: 101.
Location: composer.
First performance: Beverly Hoch, soprano; Warren Jones, piano. Midwest concert tour, 1989.
"The chief source of inspiration in my songs is the words themselves, and I try to recreate the emotion I experienced on first reading the poems. My ultimate aim is to crystalize emotion."—letter of December 3, 1990.
Hundley was one of twelve composers recognized as "standard American composers for vocalists" by the 1987 International Music Competition sponsored by Carnegie Hall and the Rockefeller Foundation.

Hunkins, Arthur B. Five Short Songs of Gladness [manuscript].
Setting: soprano, piano.
Johnson: 1052.
Location: composer; New York Puplic Library.

Iannaccone, Anthony. The Sky Is Low —The Clouds Are Mean. Boston: E. C. Schirmer, 1976.
Composed: 1962.
Setting: SATB chorus.
Johnson: 1075.
Recording: Northeastern Records. Choral Tapestries, CD-241.
The work is dedicated to Emily Lowe and the Eastern Michigan University Madrigal Singers.

Iannaccone, Anthony. This World Is Not Conclusion. Bryn Mawr, PA: Theodore Presser, 1989.
Composed: 1962.

Setting: voice, piano.
Johnson: 501.
Third of "Three Songs on Immortality."
"This madrigal is a light-hearted whimsical piece dealing with the fickle elements of weather. Its true import is revealed in the final line: 'Nature, like Us is sometimes caught Without her Diadem.' The music blends cumulative energy derived from rhythmic repetition of key words with fleeting melodic reflections of a more lyrical nature. The overall effect is very close, in spirit, to some of the lighter madrigals of the late sixteenth century.
"The actual premiere of 'The World is not Conclusion' took place in 1959 in New York City because 'Three Songs on Immortality' are piano transcriptions of three of the 'Five Songs on Immortality' for soprano and orchestra, composed in 1959. The piano-vocal version of 1962 was premiered in Carnegie Recital Hall by Maria Mastrangelo with the composer at the piano. I remember my teacher (Giannini) was upset because the printed program read 'Three Songs on Immorality.' I had worked on the original version of these songs for orchestra with Aaron Copland, with whom I was studying privately."
—letter and notes of July 2 and October, 1989.

Irvine, Jessie S., "Crimond." See "Miscellany" section. Jones, Joseph, arr. A Garland for Emily.

Irving, David. Three Emily Dickinson Songs [manuscript].
Composed: 1989.
Setting: soprano, piano.
Johnson: 101, 657, 1333.
Location: composer

First performance: An Electrix concert. Sally Munro, soprano; Graham Fitch, piano. CAMI Hall, New York City, September 9, 1989.

"I had been searching for new text material that would be immediately compelling and captivating. A friend assisted my search with a book of poems in which I first became attracted to the poetry of Emily Dickinson.

"The poems selected for 'Three Emily Dickinson Songs' illustrate a wistful, playful eccentricity that is at once enchanting yet seems only faintly to conceal a more contemplative expression that is buoyant, serene and beautiful. It is this spirit that the songs seek to express."—letter of January 14, 1990.

Irving, David. Four Songs for Soprano, French Horn, and Piano [manuscript].
Composed: 1990.
Setting: soprano, horn, piano.
Johnson: 24.
Location: composer.
First performance: Sally Munro, soprano; Francis Orval, horn; Randy Knee, piano; St. Michael's Episcopal Church, New York City, April 20, 1990.

Johns, Clayton. Nine Songs. Opus 20. Recital Publications, 1986.
Setting: soprano or tenor, [piano?].

Johnson, Hunter. Letter To the World [manuscript].
Commissioned: Bennington College, for the Martha Graham Ballet, 1940.
Composed: 1940.
Setting: originally for piano (see note below).
Johnson: 199, 214, 281, 285, 344, 373, 376, 390, 441, 728, 1320, 1672.

Location: composer.
First performance: Bennington, VT, August 11, 1940.
Originally for piano, later arranged for various combinations of instruments. In 1948 revised and scored for regular theater orchestra. In 1951, *Concert Suite for Chamber Orchestra* was extracted from the ballet score and recomposed. In 1959, scored for full orchestra.

"The mood and character of the music was largely determined by the use of many spoken lines from Emily Dickinson's poetry. The speaker is sometimes motionless, sometimes moving among the dancers. The most notable recent 'one-who-speaks' was Kathleen Turner, the actress for the 1988-1989 New York season.

"'Concert Suite' from 'Letter To The World,' full orchestra, was published in 1968 by the Galaxy Music Corporation. Galaxy was taken over by E. C. Schirmer, Boston, in 1989. The recording of 'Concert Suite' was performed by the Rochester Chamber Orchestra for the Concert Hall Society, New York. The Society later went out of business, so the recording is now out of print.

"One further note about the premiere of 'Letter' at Bennington. *Time* magazine's critic wrote that 'at the close' the audience sobbed and cheered."—letter of August, 1990.

Johnson, Hunter. Letter to the World: Concert Suite for Orchestra, from the Ballet Based on Poems by Emily Dickinson. New York: Galaxy, 1968.
Revision: Revised and scored 1948 for theater orchestra.

Recording: *Letter to the World; a Suite from the Ballet for Martha Graham.* Concert Hall Society, 1953. (CHS 1151). Rochester Chamber Orchestra.
Bibliography: Martha Graham. *Sixteen Dances in Photographs.* New York: Duell, Sloan and Pearce, 1941. "Letter to the World," pp. 113-125.
Johnson: 214, 285, 344, 390, 441.

Johnson, Hunter. Three Emily Dickinson Songs [manuscript].
Composed: (No. 92) 1956; (No. 76) 1957; (No. 63) 1959.
Setting: soprano, piano.
Johnson: 63, 76, 92.
Location: composer.
First performance: Ethel Casey, soprano; Walter Golde, piano. North Carolina Museum of Art, Raleigh, February 8, 1959.
"The songs form a group. I have always thought that her best equals the best of any of the Elizabethans, including Marlowe. Certain critics consider this [92] one of Dickinson's weaker poems because of the initially puzzling use of 'it,' especially in the fourth line. Of course 'it' refers to the state or condition of friendship, including the friend."—letters of September 1 and September 8, 1990.

Johnson, Lockrem. A Letter to Emily. Chamber opera [manuscript].
Composed: 1950.
Setting: lyric soprano, mezzo-soprano, baritone, flute, clarinet, piano, string quartet [2 violins, viola, violoncello], optional contrabass.
Johnson: 189, 318, 441.
Text: A setting of the play *Consider the Lillies*, by Robert Hupton.
Location: composer; The Jones Library.

Johnston, David A. Meditations [manuscript].
Composed: 1958.
Setting: voice, piano.
Location: composer; Library of Congress.

Jones, Joseph. See "Miscellany" section.

Joplin, Scott. See Morath, Max.

Jordahl, Robert. Death and the Maiden. Three Songs to Poems by Emily Dickinson [manuscript].
Composed: 1975.
Setting: medium voice, woodwind quartet or piano.
Duration: 4:20.
Johnson: 255, 467, 1065.
Location: composer.
First performance: Michele Martin, soprano. McNeese State University Woodwind Quartet, Spring, 1977.
"Performance notes: [255] Innocently (composed); [467] Whimsically (a little 3-part waltz); [1065] Pensively (passacaglia)."—letter of January 6, 1990.

Jordan, William. A Voice from the Front Room: Seven Poems and A Letter of Emily Dickinson [manuscript].
Composed: 1988.
Setting: voice, piano.
Johnson: Poems 94, 249, 323, 449, 829, 861, 1035; Letter 785.
Location: composer. The Jones Library.

Kaderavek, Milan. Talk Not to Me. Cincinnati: Westwood Press, 1967. Distributed by Greenwood Press.
Composed: 1967.
Setting: SATB chorus a cappella.
Johnson: 1634.

Kaderavek, Milan. Once a Child [manuscript].
Commissioned: Drake University Choir, 1976.
Composed: 1976.
Setting: SATB chorus.
Johnson: 36, 188, 251, 600.
Location: composer.
First Performance: Drake University Choir. Drake University, 1976.
"The four poems are intended to be performed as a set. Parts of [the work] have been subsequently performed by other groups."—letter of April 11, 1989.

Kagen, Sergius. Because I Could Not Stop for Death. New York: Leeds Music, 1951.
Composed: 1951.
Setting: mezzo-soprano, piano.
Johnson: 712.

Kagen, Sergius. Eight Poems by Emily Dickinson [manuscript].
Setting: voice, flute, clarinet, piano, violin, violoncello.
Johnson: 435, 650, 744, 761, 937, 1354, 1509, 1692.
Location: composer; New York Public Library.

Kagen, Sergius. I'm Nobody! New York: Weintraub Music, 1950.
Setting: high or medium voice, piano.
Johnson: 288.

Kagen, Sergius. The Mob Within the Heart. New York: Mercury Music, 1956.
Setting: voice, clarinet, chamber orchestra.
Johnson: 435, 650, 744, 761, 1509, 1692.

Martin Kalmanoff

"Isn't it incredible that so many composers of our time have reacted to basically difficult poetry of someone who died over a century ago? Does she hold the record for the most set-to-music poet in history? Emily was obviously ahead of her time. She followed her advanced aesthetic instincts rather than any rules.

"Even Thomas Higginson, who sensed that some rare quality was present in her work, thought her assonances proved she didn't know how to rhyme or scan. Thus Emily's poetry, instead of having the flowery feel of the Victorian era, had the harsher, hard-bitten feeling of a more modern style of aesthetics. For leavening, she was a throw-ahead, still retained some of the warmth & mystique of the Romantic era."—letter of October 2, 1989.

Kalmanoff, Martin. Twenty Emily Dickinson Songs [manuscript].
Composed: 1982.
Setting: voice, piano.
Johnson: 4, 12, 35, 101, 211, 249, 279, 288, 301, 324, 333, 429, 431, 605, 644, 712, 755, 791, 919, 1510.
Location: composer.

"Unlike my 'The Joy of Prayer,' which has gained widespread popularity, these Songs remain mostly unsung. Both celebrate the uniqueness of vision in human experience. I wrote my 'Twenty Dickinson Songs' almost at one sitting in 1982. It was at the request of Dr. Shirley Westwood, then on the faculty of the Cincinnati College-Conservatory of Music, for the use in a projected TV series.

"Six of my songs [Johnson: 35, 101, 301, 324, 333, 919] were premiered at The Players Club, an organization of the best American actors. They were performed in conjunction with the wonderful play about Emily D., *The Belle of Amherst* by William Luce, from whom I have a lovely letter.

"Will my songs remain? Only this I know: When I sang my songs, I found my own eternity. Emily Dickinson to a Bird: 'Why do you sing when no one listens?' Bird: 'It's my business to sing.'"—letters of October 2 and October 18, 1989.

Kavasch, Deborah. I Died for Beauty [manuscript].
Composed: 1968. Revised, 1983.
Setting: (1968) high or medium voice, piano. Revised (1983) for low voice, bass clarinet, viola.
Johnson: 449.
Location: composer.

Kavasch, Deborah. Bee! I'm Expecting You! [manuscript].
Composed: 1986.
Setting: solo soprano.
Johnson: 1035.
Location: composer.

Kay, Ulysses. Emily Dickinson Set: for Women's Chorus and Piano. New York: Leeds Music, 1965.
Composed: 1964.
Setting: SSA chorus, piano.
Johnson: 130, 829, 1067 (variant), 1760.

Kelly, Kevin. There's a Certain Slant of Light [manuscript].
Composed: 1987.
Setting: soprano, piano.
Johnson: 258.
Location: composer.
First Performance: Florence Peacock, soprano; Nan McMurray, piano. Chapel Hill, NC., June, 1988.
"An intensely dramatic song with a wide emotional range, this setting employs few traditional chords, yet conveys a strong sense of tonal center. It incorporates a quotation of the chorale 'Alle Menschen müssen sterben.'"—letter of August 7, 1989.

Kennedy, John B. Sails, Robins, and Butterflies. New York: Boosey & Hawkes, 1966.
Johnson: 52, 533, 919.

Kennedy, John B. I'm Nobody! New York: Boosey & Hawkes, 1966.
Composed: 1966.
Setting: SATB chorus.
Johnson: 288.

Kennedy, John B. It's All I Have to Bring. Melville, NY: Belwin Mills Publishing, 1973.
Setting: SSA chorus.
Johnson: 26.

Kent, Frederick James. Women's Voices. A Cycle of Nine Songs for Soprano & Piano. Bryn Mawr, PA: Elkan-Vogel, 1982.
Commissioned: Delaware Valley Composers Funded by the William Penn Foundation for Century IV.
Composed: 1982.
Setting: soprano, piano.
Johnson: 67, 249, 712.

Kent, Richard. Autumn Songs. New York: Lawson-Gould Music Publishers, n.d.
Setting: women's chorus.
Johnson: 12, 1075, 1540.

Kent Richard. Spring Songs. Cincinnati: World Library, 1971.
Setting: SSA chorus, or TTBB chorus.
Johnson: 99, 794, 812.

Kesselman, Lee R. Buzzings [manuscript].
Composed: 1976-77.
Setting: SATB a cappella.
Johnson: 1035, 1339, 1755.
Location: composer.
First Performance: Paul Rusterholz, Doctoral Recital, University of Southern California, Spring, 1978.
Recording: Macalester Concert Choir, Dale Warland, director. Macalester College, 1983. MCC 1983.
"Dickinson's poetry yields itself gratefully to musical setting. It is graceful and charming and at the same time clever and colorful in its use of language. Poetic content includes everyday subjects as well as profound and spiritual elements. Humor, often ironic and wry, is an important element of Dickinson's poetry. Her concise, finely honed style is a great asset in musical setting.
"'Buzzings' is a light-hearted suite about bees. It is wryly tonal but incorporates non-traditional choral sounds and imitations of animal sounds."
—letter of November 21, 1989.

Kesselman, Lee R. Libera Me: Requiem for 3 Poets [manuscript].
Commissioned: College of St. Theresa, Winona, MN.
Composed: 1980.

Setting: SSA chorus, flute, piano.
Johnson: 465.
Location: composer.
First Performance: College of St. Theresa Chamber Choir, Paul Rusterholz, director.
Also settings of Anne Sexton, Edna St. Vincent Millay, and the Latin Requiem Mass.

Kettering, Eunice L. The Sun. New York: C. Fischer, 1955.
Setting: SSA chorus, piano.
Johnson: 318.

Kirchner, Leon. The Twilight Stood: Song Cycle for Soprano and Piano. New York: Associated Music Publishers, 1987.
Commissioned: Spoleto Festival.
Composed: 1982.
Setting: soprano, piano.
Johnson: 435, 994, 1062, 1104, 1593, 1612.
First Performance: Beverly Hoch, soprano; Leon Kirchner, piano; Spoleto Festival, Charleston, SC, June 10, 1982.
Recording: 1983 Santa Fe Music Festival, Station KCSM, Spring, 1984.
"The work was completed in April, 1982 and was first performed by Beverly Hoch and myself in Charleston, SC (Spoleto USA) on June 10-11, and in Spoleto, Italy on July 4."—program note.
Review by Marshall Bialosky, *Notes* 45 (June 1989): 861-863. Compares Kirchner's Dickinson settings with those of Bacon, Copland, and Perle.

Kitzke, Jerome P. Emily. New York: American Composers Edition, 1983.
Commissioned: The University of Wisconsin-Milwaukee Chorale, 1983.
Composed: 1983.

Setting: SATB chorus.

Johnson: 937.

First Performance: University of Wisconsin-Milwaukee Madrigal Singers, May 7, 1983.

Texts by Emily Dickinson and James Hazard.

Kitzke, Jerome P. I Felt a Cleaving in My Mind. New York: American Composers Alliance, 1976.

Setting: SATB chorus.

Johnson: 937.

"In 'Emily,' two poems by James Hazard function as observant bookends, if you will, observing indirectly Ms. Dickinson's state of mind as revealed in her classic poem, 'I felt a Cleaving in my Mind.' Conductor Lee Spear wrote, 'James Hazard's imaginative poetry is a series of scenic flashes which frame the Dickinson poem: Amherst in winter; gazing out of Emily's window at the barren trees; the arabesques of her poetry like ribbons caught among the branches.'"—letter of May 9, 1989.

Klein, Lothar. Of Bells, Birds, and Bees: An Emily Dickinson Quilt [manuscript].

Composed: 1985.

Setting: soprano and contralto, piano.

Johnson: 1, 128, 501, 583, 824, 947, 1008, 1052, 1138, 1339, 1539.

Location: composer.

First performance: Roxolana Roslakm, soprano; Jean MacPhail, contralto; Stuart Hamilton, piano. Art Gallery of Ontario, Toronto, April 15, 1985.

"While my admiration for ED's work is unbounded, as a composer I do not believe all of her poetry is 'settable.' The richness and profundity of many of her poems are for me sufficient and perhaps only comprehensible unto themselves.

"Wishing, nevertheless, to compose a large work using her poetry, I used the Johnson compilation as my guide and inspiration. Reference to birds, bells, and bees are abundant in her work; these categories, then, thanks to the Johnson, became the starting point of my cycle. While purists may object to my using only single sentences, stitching or composing them together quilt-fashion, the thrust of the poet's use of bells, birds, and bees remains intact. The soprano and alto antiphonal exchange of lines, I think, also maintains the tender tenacity of ED's emotional thrust."—letter of May 17, 1991.

Klein, Lothar. Emily Dickinson Miscellany [manuscript].

Composed: 1988- [in progress].

Setting: soprano, piano.

Johnson: 83, 146, 249, 1431, 1483.

Location: composer.

"This is an on-going work in progress, a song being added as the spirit moves. The Miscellany uses entire poems. In both this work and the previous one, my aim was comprehensibility of imagery."—letter of December 1991.

Knowlton, Fanny Snow. A Day [manuscript].

Johnson: 318.

Kunz, Alfred. To Hear an Oriole Sing. Waterloo, Ontario: Waterloo Music Company, 1965.

Commissioned: Canadian Composers' Symposium, Canadian Music Centre, 1963.

Location: composer.

Setting: SSA chorus.
Johnson: 526.

Kyr, Robert. Maelstrom. Boston: E. C. Schirmer, 1988.
Commissioned: The Fires of London; Sir Peter Maxwell Davies, director; London, England, 1981.
Composed: 1980–81.
Setting: soprano, flute, clarinet, percussion, piano, violin, violoncello.
Johnson: 414.
First performance: Bronwen Mills, soprano; The Fires of London, Nicholas Cleobury, conductor. Queen Elizabeth Hall, London, September 21, 1983.
"'Maelstrom' was conceived as a musical drama, in which the vocalist is a heroine who tells a story about her desperate circumstances. I selected the poetry of Emily Dickinson and Dylan Thomas as the script being performed in musical discourse, rather than in physical, staged action.

"A synopsis of the 'plot' might read as follows: Act I. Scene 1. Deliberation (Emily Dickinson). The protagonist portrays herself as the victim of a situation so extreme that she is forced to deliberate between life and death: '...which anguish is the utterest, then—to perish or to live?' She vividly describes her fearful inner world, inhabited by goblins and fiends, and which closes in on her '...like a Maelstrom, with a notch.'

"The 'Maelstrom' poem exhibits characteristics I admire in all of Emily Dickinson's work: the energy of its language, the vividness of its imagery, and the intensity and urgency of the poetic vision."—letter of September, 1991.

Kyr, Robert. Toward Eternity. Boston: E. C. Schirmer, 1989.
Commissioned: Radcliffe Choral Society in celebration of its centenary anniversary.
Composed: 1988–89.
Setting: SSAA, solo oboe doubling soprano I in the second movement.
Johnson: 712.
First Performance: Radcliffe Choral Society, Beverly Taylor, conductor. Sanders Theater, Cambridge, MA, April 7, 1989, at a Women's Choral Festival celebrating the Society's hundredth anniversary.
"This poem seemed a natural choice of text for a piece about death and the reality of existence after death. It is set as a musical drama, in which half of the soprano section (doubled by a solo oboe) sings the text in a melodic setting, while the rest of the chorus declaims fragments in a half-spoken chanting style—at times, in a rhythmic stage whisper. This variety of contrasting vocal declamations emphasizes the wide range of consonant and vowel colors, as well as its rhythmic character. I was inspired by Dickinson's ability to convey the vastness of time (and space) in twenty-four lines."
—letter of September, 1991.

Laderman, Ezra. Magic Prison, for 2 Narrators and Orchestra. New York: Oxford University Press, 1970.
Setting: two narrators, orchestra.
Duration: 25:00.
Johnson: 126, 199, 288, 301, 322, 348, 463, 502, 511, 1601, 1732.
First Performance: New York Philharmonic Orchestra, Summer Festival, Lincoln Center, 1967.

Recording: From sound track of the film made by the Educational Division of the Encyclopedia Britannica, London Chamber Orchestra under the composer's direction.

Libretto in *Saturday Review*, October 28, 1967.

Dialogue for music between Emily Dickinson and Thomas Wentworth Higginson, using their own words selected and edited by Archibald MacLeish. Reviewed in The New York *Times*, June 13, June 14, 1967 and July 20, 1969. Program notes were written by Robert H. McMahan.

Ken Langer

"I hope eventually to put as many of Emily Dickinson's poems to music as possible."
—letter of January 23, 1990.

Langer, Ken. Because I Could Not [manuscript].
Composed: 1986.
Setting: bass, piano.
Johnson: 712.
Location: composer.

Langer, Ken. Funeral in My Brain [manuscript].
Composed: 1986.
Setting: soprano, piano.
Johnson: 280.
Location: composer.

Langer, Ken. I Died for Beauty [manuscript].
Composed: 1986.
Setting: soprano, piano.
Johnson: 449.
Location: composer.

Langer, Ken. I Heard a Fly [manuscript].
Composed: 1986.
Setting: soprano, piano.
Johnson: 465.
Location: composer.

Langer, Ken. My Life Closed Twice [manuscript].
Composed: 1986.
Setting: soprano, piano.
Johnson: 1732.
Location: composer.

Langer, Ken. The Insect [manuscript].
Composed: 1986.
Setting: soprano (unaccompanied).
Johnson: 1716.
Location: composer.

Langer, Ken. The Only News [manuscript].
Composed: 1986.
Setting: bass, piano.
Johnson: 827.
Location: composer.

Langer, Ken. This is My Letter [manuscript].
Composed: 1986.
Setting: bass, piano.
Johnson: 441.
Location: composer.

Langer, Ken. It's All I Have [manuscript].
Composed: 1987.
Setting: soprano, piano.
Johnson: 26.
Location: composer.

Langer, Ken. The Sun Rose [manuscript].
Composed: 1988.
Setting: soprano, piano.
Johnson: 318.
Location: composer.

Langer, Ken. The Thoughtful Grave
[manuscript].
Composed: 1988.
Setting: soprano, piano.
Johnson: 141.
Location: composer.

Langer, Ken. The Wind Tapped [manuscript].
Composed: 1988.
Setting: soprano, piano.
Johnson: 436.
Location: composer.

Langer, Ken. There Came a Wind
[manuscript].
Composed: 1988.
Setting: soprano, piano.
Johnson: 1593.
Location: composer.
"All of these songs were written with the college voice student in mind. They are challenging without being unduly difficult. Neo–classic harmonies, changing meters, and dramatic contours make them works of our time but conjunctive melodic treatment and uncomplicated accompaniments make the works accessible to both performer and listener. The purpose of each work is primarily to express the tone behind each poem."
—letter of January 23, 1990.

Langert, Jules. Three Emily Dickinson Songs. Berkeley, CA: Fallen Leaf Press, 1985.
Composed: 1967.
Setting: high voice, piano.
Duration: 6:00
Johnson: 435, 536, 605.

Langert, Jules. Three Emily Dickinson Songs [second set; manuscript].
Composed: 1971.
Setting: voice, piano.
Johnson: 280, 650, 891.
Location: composer.
"I think I chose the poems on the basis of her striking use of imagery and of the subject matter: estrangement and death, treated with irony and pathos. There is strong emotion in her work and also a great economy of language, which allows the musical setting wide scope. I continue to be moved and enthralled by many of her poems."
—letter of August, 1990.

Lardner, Borje. Three American Poems [manuscript].
Composed: 1988.
Setting: SATB chorus a cappella.
Johnson: 258.
Location: composer.
Also poems by Philip Freneau and Ralph Waldo Emerson.

Leavitt, Helen Sewall. Chartless [manuscript].
Johnson: 1052.

Roland Leich

"It was through meeting in 1939 the late Ernst Bacon, whom I greatly admired, that I first became aware of Emily Dickinson. Most of my Emily Dickinson songs have been introduced by student singers here at Carnegie Mellon University, a few at Eastman (where I did graduate study 1941-1942.)

"These songs were not commissioned. They owe their existence to a former student of mine at Dartmouth, the late John T. Maffett, their dedicatee. Knowing that I enjoyed writing songs, he brought a volume of Emily Dickinson's poems, fifteen of which I set during the spring of 1940. In 1943 Agnes Davis sang [Nos. 4 and 723] at Curtis. In 1964 Beatrice Krebs, Professor of Voice at Carnegie Mellon, sang [Nos. 83, 162, 289, 318, 322, 712, 1487, 1573] at a Pittsburgh Composers' Forum concert. Lynne Weber introduced [Nos. 528, 644, and 729] at a recital sponsored by the Pittsburgh Alliance of Composers.

"My Emily Dickinson settings can be sung individually or in groups ad lib. Although not planned as a cycle, the first fifteen [4, 115, 162, 249, 288, 367, 374, 429, 701, 723, 792, 908, 1065, 1079], all quite brief, could constitute a fairly extensive group. The last three [528, 644, 729] are definitely intended as a small cycle."

"There is little to say, technically, about my settings. During the 25 years of their gestation some changes of style did occur. I like to feel that the ideal setting of a given text 'already exists' and that one tries to capture it (as with Michelangelo and sculpture). Having indulged in almost constant editing since 1965, here's hoping they are at last 'almost ready.'"—letter of May 19, 1990.

Leich, Roland. Forty-Seven Emily Dickinson Songs, 1940-1965 [manuscript].
Composed: 1940-65.
Setting: soprano or mezzo-soprano, piano. (Johnson 970 transcribed for SATB, piano. Occasionally a choice of pitches is offered.)

Johnson: 4, 26, 35, 83, 94, 113, 115, 122, 162, 188, 196, 215, 249, 260, 266, 288, 289, 318, 322, 333, 342, 347, 367, 374, 429, 467, 528, 586, 625, 644, 695, 701, 712, 723, 729, 790, 792, 908, 970, 1065, 1078, 1079, 1080, 1487, 1521, 1558, 1573.
Location: composer.

Alan R. Leichtling

"Your book ought to reveal the extent to which Dickinson's poems have been an important literary staple of the musical world. I suspect that a sizable amount of American vocal music would not exist but for her poetry."—letter of December 22, 1990.

Leichtling, Alan R. Three Songs of Emily Dickinson. New York: Seesaw Music, 1969.
Composed: 1967; revised, 1979.
Setting: baritone, violoncello.
Duration: 6:15.
Johnson: 67, 772, 1004.
First performance: Juilliard School, New York, 1967.

Leichtling, Alan R. A Book of Madrigals. New York: Seesaw Music, 1975.
Composed: 1975.
Setting: SATB chorus a cappella.
Johnson: 605, 1624.
First performance: Alan Leichtling, conductor. Madrigal Chorus of Grinnell College, Grinnell, IA, 1976.

Leichtling, Alan R. My Lady Anita's Song Book. New York: Seesaw Music, 1977.
Composed: 1976-77; orchestral version, 1977.
Setting: coloratura soprano, piano.
Johnson: 568, 1474, 1548.

Leichtling, Alan R. Six Poems of Emily Dickinson, Op. 47. New York: Seesaw Music, 1979.
Composed: 1979.
Setting: soprano, oboe.
Johnson: 605, 1081, 1084, 1270, 1276, 1331.
First performance: Faculty recital, East Carolina University, Greenville, NC, 1979.

Leichtling, Alan R. A Second Book of Madrigals. New York: Seesaw Music, 1981.
Composed: 1980.
Setting: SATB chorus, a cappella.
Johnson: 328, 629.

Leisner, David. Simple Songs, for Medium Voice and Guitar. New York: Associated Music Publishers, 1984.
Composed: 1982.
Setting: medium voice, guitar.
Johnson: 76, 435, 1035, 1339, 1510, 1654.
First Performance: Boston, Longy School of Music, March 20, 1982.
Reviewed by John McInerney in *Musical America* (September, 1982): 22.

Leisner, David. Confiding, for High Voice and Piano. A Cycle of 10 Songs to Women's Poems [manuscript].
Composed: 1985-86.
Setting: high or medium voice, piano. Arranged for high voice and guitar (1985-86).
Johnson: 217, 249, 441, 829.
Location: composer.
First Performance: Jordan Hall, Boston, March 30, 1987.
"The cycle of ten songs, all set to poems by women, deals with various kinds and stages of confiding. The first and last songs [217, 441] act as prelude and postlude. Actually, it's no surprise that Emily Dickinson has been set to music by so many composers. Her poetry is lyrical and has a densely packed power and emotional urgency."—letter of April 14, 1989.
Includes settings of poems by Gene Scaramellino, Elissa Ely, and Emily Brontë.

Lenel, Ludwig. Five Poems by Emily Dickinson [manuscript].
Composed: 1981, revised 1984.
Setting: chamber chorus (12-16 voices), flute, percussion.
Johnson: 230, 653, 703, 913, 1065.
Location: composer.

First Performance: Muhlenberg Chamber Chorus; Elaine Martin, flute; Earl Blackburn, percussion. Muhlenberg College, October 27, 1985.

"The poems should be sung, because of their character of intimacy, by a small ensemble (I specified 12-16 voices) with a small transparent accompaniment of a solo flute & vibraphone, suspended cymbal and tam-tam. The poetry obviously lends itself to musical treatment."—letter of September 2, 1990.

Lenk, Thomas Timothy. Two Songs on Poems by Emily Dickinson [manuscript].

Setting: tenor, B-flat clarinet, violoncello.

Johnson: 288, 441.

Location: American Music Center.

"My settings of two poems by Emily Dickinson, composed while I was a graduate student at American University, are perhaps a bit naive, especially in their use of the atonal idiom with which I was only beginning to become familiar. Nonetheless, the settings do illustrate my feelings toward the texts in sum. I suppose I viewed these poems as both the realization of solitude and a reconciliation, even pleasure, with it."—letter of September 5, 1989.

Lerdahl, Fred. Beyond the Realm of Bird [manuscript].

Commissioned: (1259) Department of Music, University of Chicago, in honor of Paul Fromm's 75th birthday.

Composed: 1981-84.

Setting: soprano, chamber orchestra.

Johnson: 378, 517, 1259.

Location: composer.

First performance: [1259] University of Chicago Contemporary Ensemble, 1982. "The completed cycle was first performed at Tanglewood, MA in 1985."

"I eventually added two more songs and arranged all three [378, 517, 1259] for small orchestra. 'Beyond the Realm of Bird' sets three relatively unknown poems. All three are mystical contemplations of nature. The title comes from a line in the first poem [1259], and signifies a reaching out beyond the material world. The second poem [517] is nominally about the wanderings of a butterfly, more deeply about inner transformation. The third [378] moves from despair to transcendence.

"For me poetry is just the starting point. Here I found close musical equivalents for the structure of the poems, which I then clothed in sumptuous, unDickinsonian garb of harmony and instrumentation. Beneath the romantic surface, however, lies a good deal of calculation: every aspect of the musical language is tightly and elaborately controlled. I believe this control enhances rather than contradicts the intense expression."—letter of October, 1990.

Levy, Frank. This is My Letter to the World. New York: Seesaw Music, 1960.

Composed: 1960.

Setting: SATB chorus.

Johnson: 441.

"My choice of text was based on two factors: 1. The conciseness of expression in Emily Dickinson's verse lent itself to the structured modal style of my composition; 2. the verses were and are still in the public domain. In more general terms I would hazard to speculate that the curious blending of austerity and a certain extravagance of imagery make this poet's work both appealing and suitable to many composers."—letter of July 24, 1989.

Lidov, Davis. I Have No Life But This [manuscript].
Composed: 1970.
Setting: tenor, piano.
Johnson: 1398.
Location: composer.

Lighty, Alan K. Music From Amherst [manuscript].
Composed: 1979.
Setting: soprano, flute, bassoon, harp, piano, violin, violoncello.
Johnson: 157, 253, 402, 415, 1003, 1005, 1480.
Location: composer.

Lindenfeld, Harris. Three Dickinson Songs. New York: American Composers Edition, 1978.
Setting: soprano, E-flat clarinet, piano.
Johnson: 435, 449, 1624.
First Performance: Carnegie Recital Hall, New York, May 20, 1982.

Locklair, Dan. Two Soprano Songs [manuscript].
Composed: 1982.
Setting: soprano, piano.
Johnson: 258
Location. E. C. Kirby, Ltd. (Ricordi), c/o Hal Leonard, attn. Steve Rauch, P.O. Box 13819, Milwaukee, WI 53213.
First Performance: Reynolds House Museum of American Art, Winston-Salem, NC, February 17, 1983.

Lockwood, Normand. Three Verses of Emily Dickinson [manuscript].
Composed: 1980.
Setting: (Nos. 1, 2) soprano, piano. (No. 3) SATB chorus.
Johnson: 155, 712, 1760.
Location: Normand Lockwood Archive, Music Library, University of Colorado, Boulder, CO.
"The death of Lockwood's daughter, Angi, in 1980, brought about the choral arrangement of the third song, and that version is designated to her memory."—letter of September 10, 1989, from Kay Lockwood.

Lorenz, Ellen Jane. Bring Me the Sunset in a Cup [manuscript].
Commissioned : The University of Dayton for their Dickinson Festival, 1986.
Composed: 1986.
Setting: high voice, piano.
Johnson: 126.
Location: composer; The Jones Library.
"I have loved Emily's poetry since I first 'met' her in high school sixty-four years ago."—letter of July 3, 1989.

Luening, Otto. Nine Songs to Poems of Emily Dickinson for Soprano and Piano. New York: Galaxy, 1961.
Composed: 1942-51.
Setting: soprano, piano.
Johnson: 113, 139, 254, 919, 937, 1073, 1181, 1206, 1596.
First Performance: Vermont Composers Conference, Bennington, VT: August 21, 1951.
Recording: (Johnson 919, "If I can stop one Heart from breaking.") *Phalen Tassie Sings American Contemporary Songs.* Pianist, Le Roy Miller. Lakeport, CA: Music Library MLR 7117, 1967.

"Professor Luening's 'Nine Songs to Poems of Emily Dickinson' were composed from 1942 to 1951. They appeared with remarks by the composer in *Parnassus Poetry in Review*, X/2 (Fall/Winter 1982): 225-250." —letter of May 7, 1989 from Emily Good, Assistant to Otto Luening.

Luther, Martin. See "Miscellany" section: Gould, John A., arr. I Heard A Fly Buzz—When I Died.

Lutkin, Peter C. If I Can Stop One Heart From Breaking. In: *The American Student Hymnal*, ed. by Henry Smith (London: The Century Co.; New York: Appleton-Century, 1928) and *The New Hymnal for American Youth*, ed. by Henry Smith (New York: Appleton-Century, 1930).
Composed: 1928.
Setting: voice, piano.
Johnson: 919.

Macaulay, Janice. Three Love Poems of Emily Dickinson For Treble Voices [manuscript].
Composed: 1980.
Setting: women's chorus.
Johnson: 249, 738, 1290.
Location: composer.
First Performance: Cornell University Chorus, Sage Chapel, March 20, 1981.

Macaulay, Janice. Seven Love Poems of Emily Dickinson [manuscript].
Composed: 1982.
Setting: soprano, piano.
Johnson: 249, 673, 738, 1290, 1643, 1670, 1732.
Location: composer; American Music Center.

First Performance: Patrice Pastore, soprano; Christopher Been, piano. Barnes Hall, Cornell University, March 8, 1983.
"I chose seven poems by Emily Dickinson that reflect various aspects of love. The order of the poems progresses emotionally from the celebratory and ecstatic moods of the first two songs, 'Extol Thee—could I? Then I will' and the well-known poem 'Wild Nights—Wild Nights!' to the contrasting moods of pain and playfulness in the third and fourth, 'The most pathetic thing I do' and 'You said that I "was great"—one Day.'

"The dark and disturbing poem 'In Winter my Room' forms the emotional climax (or nadir) of the cycle, which concludes with the reflective poems 'My life closed twice before its close' and 'The Love a Life can show Below.' While composing the last song I had in mind the final piece of Brahms's 'Neue Liebeslieder Walzer.' I tried to capture in my setting of Dickinson's lovely poem the mood of beautiful serenity that Brahms created for Goethe's poetry in opus 65, number 15, 'Zum Schluss: Nun, ihr Musen, genug.'"—letter of August 27, 1989.

MacDermid, James G. Charity. Chicago: Forster Music Publisher, 1921.
Composed: 1908.
Setting: voice, piano.
Johnson: 919.
Location: The Jones Library.
Copyright in 1908 by the composer, who issued it under the title "Songs" in 1908. MacDermid added his own text to that of Emily Dickinson.

Manzoni, Giacomo. Dieci versi di Emily Dickinson. Milan: G. Ricordi, 1989. (Boosey & Hawkes, sole U.S. agent.)
Composed: 1989.
Setting: soprano, 2 harps, 10 strings.
Johnson: 1695.
First performance: Biennale Musicale, Venice, May 26, 1989.

Marcello, Joseph. An Heir of Heaven: The Spiritual Journey of Emily Dickinson; a Diary of Operatic Meditations [manuscript].
Composed: 1988.
Setting: soprano, flute, clarinet, harp, piano, viola, violoncello.
Johnson: 193, 249, 288, 376, 712, 919.
Location: composer; The Jones Library.
First Performance: Greenfield Community College, April 22, 1988.

Marzo, Eduardo. Autumn [manuscript].
Setting: voice, piano.
Johnson: 12.

Matsunaga, Michiharu. An Invisible Cosmos [Fukashi uchu]. Tokyo: Japanese Federation of Composers, 1986.
Composed: 1986.
Setting: shakuhachi [Japanese flute], harp, violoncello.
English words for the Dickinson poems are recited in the work.

Mayer, Stephen. Six Poems of Emily Dickinson [manuscript].
Composed: 1972. Revised, 1986.
Setting: baritone, piano.
Johnson: 321, 528, 569, 653, 861, 1003.
Location: composer.
First performance: (1972) Robert Kuehn, baritone; Stephen Mayer, piano. Carnegie Recital Hall, New York, 1975. (Revised, 1986) Robert Kuehn, baritone; Stephen Mayer, piano. Carnegie Recital Hall (Weill Concert Hall), New York, June 1987.
"Emily Dickinson is pretty much my ideal of an artist, particularly (aside from the quality of her work) in respect to her integrity and ability to steer her own course without recognition of any sort. The poems and selections have generally to do with an artist's vocation." —letters of March 11 and December 6, 1991.

McAfee, Don. I'll Tell You How the Sun Rose. Philadelphia: Elkan-Vogel, [n.d.]
Setting: SSA chorus, piano.
Johnson: 318.

McFarland, Ron. Emily Dickinson's American Garden Song Book [manuscript].
Commissioned: Maria Ravetti, soprano, 1986.
Composed: 1986.
Setting: soprano, piano.
Johnson: 2, 18, 31, 81, 994, 1423, 1448, 1755.
Location: composer.
First performance: Barbara Emerson, soprano; Ron McFarland, piano. San Francisco Musical Club, 1988.
Duration: 8:00

McFarland, Ron. A Dickinson Dialogue [manuscript].
Commissioned: Music Department, Mt. Tamalpais High School, 1974.
Composed: 1974.
Setting: SATB chorus, orchestra [2.2.2.2, 2.2.2.1, organ, strings]. Another version for SATB chorus, solo soprano, piano.
Johnson: 258, 712.
Location: composer.

First performance: Mt. Tamalpais High School chorus, Robert Greenwood, conductor.
Duration: 6:00

McKay, George Frederick. Indian Summer. New York: G. Schirmer, 1967.
Setting: SSA chorus, piano.
Johnson: 130.

McNeil, Jan Pfischner. And When a Soul Perceives Itself [manuscript].
Composed: 1975.
Setting: soprano, string quartet.
Johnson: 465, 530, 543, 632, 1035, 1052.

McNeil, Jan Pfischner. Seven Snow Songs [manuscript].
Composed: 1978.
Setting: medium voice, piano.
Johnson: 126.

Meachem, Margaret M. Three Humorous Songs [manuscript].
Composed: 1985.
Setting: soprano, piano.
Johnson: 108, 229, 1405.
Location: composer.
The manuscript is unfinished; no. 108 is a work in progress. "The piano makes use of constantly changing rhythms, partly to convey the humor and in the case of the Bees a whirling accompaniment in the piano and accentuation of Miss Dickinson's use of the consonants (Buzz and Fuzz). In the Bog song, dissonances and counterrhythms suggest the reaction of the fate of the victim."—letter of August 26, 1989.

Medley, Marsha Maria. Four Songs on Poems by Emily Dickinson. More Songs on Poems by Emily Dickinson.

BMI suggested Marsha Medley's songs but had no further information.

Mennin, Peter. Reflections of Emily: Choral Cycle on Poems of Emily Dickinson for Three-Part Chorus of Treble Voices with Harp, Piano, and Percussion. New York: G. Schirmer, 1979.
Commissioned: National Endowment for the Arts for the Newark Boys Chorus, Terence Shook, Music Director.
Composed: 1978-79.
Setting: SSA chorus, harp, percussion, piano.
Duration: 25:00.
Johnson: 157, 172, 260, 441, 549.
First Performance: Newark Boys Chorus. Alice Tully Hall, Lincoln Center, January 18, 1979.

Meyerowitz, Jan. Emily Dickinson Cantata [manuscript].
Composed: 1947.
Setting: soprano, orchestra.
Johnson: 47, 205, 207, 259, 461, 918, 1760.
Location: composer; New York Public Library.

Meyerowitz, Jan. Eastward in Eden: A Lyric Drama in Four Acts [on a text] by Dorothy Gardner [manuscript].
Composed: 1954.
"I wrote the opera *Eastward in Eden* after the play by Dorothy Gardner. It was first performed at Wayne University Theatre, Detroit, then at Hunter College, given by the Mannes School. Boris Goldovsky did numerous performances of the 2nd act, as 'The Meeting.' He wanted to take the whole work on his tour, but did not get enough interest, not even in Amherst.

The scores are in the Goldovskys' possession."—letter of September, 1989, Labaroche, France.

Mollicone, Henry. Five Poems of Love.
Boston: E.C. Schirmer, 1971.
Commissioned: Wheelock College Glee Club, Lee Collins, director, 1966.
Composed: 1966.
Setting: SSAA chorus, piano or harp. Also available with harp soli.
Johnson: 136, 213, 245, 271, 498.

Mollicone, Henry. I Never Saw a Moor [manuscript].
Composed: 1988.

Setting female voice, piano.
Johnson: 1052.
Location: composer.
First performance: Frederica Von Stade, soprano. Kennedy Center, Washington, 1988.
"I have sketches to more settings of Ms. Dickinson's poetry, not yet completed. I am attracted to the beautiful simplicity and imagery, and the eloquence and economy of expression."—letter of September, 1990.

Moore, Dorothy Rudd, arr. See Hageman, Richard. Charity.

Max Morath

"I draw to your attention an unusual group of settings by the composer-pianist-entertainer Max Morath. Some of them were performed at a concert here in Spokane by Fennessy with the composer at the piano. The unusual aspect of Morath's settings is that they are newly created vocal lines 'floated over' piano rags by Joplin."—letter of March 20, 1990, from Travis Rivers, "The Spokesman-Review," *Spokane Chronicle*, Spokane, WA.

"The first time I listened to your tape I simply tapped and hummed and smiled, for Joplin's rags are joyful and the tunes you have laid—so gently and carefully—on top of them are so appropriate. Had the opening lyric been an iambic trimeter version of 'Thirty days hath September' I would have clapped anyway. But on listening and reflecting, I find even more pleasure in hearing what your settings have released from the texts.

"There is a light, nearly humorous quality to Dickinson, extremely subtle and often obscured. 'I Never Saw a Moor' begains like a plaint, but spins lightly around as it sets its terms and develops its analogy. The rag tune and rhythm work seamlessly with such word play. 'I'll Tell You How the Sun Rose' also fits neatly in mood, light and playful, with the flock of little yellow boys and girls led away by the gray Dominie. Most interesting is the choice of 'If You Were Coming in the Fall.' It too is light—especially when the last stanza is omitted!—although there's a bit of bittersweet there as well.

"I am intrigued at how you chose those poems. They all seem related in one sense, the speaker as observer, who looks at the natural world and uses it as a source of meditation and instruction for problems of the heart: God and humanity, separation and isolation. But I wonder, was there anything more that brought you to these three? I will certainly teach your settings in my classes next year. One final word on the tape:

Kathy Morath—a relative surely—has a lovely voice that certainly enhanced the sense of joy I felt in hearing the cycle."—letter of July 3, 1991, from John A. Gould to Max Morath.

"I composed these pieces for a concert in Sedalia, Mo., under the auspices of the Scott Joplin Festival, held there every June for the last few years. (Joplin's first publication was in Sedalia in 1899.) The medley was included in a concert by myself and Ann Fennessy, soprano, entitled 'The Legacy of Scott Joplin.' (I didn't get around to copyright until 1990.) I think Mr. Travis Rivers' comment is quite accurate—the Dickinson melodies 'floated over' the rags. They are NOT an attempt to set Dickinson to rags themselves. I think that would be impossible, or impossibly contrived. I'll admit to a fanciful thought that triggered this work. I have always 'heard' legato melodies within rags, especially Joplin's rags. I wondered what he might have written if he could have collaborated with some late-19th-century American poets. With Dickinson, the dates work—Joplin, born 1868, and her work published, I believe, in 1890, 1891, and 1896. I am a lover of Dickinson but no expert, but I find her brevity and simplicity match beautifully the brevity and plainness of ragtime themes—again, especially those of Joplin."—letter of May 16, 1991, from Max Morath.

Morath, Max. In Separate Rooms: An American Song Cycle [manuscript].
Composed: 1989.
Setting: soprano, piano.
Johnson: 318, 511, 1052 (two versions).
Location: composer.
First Performance: Ann Fennessy, soprano; Max Morath, piano. Scott Joplin Festival, Sedalia, MO, June 3, 1989.

Muczynski, Robert. I Never Saw a Moor. New York: G. Schirmer, [n.d.].
Setting: SATB chorus.
Johnson: 1052.

Mueter, John. It Is a Lonesome Glee. A Cycle of Ten Songs on Poems of Emily Dickinson. Kansas City, MO: JAM Music, 1988.
Composed: 1988.
Setting: soprano, piano.
Johnson: 249, 735, 739, 757, 774, 824, 839, 932, 1037, 1053.

First Performance: Jean Herzberg, soprano; Garik Pedersen, piano. Ellis Recital Hall, Southwest Missouri State University, February 2, 1989.

"The poetry of Emily Dickinson has been an inspiration to many American composers. Her verse has qualities that lend themselves easily to a musical setting, namely: a wealth of strong imagery, sentiments which are at once personal and universal, an economical verbal expression.

"The ten poems selected for this cycle exhibit various facets of Emily Dickinson's emotional world, from the sensation of a mystical oneness with the universe to sheer exuberance in the perception of the everyday; an intense introversion and aloneness that engendered fancies of an ecstatic/erotic nature, as well as an objective and philosophical view of the meaning of life."—letter of February 23, 1990.

Murray, Bain. Safe in Their Alabaster Chambers. New York: Galaxy Music, 1968.

Commissioned: Robert Shaw, 1962.

Composed: 1962.

Setting: mixed chorus SATB, English horn, violoncello; optional accompaniment for organ.

Duration: 5:20.

Johnson: 216.

First performance: First Unitarian Church Choir, Cleveland, OH, 1962.

Recording: Kulas Choir, Robert Shaw, director; Harvey McGuire, English horn; Warren Downs, cello. Composers Recordings CRI 182/182SD, 1964.

"Robert Shaw, along with heading the Robert Shaw Chorale and being Associate Conductor of the Cleveland Orchestra, was also minister of music at the First Unitarian Church of Shaker Heights. At that time, the philosophy of the church was to integrate musical selections with sermon topics as closely as possible. Shaw was about to give a sermon on the poetry of Emily Dickinson—its transcendental qualities intrigued him—and he asked me to write a new piece for that event. I chose the early imagistic 'Safe in Their Alabaster Chambers,' which contrasts the brief, temporal existence of man and his civilizations with the eternity of the universe. In this setting the English horn and cello act as a kind of pastoral ritornello which weaves through the vocal texture and attempts to bring out the bleak, mystical quality of the poem. The premiere occurred on April 29, 1962, as part of a service in which Robert Shaw preached a sermon on the 'Prophets of the American Spirit— Emily Dickinson.' "—letter of December 12, 1990.

Niles, John D. Gifts. Poems and Translations, 1962-1969 [manuscript].

Composed 1962-69.

Setting: voice, guitar chords.

Johnson: 465, 812, 1233, 1528, 1540.

Location: composer.

"I'm amazed and a bit taken aback that you have discovered this. It's a young book, and a homemade production. The Dickinson song settings have not been performed; to tell the truth, I'd forgotten that I made them. I do not consider myself a composer, just someone interested in the musical possibilities of poetry."—letter of April 24, 1989.

Nixon, Roger. Six Moods of Love; a Song Cycle for Soprano and Piano. New York: Independent Music Publishers, 1950.

Composed: 1950.

Setting: soprano or mezzo-soprano, piano.

Duration: 17:00.

Johnson: 1053 (and texts by other poets).

Recording: Dorothy Renzi, soprano; Raylene Pierce, piano. Fantasy 5009, 1959.

Nowak, Lionel. Three Songs [manuscript].

Composed: 1942.

Setting: medium voice, piano.

Johnson: 324, 425, 1593.

Location: composer; Bennington College Music Library.

"Their writing may have sprung from the summer of 1940 when I accompanied soprano Ethel Luening (then wife of Otto Luening) in many of the Dickinson settings by Ernst Bacon. The natural ease and fluency of his writing may well have accounted for the simplicity in my setting of two of the set. Despite the austerity in much of Emily, I have often found an ineffable charm and lightness which I tried to project, especially in 'Sabbath' [324]." —letters of April 16 and May 14, 1989.

Nowak, Lionel. Summer Is Away. Nine Songs on Poems of Emily Dickinson. New York: American Composers Edition, 1976.
Composed: 1976.
Setting: low voice, flute, clarinet, bassoon, piano, violoncello.
Johnson: 249, 1186, 1233, 1259, 1503, 1518, 1536, 1548, 1695.
First Performance: Richard Frisch, Baritone; Maurice Pachman, bassoon; Gunnar Schonbeck, clarinet; Sue Kahn, flute; Lionel Nowak, piano; Michael Finckel, violoncello. Bennington College, October 27, 1976.

Obrecht, Eldon. Three Dickinson Songs [manuscript].
Commissioned: Dr. Richard Kerber, University of Iowa.
Composed: 1985.
Setting: voice, clarinet, piano.
Johnson: 276, 321, 808.
Location: composer; The University of Iowa Library.
First Performance: Carol Meier, soprano. Richard Kerber, clarinet; Eldon Obrecht, piano. University of Iowa, May, 1985.
"Dr. Richard Kerber, a member of the faculty of the University of Iowa College of Medicine, is a good clarinetist. He commissioned my songs as a wedding anniversary present for his wife, Dr. Linda Kerber, Professor of History. The Kerbers had enjoyed

reading Dickinson poems together in their student days."—letter of September 24, 1990.

Olan, David. After Great Pain. Five Poems of Emily Dickinson. New York: American Composers Edition, 1982.
Composed: 1982.
Setting: soprano, electronic tape.
Duration: 9:45
Johnson: 178, 341, 405, 673, 1053.
Recording: Composers Recordings CRI CD 565 (1988). Judith Bettina, soprano.

Olin, Esther M. Elegy on Three Dickinson Poems [manuscript].
Composed: 1972.
Setting: soprano, percussion, piano.
Duration: 5:02.
Johnson 258, 449, 1732.
Location: composer.
First Performance: Isabelle Schwartz, soprano; Robert LeBlanc, piano; John Vidacovich, percussion. Loyola University College of Music, April 5, 1972.
"These three songs are in extended serial compositional style, and are minimalist in sound. The timbral possibilities of the various set-forms are explored, using soprano and piano in Songs 1 [449] and 2 [1732]. In Song 3 [258], timpani and cymbal timbres are additionally integrated. Large leaps and the articulative demands of the vocal part call for a coloratura soprano of considerable versatility."—letter of January 9, 1990.

O'Meara, Mollie. Songs of Life, Death, and Love Beyond Death [manuscript].
Composed: 1977.

Setting: mezzo-soprano, percussion (xylophone, chimes, snare drums, timpani), violin, violoncello.

Johnson: 491, 549, 749, 809, 1121, 1287.

Location: composer.

First Performance: Central Ohio Composers Alliance, October, 1984.

"These songs are character pieces: the music, which is atonal but not serial, describes the moods and rhythms of the poetry. Each piece employs a different combination and use of the six instruments. Metres change with the metres of the poems. The vocal part calls for a mezzo with a wide range, and ability to read and sing intervals rather than melody; some sprechstimme is used. The pieces form a complete cycle, as the first poem is repeated at the end,

though the music is somewhat different."—letter of September 5, 1990.

O'Meara, Mollie. Two Emily Dickinson Songs [manuscript].

Composed: 1977.

Setting: soprano, violin.

Johnson: 480, 1333.

Location: composer.

"'Why Do I Love You?' [480] and 'A Little Madness' [1333] are scored for piano and violin. The first is tonal, and uses conventional melody shared between the instruments. The second employs mostly sprechstimme in the vocal part while the violin accompaniment is jazz-like in its melodic and rhythmic lines."—letter of September 5, 1990.

Alice Parker

"Emily Dickinson lived in an age when the role of women was fixed by seemingly immutable laws. The depth of her response—not in headlines and confrontation but in the quietness of her life and the explosion of her art—has made her poems speak increasingly clearly to a generation raised on protest marches and radical feminism. For, of course, she does far more than protest injustice: she posits a way of life that honors all creation, that sees the humanity behind religious cant, that encompasses birth, love, death, eternity, with broad vision tempered by a piquant wit. Her theme is life itself, lived fully and consciously."—letter of June 16, 1989.

Parker, Alice. Commentaries. A Cantata for Two Choruses of Women's Voices and Full Orchestra, Based on Five Poems of Emily Dickinson and Southern Folksongs, Hymns and Spirituals. New York: [n.p.], 1978.

Commissioned: Meredith College, Raleigh, NC., 1978.

Composed: 1978.

Setting: two women's choruses, orchestra.

Johnson: 89, 387, 502, 850, 1574.

First Performance: Meredith Chorale, North Carolina Symphony, Consortium of Women's College Choruses, conducted by Alice Parker, Meredith College, Raleigh, NC, April 16, 1978.

"In this work Emily Dickinson's poems serve as contrapuntal commentary on sacred and secular texts of the same era, principally from the south. Her conception of a life as a 'Waiting,' a 'Journey to the Day,' is paralleled in the sentimental dialogue of the 'pilgrim stranger' hymn. This text, with its familiar melody called 'Warrenton' or 'Nettleton,' was found in *Genuine Church Music*, Winchester, Virginia, 1835.

"Her paradoxical defintion of love as 'the sweetest Heresey' is balanced by an Appalachian love song with old English roots ('O waly, waly'). The singer laments her lost love with unaccustomed frankness: 'To think so fair a lady as I am Should be in love, and be denied.' Love ends in loneliness—and Emily Dickinson's heartfelt cry is a hymn. Who else would use common meter to ask 'Say, Jesus Christ of Nazareth—Hast Thou no Arm for Me?' Despair itself is turned to love in the magnificent cadences of the Spiritual, which transforms moaning into 'the Holy Ghost, Comin' down from above.' Her epigram on Time balances evanescence and eternity with the incredible line 'There are that resting, rise.' The folk answer is a Quaker hymn, origin unknown, which draws from earth's lamentations an unquenchable faith: 'How can I keep from singing?'

"And we close, as often happens, with the Promised Land. Emily's bird flies up, needing neither ladder nor baton; and her cherubim are wafted by His 'Come unto me.' As before, the commentary works two ways, and the delightful lilt of the tune 'Mt. Sion,' from the *Kentucky Harmony*, 1815, is reflected in its cheerful refrain: 'Then let your songs abound / Let every tear be dry; / We're marching through Emmanuel's ground / To fairer worlds on high.'"—letter of June 16, 1989, with notes from *Commentaries*, April, 1978.

Parker, Alice. Echoes from the Hills. A Song Cycle On Seven Poems [manuscript].

Commissioned: Mohawk Trail Concerts, 1979.

Composed: 1979.

Setting: soprano, flute, clarinet, horn, string quartet (2 violins, viola, violoncello).

Johnson: 26, 76, 279, 722, 766, 1420, 1634.

Location: composer.

First Performance: Mohawk Trail Concert, August 17, 1979.

Recording: Musical Heritage Society MHS 827161.

"The music springs from the poems of Emily Dickinson, who lived in nearby Amherst: her 'hills' flow north to Charlemont, the composer's home. The brevity, frankness, wit and weight of the poems is reflected in the songs, which flow with a thoroughly vocal lyricism. We approach the hills lightly and easily, through the meadows, bearing the song as a gift: 'It's all I have to bring today / This, and my heart beside. / This, and my heart, and all the fields / And all the meadows wide.'

"Then the mood turns slow and mysterious, with bird calls and winds and bugles: 'Talk not to me of Summer Trees / The foliage of the mind / A Tabernacle is for Birds / Of no corporeal kind.'

"With the third song we are in the 'Sweet Mountains' which 'tell me no lie'. With broad affirmation, she salutes their permanence, and prays: 'My Strong Madonnas—cherish still / The Wayward Nun—beneath the Hill / Whose service is to you.'

"A bright wit and whimsy suffuse Emily Dickinson's boast 'My Faith is

Three Songs

By

Pippa's Song .30
Dance of The Faries .60
Have You got a Brook in
your Little Heart .50

Miss Etta Parker

Copyright 1896 by Miles & Thompson   Boston

Cover of *Three Songs by Miss Etta Parker* (including "Have You Got a Brook in Your Little Heart"). Boston: Miles & Thompson, ©1896.

larger than the Hills,' matched by the quirky 7-8 rhythms in the music. She foresees the end of the world, but for her: 'How dare I, therefore, stint a faith / On which so vast depends / Lest Firmament should fail for me / The Rivet in the Band.'

"Then slow, sustained anguish: after the wakeful night, she hears the birds, and flings out a question that will receive reply only 'when Flesh and Spirit sunder' in Death: 'Why Birds, a Summer morning / Before the Quick of Day / Should stab my ravished spirit / With Dirks of Melody.'

"The next-to-last song images a ship putting out to sea—Eternity—exultantly catching the full wind as it leaves the shore: 'Bred as we, among the mountains / Can the sailor understand / The divine intoxication / of the first league out from land?'

"And finally, Death again: this time the journey, with horses, a wild carriage ride to Judgement, and a final goodbye: 'Tie the strings to my life, my Lord / Then, I am ready to go! / Goodbye to the Life I used to live / And the World I used to know. / And kiss the Hills for me, just once / Then —I am ready to go!' "

Parker, Alice. Three Seas [manuscript].
Commissioned: Holton Arms School, Bethesda, MD, 1989.
Composed: 1989.
Setting: SSAA chorus, 2 flutes, bassoon, harp.
Johnson: 695, 1198, 1695.
Location: composer.
First performance: Holton Arms School Choir, Alice Parker, conductor. Holton Arms School, March 1989.

Parker, Etta. Have You Got a Brook in Your Little Heart? Boston: C. W. Thompson, 1896.
Composed: 1896.
Setting: voice, piano.
Johnson: 136.
Also published in *Three Songs.* Boston: Miles & Thompson, 1896. Emily Dickinson's words were used by permission of Lavinia Dickinson, her sister.

Pasatieri, Thomas. Far from Love. Melville, NY: Belwin-Mills, 1976.
Setting: soprano, clarinet, piano, violin, violoncello.
Duration: 22:00.
Johnson: 130, 463, 494, 549, 622, 644, 739, 995, 1021, 1065, 1099, 1398, 1593.

Pasatieri, Thomas. Reflections. Melville, NY: Belwin-Mills, 1977.
Composed: 1975.
Setting: voice, piano.
Johnson: 739.

Patterson, Janie Alexander. Not in Vain. Philadelphia, PA: Theodore Presser, 1944.
Composed: 1944.
Setting: low voice, piano.
Johnson: 919.

Pender, Nicholas Scott. From the Letters of Emily Dickinson [manuscript].
Composed: 1988.
Setting: SSAA women's chorus, 2 horns, piano.
Duration: 13:00.
Johnson Letters: 216, 225, 234, 388.
Location: composer.
First Performance: The DaCamera Singers, Ernest Liotti, conductor, Jean

Crichton, mezzo-soprano; Adam Tillett, Jennifer Smith, horns; Scott Pender, piano. Bradley Hills Presbyterian Church, Bethesda, MD, June 25, 1989.

Pengilly, Sylvia. Three Poems of Emily Dickinson [manuscript].

Composed: 1973.

Setting: soprano, piano.

Johnson: 214, 341, 1068.

Location: composer.

First Performance: Mary deFord, soprano; Jerry Davidson, piano. Cleveland Composers' Guild, Cleveland State University Auditorium, May 13, 1973.

"During 1972, when I was an instructor in Theory at Kent State University, I became friends with Tom and Gina Davis, of the English department. Their great gift to me was to introduce me to American literature and poetry that had previously been unknown to me. Their Christmas gift to me in 1972 was the Thomas H. Johnson edition of the complete poems of Emily Dickinson, together with a critical biography, *This Was a Poet* by George Frisbee Whicher. These books kindled my interest and gave me a profound respect for Miss Dickinson's craft, to the extent that I decided to set three of her poems to music. These songs, together with my rough compositional sketches, comprised my Christmas gift to Tom and Gina in 1973.

"Technically, they were composed using twelve-tone serial procedures, my feeling being that the subtleties of this style would best express the delicate imagery of Miss Dickinson's poetry."—letter of February 4, 1990.

Perera, Ronald. Five Summer Songs on Poems of Emily Dickinson. Boston: E. C. Schirmer, 1976.

Composed: 1969, 1972.

Setting: mezzo-soprano, piano.

Johnson: 86, 99, 307, 337, 1755.

Jane Manning discusses these songs in her *New Vocal Repertory*. London: Macmillan; New York: Taplinger, 1986.

Perle, George. Thirteen Dickinson Songs. Newton Centre, MA: Gunmar Music, 1981-1984. 3 vols.

Composed: 1977-78.

Setting: soprano, piano.

Duration: 36:00.

Johnson: 130, 134, 144, 256, 277, 289, 436, 516, 536, 585, 777, 949, 1593.

First Performance: Bethany Beardslee, soprano; Morey Ritt, piano. Fifth Annual Arts Song Festival of the Westminster Choir College, Princeton, NJ, June 19, 1978.

Recording: Composers Recordings, CRI SD 403, 1979. Bethany Beardslee, soprano; Morey Ritt, piano. Nos. 1-4 reissued on *Music of George Perle*, Composers Recordings ACS 6015 CRI, 1986.

Bibliography: Ann Willison. "Composer as Interpreter of the Poems of Emily Dickinson." Seminar Paper, Department of Comparative Literature, Indiana University, 1990. Comparative study of settings by Perle, Bacon, Copland, and Getty.

See also Marshall Bialosky's review of Kirchner's songs, *Notes* 45 (June 1989): 861-863, which compares settings by Bacon, Copland, and Perle.

Perry, Julia. By the Sea. New York: Galaxy Music, 1950.
Composed: 1950.
Setting: soprano or tenor [and piano?].

Persichetti, Vincent. Emily Dickinson Songs, Opus 77. Bryn Mawr, PA: Elkan-Vogel, 1958.
Composed: 1958.
Setting: mezzo-soprano, piano.
Johnson: 101, 288, 333, 729, 758, 919.

Persichetti, Vincent. If I Can Stop One Heart from Breaking. Bryn Mawr: Elkan-Vogel, 1956.
Setting: mezzo-soprano, piano.
Johnson: 919.

Pierce, Brent. Solitude of Space: Choralography, Mixed Chorus. New York: Walton Music, 1975.
Composed: 1975.
Setting: 8-part mixed chorus (SSAATTBB), piano.
Johnson: 1695.
Included is a chart illustrating head, face, arm, and foot positions.

Pierce, Brent. Who Are You? New York: Walton Music, 1975.
Composed: 1975.
Setting: SATB chorus.
Johnson: 288.
Includes choralography chart, as above.

Pilz, Gerhard. The Brain is Wider than the Sky. Vienna: Rockband The Prize, 1988.
Composed: 1988.
Setting: Guitars, bass, keyboards, drums.
Johnson: 362
First performance: Rockband The Prize, in Feldkirch, Austria, 1988.
Recording: Studio Karrow, Bregenz, LC-NR 7982.

"At first sight it seems odd that in this case I have packed lyrics of Emily Dickinson into Rockmusic. It is her open mind that inspired me. Surely Emily Dickinson was ahead of her time. There are not many poets who have created such immortal works. Perhaps it is [chance], or a flair for something new, that this synthesis of lyrics and music had come together." —letter of June 3, 1991.

"I was surprised to hear that such a great number of musicians have put Emily Dickinson's words to music. So we are proud to belong to them, although her poems are not that well known in Austria. But the positive reaction of the audience shows us that a lot of people are sick of hearing always the same lyrics in modern music."—letter of November 15, 1991.
The composer is also working on a setting of "Snake" (1740) and "There's Been a Death" (389).

Pinkham, Daniel. An Emily Dickinson Mosaic. New York: C. F. Peters, 1963.
Commissioned: Mount Holyoke College, 1962.
Composed: 1962.
Setting: women's chorus, piano or orchestra.
Duration: 10:00
Johnson: 632, 677, 680, 1118, 1354, 1355.
First Performance: South Hadley, MA, Mount Holyoke College. Glee Club Commencement, June 1, 1962.

Pinkham, Daniel. Safe in Their Alabaster Chambers. Boston: E. C. Schirmer, 1974.
Composed: 1972.
Setting: medium voice, electronic tape.
Johnson: 130, 216, 258.

Pinkham, Daniel. Getting to Heaven. Boston: Ione Press, 1987.
Composed: 1987.
Setting: SATB, soprano solo, harp, contrabass quintet.
Johnson: 4, 150, 157, 324, 947, 1278.
First Performance: "A Concert for the Hymnbook," Boston, October 24, 1987.

Pinkham, Daniel. Down an Amherst Path. Boston: Ione Press, 1989.
Composed: 1989.
Setting: TTBB chorus a cappella.
Johnson: 204, 328, 783, 1035, 1053, 1710.
First Performance: Yale University, Sprague Hall, June 3, 1989.
"The Board of the Boston Gay Men's Chorus, who asked me to submit a text which was 'life affirming,' found 'It is as a Quiet Way' especially appropriate, considering the large number of their colleagues who had died of AIDS. ED's concern with death and eternity is often expressed magically, as 'This World did drop away As Acres from the feet.'"—letter of May 28, 1989.

Pisk, Paul A. Sunset, Opus 81. New York: American Composers Edition, 1954.
Composed: 1954.
Setting: SSAA chorus.
Johnson: 221.

Potter, Virginia. The Heart Asks Pleasure First [manuscript].
Composed: 1926.
Setting: voice, piano.
Johnson: 536.
Location: composer.

Rands, Bernard. Canti dell'eclissi. London: Universal Edition, 1991.
Commissioned: Philadelphia Orchestra, "Meet the Composer" orchestral composer-in-residence program.
Composed: 1991.
Setting: bass solo, large orchestra (3.3.4.4., 4.3.4.1., 2 harps, celesta, piano, electric organ, timpani, 4 percussionists, strings).
Johnson: 415.
First performance: Thomas Paul, bass; Philadelphia Orchestra; Riccardo Muti, conductor. (Scheduled for 1992-93 season.)
"I have set Dickinson's poem as one of 13 texts dealing with the eclipse of the sun and moon. *Canti dell'eclissi* is the third and final part of a trilogy, including *Canti lunatici* and *Canti dell' sole.*"—letter of September, 1991.

Rasely, Charles W. Hope Is a Thing with Feathers. Allegany, NY: Music 70/80, 1982.
Composed: 1969; SATB arrangement 1982.
Setting: SATB a cappella.
Johnson: 254.
First Performance: St. Bonaventure University Concert Choir, St. Bonaventure University, New York, 1986.
"An opening phrase of the music occurred to me almost immediately. Then the remaining sections fell into place and came into being as an SSA arrangement. However, the editor of *Music 70/80* felt it should be an unaccompanied SATB, which is what finally evolved for publication." —letter of July 25, 1990.

Rasely, Charles W. I Never Saw a Moor.
Oneida: Plymouth Music, 1976.
Composed: 1971.
Setting: SATB a cappella.
Johnson: 1052.
First Performance: St. Bonaventure University Chamber Singers, 1982 Concert at the University, St. Bonaventure, New York, 1982.
"After reading the poem several musical ideas came to mind which seemed to illustrate, in a musical sense, the ideas of the poet. When word images are potent and condensed, as are those of Emily Dickinson, the music seems to write itself. In this case the composition took all of four hours to complete."—letter of July 25, 1990.

Raum, Elizabeth. The Passing [manuscript].
Composed: 1983.
Setting: soprano or mezzo-soprano, piano.
Johnson: 712.
Location: composer.
"I always felt this poem to be quite moving. I feel the music suits its funereal quality, but turns hopeful at the end. I write in tonal style."—letter of January, 1990.

Raymond-Ward, Adeline. A Day.
Boston: Charles W. Homeyer, 1913.
Composed: 1913.
Setting: voice, piano.
Johnson: 318.

Reinagle, A.R., "St. Peter." See "Miscellany" section. Jones, Joseph, arr. A Garland for Emily.

Rericha, Robert J. There's a Certain Slant of Light [manuscript].
Composed: 1985.
Setting: voice, guitar.
Johnson: 258.

Location: composer.
First Performance: East Cleveland Community Theatre, June, 1988.
"I chose Miss Dickinson's poems because they seem to have a certain quality that turns them into music when they are read. I am planning to set more of her poems in the near future. I do regret that our lifetimes were not concurrent so that I could have met this special woman."—letter of March, 1990.

Richter, Marga. Three Songs to Poems of Emily Dickinson. New York: G. Schirmer, 1984.
Commissioned: Mädchenchor, Hannover, December, 1982.
Composed: 1982.
Setting: four-part women's chorus.
Johnson: 442, 445, 585.

Riegger, Wallingford. Eternity. New York: H. Flammer, 1945.
Setting: women's chorus, flute, bassoon, 2 horns.
Johnson: 695.

Riley, Dennis. Seven Songs on Poems of Emily Dickinson, for Soprano and Orchestra. New York: C.F. Peters, 1987.
Composed: 1978-81.
Setting: soprano, orchestra; soprano, piano.
First performance [piano version]: Catherine Aks, soprano; Walter Hilse, piano. Carnegie Recital Hall, New York City, March 20, 1982.
Duration: 15:00.
Johnson: 6, 12, 47, 99, 288, 321, 657.

Riley, Dennis. Three Little Commentaries [manuscript].
Composed: 1981.
Setting: SAB chorus, string ensemble.

Riley, Dennis. Three Little Commentaries [manuscript].
Composed: 1981.
Setting: SAB chorus, string ensemble.
Johnson: 288.
Location: composer.

Rizzetto, Jay. Five Poems of Emily Dickinson for Trumpet and Narrator. Oakland, CA: Pasquina Publishing, 1978. (Sales agent, North Easton, MA: King Music Sales.)
Composed: 1978.
Setting: Narrator, solo trumpet.
Johnson: 214, 258, 441, 712, 790.
First Performance: Diane Rizzetto, narrator; Jay Rizzetto, trumpet. Eastern Nazarene College, Quincy, MA, 1978.
"At the time I was performing quite a few trumpet recitals around the Boston area and thought it would be interesting to include in a performance my wife, Diane, who had considerable stage skills. I searched for a work that we could do together and was quite disappointed by what I found.

"I informed Diane that I would write a piece for us. Diane was at this time a master's degree candidate in American Literature at Brown University and was writing her thesis on Emily Dickinson. She had been reading Emily's poems to me for the past year and I decided that some of these poems might work out. Diane's suggestions were immensely helpful, and I was lucky to have a Dickinson scholar so close at hand!

"The poems are read in a dramatic manner. The work is tonal and written in traditional music notation. The trumpet uses different mutes throughout the work."—letter of February 26, 1990.

Rogers, William Keith. Three Songs from Emily Dickinson. Scarborough, Ontario: Berandol Music, 1969.
Composed: 1948.
Setting: SATB chorus.
Johnson: 536, 585, 1672.

Rorem, Ned. Love's Stricken "Why?" [manuscript].
Composed: 1947.
Setting: mezzo-soprano, piano.
Johnson: 1368.
Location: composer, Library of Congress.

Rorem, Ned. Poems of Love and the Rain; A Song Cycle for Mezzo-Soprano and Piano. Oceanside, NY: Boosey & Hawkes, 1965.
Commissioned: Ford Foundation.
Composed: 1962-63.
Setting: mezzo-soprano, piano.
Duration: 28:00.
Johnson: 1368.
Recordings:
  Regina Sarfaty, mezzo-soprano; Ned Rorem, piano. Composers Recordings CRI 202 [1965?].
  Beverly Wolff, mezzo-soprano; Ned Rorem, piano. Phoenix PHCD 108, 1989; reissue of Desto DC 6480, 1969.
Also includes texts by Donald Windham, W.H. Auden, e.e. cummings, Howard Moss, Theodore Roethke, J. Larson, and Kenneth Pitchford.

Rorem, Ned. Women's Voices. Eleven Songs for Soprano and Piano. New York: Boosey & Hawkes, 1979.
Composed: 1975.
Setting: soprano or mezzo-soprano, piano.
Duration: 22:00.
Johnson: 115.

First Performance: Joyce Mathis, mezzo-soprano. Alice Tully Hall, New York, 1976.

Also includes texts by E. Wylie, C. Rossetti, A. Bradstreet, M. E. Coleridge, and others.

Rorem, Ned. After Long Silence. New York: Boosey & Hawkes, 1982.
Composed: 1982.
Setting: voice, oboe, strings.
Johnson: 341.

Rorem, Ned. Swords and Plowshares [manuscript].
Composed: 1990.
Setting: four voices, orchestra.
Johnson: 67, 1755.
Location: composer.

Roy, William. This Little Rose. New York: G. Schirmer, 1947.
Setting: voice, piano.
Johnson: 35.
Reprinted in *Songs by 22 Americans; A Collection of Songs by Outstanding American Composers,* compiled by Bernard Taylor. New York: G. Schirmer, 1960.

Roy, William. Spring. New York: G. Schirmer, 1948.
Setting: voice, piano.
Johnson: 844.

Ruggiero, Charles H. Songs from Emily Dickinson [manuscript].
Composed: 1974.
Setting: soprano, chamber ensemble.
Duration: 25:00.
Johnson: 258, 280, 380, 436, 1062, 1078, 1612.
Location: American Music Center.
"This song cycle is an early work of mine, but I'm still happy with much of it."—letter of April 12, 1989.

Ruiter, Wim de. Four Songs on Poems by Emily Dickinson. Amsterdam: Donemus, 1983.
Composed: 1983.
Setting: soprano, flute/piccolo, oboe, clarinet, bassoon, horn, piano, violin, viola, violoncello.
Johnson: 386, 1540, 1618, 1670.
Location: Library of Congress.

Sacco, John. Three Songs. Boston: Boston Music, 1941.
Composed: 1941.
Setting: voice, piano.
Johnson: 1052.

Samuel, Gerhard. What of My Music. St. Louis, MO: MMB, 1974.
Composed: 1974.
Setting: soprano, percussion (3 players), double-bass ensemble (30 players).
Johnson: 261.
Recording: *80 Trombones and 30 Basses.* Nelga Lynn, soprano. Composers' Recordings CRI SD 422, 1980.

Samuel, Gerhard. Put Up My Lute! St. Louis, MO: MMB, 1979.
Composed: 1979.
Setting: cello solo, percussion (3 players).
Johnson: 261.

Samuel, Gerhard. Hope Is the Thing with Feathers. St. Louis: MMB, 1980.
Composed: 1980.
Setting: soprano, percussion (1 player), violin.
Johnson: 254.

Samuel, Gerhard. As Imperceptibly as Grief. St. Louis: MMB, 1987.
Composed: 1987.
Setting: 3 percussion soli, orchestra.
Johnson: 1540.

Samuel, Gerhard. Three Songs. St. Louis: MMB, 1991.
Composed: 1991.
Setting: high voice, piano.
Duration: 2:00.
Johnson: 145, 156, 158.

Saya, Mark. Three, By Emily [manuscript].
Composed: 1978.
Setting: soprano, piano.
Duration: 4:00.
Johnson: 288, 362, 1755.
Location: composer.
"The first song [288] is playful and eccentric, the second [1755] very lyric, the third [362] quite dramatic. All are serially constructed. The row—D, C, E, F, B, A, F sharp, G, E flat, D flat, A flat, B flat—clearly has tonal possibilities, which I employed most noticeably in the second song."—letter of January 17, 1990.

Schevill, James Erwin. Emily Dickinson [manuscript].
Setting: mixed chorus, chamber ensemble.
Johnson: 126, 258, 435, 632, 1082.
Location: composer.
See also Bielawa. A Dickinson Album.

Schröter, L. "Freut euch des Lebens."
See "Miscellany" section. Jones, Joseph, arr. A Garland for Emily.

Schudel, Thomas. Three Songs on Poems of Emily Dickinson [manuscript].
Composed: 1980.
Setting: soprano or tenor, piano.
Johnson: 258, 1593, 1732.
Location: composer.
"I am working on a longer chamber piece for soprano, flute, oboe, clarinet, percussion, piano, and viola, on several poems of Emily Dickinson, but it has no title yet."—letter of August, 1991.

Schwartz, Paul. Three Choruses on Poems by Emily Dickinson. New York: Rongen Music, 1981.
Composed: 1981.
Setting: SATB chorus, piano.
Johnson: 386, 861, 1685.

Sclater, James S. Four Songs on Texts of Emily Dickinson.
Clinton, MS: Mt. Salus Music, 1977.
Composed: 1976.
Setting: soprano, clarinet.
Johnson: 1035, 1037, 1738, 1755.

Sclater, James S. Songs of Time and Passing. Clinton, MS: Mt. Salus Music, 1977.
Setting: high voice, piano.
Johnson: 1053, 1065, 1121, 1149, 1445.

Seeboth, Max. I Never Saw a Moor [manuscript].
Setting: SATB chorus, contralto solo.
Johnson: 1052.
Location: Amherst College Library.
Manuscript given to Amherst College by Millicent Todd Bingham in the 1950s.

Shearer, C.M. Of All the Souls. San Antonio, TX: Southern Music, 1982.
Composed: 1982.
Setting: SATB chorus.
Johnson: 664.
"This piece was written for the Texas University Interscholastic League State Choral Sight-Reading Contest. It was first sightread by about fifty choirs throughout the state. It has subsequently been performed by high-school and college choirs."—letter of April, 1989.

Shore, Clare. Four Dickinson Songs.
Washington, D.C.: Sisra Publications,
1984.
Composed: 1981-82.
Setting: soprano, harpsichord.
Johnson: 193, 288, 434, 794.
First Performance: Deanna McBroom,
soprano; Roye Linn Kulik, harpsi-
chord. Charleston Spoleto Festival,
June 1, 1984, Charleston, SC.
"The songs are of medium difficulty and
are written in a rather chromatic, con-
trapuntal style."—letter of July 11,
1989.

Silsbee, Ann L. An Acre for a Bird.
New York: American Composers
Edition, 1982.
Commissioned: Peter Perrin, Alliance for
American Song.
Composed: 1982.
Setting: soprano, mezzo-soprano, and
tenor soloists, piano, percussion.
Johnson: 1677.
First Performance: New York Motet
Choir, Stephen Sturk, conductor.
Merkin Hall, New York, at concert
"Six Decades, 1922-1982," June 21,
1983.
"Taking its cue from the opposition in
the poem of apparent serenity ('On
my volcano grows the grass a medita-
tive spot') with boiling intensity ('How
red the fire rocks below'), the men's
voices undermine the attempt at a
lyrical unfolding of the text in the
women's voices by their incessant
nervous aleatory repetition."—letter
of May 14, 1989.

Silverman, Faye-Ellen. In Shadow. New
York: Seesaw Music, 1973.
Composed: 1972.
Setting: soprano, clarinet, guitar.
Johnson: 101, 348, 1760.

First performance: Katherine Hoffman,
soprano; Dennis Turchek, guitar; Ann
Owen, clarinet. New York City,
February 8, 1973.

**Silverman, Faye-Ellen. Echoes of
Emily.** New York: Seesaw Music,
1979.
Composed: 1979.
Setting: contralto, English horn.
Johnson: 476, 777.
First performance: Ann Zibelman, alto;
James Ostryniec, English horn. Bal-
timore, MD, October 16, 1979.

Sims, Jo Ann. That I Did Always Love
[manuscript].
Composed: 1989.
Setting: soprano, piano.
Johnson: 549.
Location: composer.
First Performance: Jo Ann Lacquet Sims,
soprano; Greg Upton, piano. Faculty
Recital, Department of Music, The
University of Mississippi, February 5,
1990.

Siskind, Paul A. Some Epigrams. Minne-
apolis, MN: Sweet Child Music, 1986.
Composed: 1986.
Setting: high or medium voice, piano.
Duration: 9:00.
Johnson: 288.

Siskind, Paul A. Some More Epigrams.
Minneapolis, MN: Sweet Child Music,
1989.
Composed: 1989.
Setting: high or medium voice, piano.
Duration: 10:00.
Johnson: 1389.
"'Some Epigrams' and 'Some More Epi-
grams' are two collections totaling
eleven short songs; besides Emily Dick-
inson, the poets include David Igna-
tow, Langston Hughes, Stephen Crane,

John Keats, David Marc Fischer, Alfred Lord Tennyson, and Bob Kaufman. The songs are connected solely by the terse, epigrammatic nature of the poetry, rather than by any underlying musico-dramatic concept. The performer is thus free to select those songs he or she finds most attractive or appropriate for his or her vocal range or programming needs. The songs convey a wide variety of quickly-changing moods, reflecting the sometimes quirky aspects inherent in the poems."—letter of January 17, 1990.

Leo Smit

"Since August 1988, when I bought a copy of her complete poems in the 'urtext' edition, Emily Dickinson has been running my life. Opening the book of poems at random, I read, 'I was a Phoebe—nothing more' [1009]. Turning some pages, I noticed the phrase 'perfect Mozart' in a poem that began 'Better—than music!' [503]. Continuing to jump from poem to poem, I found many references to music, some direct, others metaphoric, and to birds, her symbols for life and creativity. Within minutes I had decided to compose a cycle of songs for mezzo-soprano (representing the poet) and piano.

"That was just the beginning, for upon completion of the twelve songs ('The Celestial Thrush'), I had planned several more cycles, each devoted to an important subject, such as memories and fantasies of childhood, love and renunciation, religious struggles, death and immortality, and last, pride in her own poetic powers, thus touching upon the crucial events and concerns of her life. Digressing briefly, I set five of her poems on death and dying for a cappella chorus ('The Last Hour'), in memory of a dear friend who was soon to be 'called back.'

"Since that 'mighty afternoon' in August, when I encountered the electric mind and effusive heart of this glorious woman, I have set some seventy-seven poems hoping to send her my musical responses to the deep thoughts and questions she propounded. A few months after falling under the spell of the great poet, I dreamed I was in her house, playing on her twangy square grand piano, knowing she was in her upstairs bedroom listening through the narrowly opened door. When I finished, I turned around, sensing a presence, and saw a slight girl in white, enveloped by a fiery mist. She silently pressed two hyacinths into my hand and vanished. I still have not awakened from my dream."—letter of May 24, 1989.

Smit, Leo. The Last Hour. In Memory of Harriet Greif [manuscript].
Composed: 1988.
Setting: mixed chorus a cappella.
Johnson: 158, 182, 279, 441, 919.
Location: composer.

Smit, Leo. A Love [manuscript].
Composed: 1989.
Setting: solo female violist/reciter.
Johnson: 663.
Location: composer.
"[I am now] well into No. 663 ('Again— his voice is at the door'), a terrifying

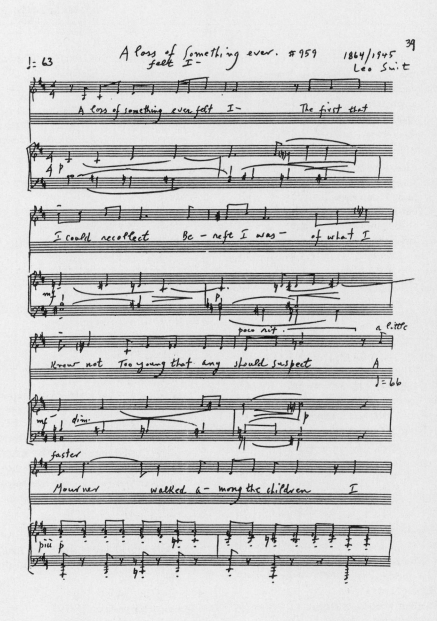

Leo Smit. "A Loss of Something Ever," from *The Ecstatic Pilgrimage*,
Cycle I. Autograph manuscript, 1989. Reprinted by permission of the
composer.

poem (what a climax!) which I shall call 'Under a Tender Moon.' This version will replace the one for female violist/reciter. The new setting is for soprano, horn, viola, and harp."—letter of March 10, 1990. [See "Under a Tender Moon," below.]

Smit, Leo. The Ecstatic Pilgrimage. Five Song-cycles for Mezzo-soprano and Piano [manuscript].

Cycle I: Childe Emilie (memories and fantasies of childhood).

Johnson: 9, 61, 425, 486, 508, 586, 588, 600, 613, 637, 728, 959, 1010, 1738.

Cycle II: The Celestial Thrush (songs of music and birds).

Johnson: 83, 250, 326, 500, 503, 1005, 1009, 1585, 1591, 1600, 1761, 1775.

Cycle III: The Marigold Heart (songs of love and renunciation).

Johnson: 186, 249, 301, 322, 336, 456, 461, 537, 599, 659, 754, 1072, 1398, 1637, 1643.

Cycle IV: Beyond Circumference (songs of death, faith and immortality).

Johnson: 193, 277, 341, 344, 374, 376, 378, 410, 449, 465, 502, 524, 531, 547, 692, 947, 1030, 1297, 1612, 1632, 1638.

Cycle V: The Purple Diadem (the poet speaks).

Johnson: 431, 448, 505, 544, 569, 657, 883, 1162, 1247.

Composed: 1989.

Setting: mezzo-soprano, piano or chamber choir.

Johnson: (see Cycles above).

Location: composer.

First Performance: Unitarian Church, Buffalo, NY., October 29, 1989 (Selections).

Smit, Leo. Under a Tender Moon [manuscript].

Commissioned: New York State Music Teacher's Association, 1990.

Composed: 1990.

Setting: soprano, horn, harp, viola.

Johnson: 663.

Location: composer.

First performance: Neva Pilgrim, soprano. Syracuse University, October 27, 1990.

New commission and setting for "A Love" (1989) cited above.

Smit, Leo. Light and Landscapes [in progress; manuscript].

Composed: 1990-.

Setting: voice, piano.

Johnson (to date): 258, 812, 1000, 1278.

Location: composer.

"Am waiting word from a publisher re my 'Childe Emilie' cycle. I have now set eighty songs. Previewed 'Childe Emilie' June 9th, at St. Peter's Church in NYC, and June 19th at the Cleveland Museum of Art. Both with Rosiland Rees, soprano."—letter of August 7, 1991.

Smith, Russell. Three Songs from Emily Dickinson. New York: F. Colombo, 1963.

Composed: 1963.

Setting: SSA chorus.

Johnson: 47, 586, 1042.

Snyder, Randall. Blue Sea, My River Runs to Thee [manuscript].

Composed: 1966.

Setting: SATB chorus, woodwind ensemble.
Johnson: 162.
Location: composer.

Snyder, Randall. Songs of Life and Death [manuscript].
Composed: 1966.
Setting: high voice, piano.
Johnson: 76, 162, 182, 214, 258, 288, 650, 812, 816, 1078.
Location: composer.
"All my Dickinson settings were composed while I was an undergraduate student at Quincy College, a small college in Quincy, Illinois, located on the Mississippi River. Her poetry was a graceful start for a beginning composer. I look back on these Neo-Classic settings of my youth with nostalgia and affection."—letter of July 5, 1989.

Snyder, Randall. Two Poems by Emily Dickinson. West Hollywood, CA: Brightstar Music Publications, 1974.
Composed: 1974.
Setting: SATB chorus, baritone solo, flute, oboe, 3 clarinets, bassoon, 2 horns, trumpet, tuba, percussion.
Johnson: 254, 1593.
Reissued: Greeley, CO: Western International Music, 1988.

Sørensen, Bent. Garnet to Garnet. Copenhagen: Wilhelm Hansen, 1985.
Composed: 1985.
Setting: female voice, guitar/electric guitar, percussion (1 player).
Location: Danish Music Information Centre.
First performance: May 1, 1986.
Johnson: 1072.
Emily Dickinson's poem is combined with a quotation from Shakespeare's *Macbeth*.

Soule, Edmund Foster. Parting [manuscript].
Composed: 1948.
Setting: soprano, piano.
Johnson: 1732.
Location: composer.
First Performance: Eugene, OR, 1974.

Soule, Edmund Foster. A Book of Emily; or Thirteen Ways of Looking at Miss Dickinson [manuscript].
Composed: 1978.
Setting: high voice, piano.
Johnson: 47, 111, 214, 280, 288, 364, 441, 479, 712, 919, 1052, 1133, 1173.
Location: composer.
Dedication: In remembrance of the teaching of Estelle Carver, c. 1924-1927, and Hannah Kirk, 1931-1933.
First Performance: Priscilla Woodley, soprano. St. John's University Faculty Recital, April 9, 1984.
"I have read all of Miss Dickinson's poetry, and I am constantly searching for good texts to set. (I seem to be a born composer of songs in an era when solo songs are in little demand.) My feeling is for lyric poetry, and there are at this time almost no lyric poets. Most of the stuff I look through are pieces of visually organized prose. One song of mine is published in a voice-method book."
—letter of July 1, 1989.

Speaks, Oley. Charity. New York: G. Schirmer, 1911.
Composed: 1911.
Setting: high or medium voice, piano.
Johnson: 919.

Sprenkle, Elam Ray. Simple Songs on Nine Tableaux on the Poetry of Emily Dickinson [manuscript].
Composed: 1981-82. Revised 1991.
Setting: mezzo-soprano, piano.

Johnson: 70, 214, 254, 258, 321, 322, 449, 712.

First performance: Baltimore Museum of Art, 1982.

Location: composer.

Sprenkle, Elam Ray. Six Songs for Mezzo-soprano and Brass Quintet [manuscript].

Composed: 1981.

Setting: mezzo-soprano, brass quintet.

Duration: 15:50.

Johnson: 70, 254, 318, 321, 322, 712.

Location: composer.

Recording: Elaine Bonazzi, mezzo-soprano; Annapolis Brass Quintet. Sedro Woolley, WA: Crystal Records S219, 1985.

Springer, Philip. Come Slowly, Eden! Boston: Boston Music, 1986.

Commissioned: Norman Rosten for his play *Come Slowly, Eden!*

Composed: 1966.

Setting: dramatic soprano or mezzo-soprano, piano.

Johnson: 211.

First Performance: University of Illinois at Urbana, November 12, 1986.

"My song 'Come Slowly, Eden!' was commissioned by the poet Norman Rosten for his play of the same title in 1966. It is my first art song and is written using a tone-row technique of my own making."—letter of July 12, 1989.

Starer, Robert. I'm Nobody! New York: Music Corporation of America, 1968.

Commissioned: Sarah Lawrence Chorale, Harold Aks, musical director.

Composed: 1968.

Setting: SSA chorus a cappella.

Johnson: 288.

First Performance: Sarah Lawrence Chorale, Carnegie Hall, NY, 1968.

Starer, Robert. On the Nature of Things. New York: Music Corporation of America, 1969.

Commissioned: Collegiate Chorale, Abraham Kaplan, director, 1969.

Composed: 1969.

Setting: SATB chorus a cappella.

Johnson: 650.

First Performance: Ulster County Community College, Stone Ridge, NY, 1976.

Recording: Collegiate Chorale, Desto DC7106.

"Emily Dickinson's poetry is extraordinarily musical, so attractive to the musician's ear that I am not surprised so many composers have set it to music. In her poetry every sentence is filled with meaning, every word is precisely right, her imagery is suitable to musical setting and, above all, the rhythm of her language is so musical. The three poems that I have set—all of them for chorus—I carried in my mind for a long time before the right occasion arose to use them."—letter of May 8, 1989.

Starer, Robert. "Hope" Is the Thing With Feathers. New York: Music Corporation of America, 1977.

Commissioned: Ulster County Community College, Stone Ridge, NY.

Composed: 1976.

Setting: SATB chorus a cappella.

Johnson: 254.

First Performance: Ulster County Community College, Stone Ridge, NY, 1976.

Steiner, Gitta. Five Poems for Mixed Chorus. New York: Seesaw Music, 1971.
Composed: 1958-65.
Setting: SATB chorus.
Johnson: 47, 134, 162, 463.
"I am also a Dickinson scholar. I have her complete works and have read almost all the biographies of her. I also visited her home in Amherst, Mass., two years ago. I studied with jazz musician Lennie Tristano when I was 20 years old and we were avid readers of her poetry. That is where it all began for me."
—letter of November 20, 1989.

Steiner, Gitta. 4 Choruses of Emily Dickinson. New York: Seesaw Music, [n.d.].
Composed: 1958-65.
Setting: SATB chorus.
Johnson: 31, 113, 288, 1398.

Steiner, Gitta. Four Settings to the Poems of Emily Dickinson [manuscript].
Composed: 1958-65.
Setting: SATB chorus.
Johnson: 12, 30, 95, 347.
Location: composer.

Steiner, Gitta. I Envy Seas, Whereon He Rides. New York: Seesaw Music. [n.d.].
Composed: 1958-65.
Setting: soprano, piano.
Johnson: 498.
First performance: Memphis State University, November 6, 1986.

Steiner, Gitta. Ten Songs from the Poems of Emily Dickinson [manuscript].
Composed: 1958-65.
Setting: SATB chorus, or soprano, piano.

Johnson: 31, 258, 277, 288, 498, 511 (2), 959, 1736, 1754.
Location: composer.
First performance: New School for Social Research, New York City, November 2, 1975.
"There are two musical versions of 'If you were Coming in the Fall' [511]."
—letter of November 20, 1989.

Steiner, Gitta. Four Songs. New York: Seesaw Music, 1970.
Composed: 1970.
Setting: medium voice, piano.
Johnson: 249.

Steiner, Gitta. Three Songs. New York: Seesaw Music, 1970.
Composed: 1960.
Setting: medium voice, piano.
Johnson: 498.
With two James Joyce poems.

Stolba, K Marie. A Word [manuscript].
Commissioned: Cathy Jackson.
Composed: 1985.
Setting: voice, piano.
Johnson: 1212.
Location: composer.
First performance: Cathy Jackson, Senior Recital, Neff Hall, Indiana University-Purdue University, Fort Wayne, IN, 1985.

Stolba, K Marie. This World Is Not Conclusion [manuscript].
Composed: 1986.
Setting: voice, piano.
Johnson: 501 (see note, below).
Location: composer.
First performance: Fort Wayne Alumnæ of Sigma Alpha Iota, 1986.
"I did not use the Johnson edition of the poem, but that in the *Collected Poems of Emily Dickinson, Original Editions*, Ed. Todd and Higginson, 1982, Book

IV, 'Time and Eternity,' I, p. 183. The lyrics are not identical [to Johnson No. 501]. This setting is untitled but the first line is: 'This world is not conclusion.'"—letter of May 9, 1990.

Strongin, Theodore. Some Days [manuscript].
Setting: medium voice, piano.
Johnson: 1157.
Location: New York Public Library.

Stucky, Steven. Nature, Like Us [manuscript].
Composed: 1971.
Setting: SATB chorus a cappella.
Johnson: 828, 1075, 1619, 1755.
"Two settings [1619 and 1755] were published in 1972 by Chor Publications, no longer in business. The two poems were part of a four-poem cycle ('Nature, Like Us'), composed in 1971."—letter of August 21, 1991.

Sullivan, Arthur S. See "Miscellany" section: Gould, John A., arr. Abraham To Kill Him.

Sydeman, William. Three Songs After Emily Dickinson. Boston: Ione Press, 1970.
Composed: 1961.

Setting: soprano or tenor, violoncello.
Johnson: 214, 254, 465.
First performance: Carnegie Recital Hall, New York, 1961.
"The Dickinson songs are particularly lyrical and are almost Mahleresque in style. They have recently been performed in Newark City, where I now reside."—letters of July, 1989 and January, 1991.

Taggard, Genevieve. I'm Nobody! [manuscript].
Composed: 1953.
Johnson: 288.
Recording: East Jamaica, VT: River Press, FRLP-466, 1953. (Also includes a setting of e. e. cummings.)

Tallis, Thomas. See "Miscellany" section. Jones, Joseph, arr. A Garland for Emily.

Talma, Louise. One Need Not Be a Chamber—to Be Haunted. New York: Carl Fischer, 1986.
Composed: 1941.
Setting: medium voice, piano.
Johnson: 670.
First performance: Alica Anderson, soprano; Louise Talma, piano. WYNC Festival, New York City, February 12, 1949.

Barry Taxman

"To catalogue all my E. D. songs would be overwhelming. So I have listed the most important ones. None of the songs are part of a cycle, and I do not group them by subject since I feel that would be against the spirit of the poetry. I realized there have been so many performances at random of various songs over the years there is no way of listing first performances. I do not 'date' my songs but leave them to the ages. 'He asked me why / I chose so fine / I could not say / Or spirit define. / I chose the brooks / I chose the seas; / For lack of direction / I chose the bees.'"—letter of December 2, 1990.

Taxman, Barry. Songs to Poems of Emily Dickinson [manuscript].
Composed: 1960-90.
Setting: high voice, piano.
Johnson: 4, 13, 26, 30, 31, 32, 33, 41, 47, 52, 74, 77, 86, 89, 90, 92, 94, 95, 99, 101, 108, 111, 125, 134, 136, 150, 155, 162, 172, 201, 211, 232, 245, 249, 254, 265, 347, 431, 441, 526, 528, 533, 549, 636, 647, 794, 884, 903, 1026, 1045, 1052, 1065, 1078, 1199, 1332, 1398, 1463, 1510, 1540, 1544, 1547, 1605, 1619, 1624, 1627, 1732, 1736, 1743, 1754, 1755, 1760, 1767.
Location: composer.

Thygerson, Robert. Emily Dickinson. Richmond, IN: Richmond Music, 1980.
Composed: 1980.
Setting: SSA chorus, piano.
Johnson: 1540.

Towner, Earl. Not in Vain [manuscript].
Johnson: 919.

Vehar, Persis. Emily D [manuscript].
Commissioned: Shanti Chamber Music Ensemble, 1980.
Composed: 1980.
Setting: soprano, flute, oboe, piano.
Duration: 8:30.
Johnson: 101, 712, 1064, 1540.
Location: composer; American Music Center.
First performance: Rachel Lewis, soprano; Rhonda Schwartz, flute; Ronal Richards, oboe; Marcella Branagan-Faine, piano. Kleinhans Music Hall, Buffalo, NY, May 7, 1980.
Broadcast on WNED-FM radio, Buffalo, New York, on program "Interview with composer Persis Vehar" by Leila Lustig, May 12, 1985.

Vehar, Persis. Three from Emily. Geneseo, NY: Leyerle Publications, 1987.
Composed: 1984.
Setting: high voice, piano, violoncello.
Johnson: 4, 792, 1510.
First performance: Elizabth Holt Brown, soprano; Susan Krystaf, violoncello; Marjorie Lord, piano. The Chromatic Club of Buffalo, NY, October 28, 1984.
Broadcast on WNED-FM radio, Buffalo, NY, on program "Music in Buffalo," fall, 1986.
"Much of my historical knowledge of the period came from my nonagenarian grandmother, Persis Race, who was born in the 19th century and lived most of her life on the Massachusetts-New York border. Having been raised in the Albany, NY, area myself with 'rugged individualist' ancestors on both sides who fought in the American Revolution, I know very well, as John Dwyer writes in a review, 'the turn of mind and introspective moods of 19th-century New England.'"—letter of July 10, 1989.

Vernon, Sean. I Felt a Funeral in My Brain [manuscript].
Composed: 1985.
Setting: voice, six-string guitar.
Johnson: 280.
Location: composer.
First performance: Sean Vernon, voice and guitar. Danforth Chapel, University of Iowa, October 21, 1986.
"I've always thought Dickinson unequaled in her ability to create vivid, believable scenes of her own death. This poem is a dazzling example. I took my musical cue from

the two middle lines of the second verse: 'A Service, like a Drum / Kept Beating—Beating,' and built the setting around a steady, pounding bass line in the key of E major, which I consider the darkest of the major keys. The first four stanzas end on a B-Major chord, played at the 7th fret with an open first string, for an eerie effect; the last ends on a full B-Major chord, struck five times in quick succession, like a tolling bell."—letter of February 9, 1990.

Vernon, Sean. After Great Pain a Formal Feeling Comes [manuscript].
Composed: 1989.
Setting: Voice, piano.
Johnson: 341.
Location: composer.
First performance: Sean Vernon. Bowne Theater, Drew University, Madison, NJ, February 22, 1990.
"I originally set this poem in the key of C Major, with a slow, stately, dirge-like tone. But there's a cheerfulness, an optimism, about C Major which is hard to suppress, even with words as bleak as Dickinson's here. I ended up at A Minor—to my ear, a key of melancholic resignation—and used extremely spare fingering, trying for the feel of a stark winter landscape." —letter of February 9, 1990.

Vries Robbe, Willem de. Poems. Amsterdam: Donemus, 1973.
Composed: 1973.
Setting: voice, flute, vibraphone.
Johnson: 251, 386, 1065, 1585, 1672, 1690, 1726, 1755.

Walker, Christopher R. H. Hope Is the Thing with Feathers [manuscript].
Composed: 1991.
Setting: voice, piano.
Johnson: 254.
Location: composer.

Walker, George. I Went to Heaven. Boston: General Music Publishers, 1971.
Composed: 1953.
Setting: soprano or mezzo-soprano, piano.
Johnson: 374.
Recording: *Music by Lockwood & Walker*. Phyllis Bryn-Julson, soprano; George Walker, piano. Composers Recordings SD 488 CRI, 1983.
"The succinct verses of Emily Dickinson, with their brilliant, fanciful images and predictable metrical patterns, are immensely enticing as material for short lyrical songs."—letter of September 5, 1990.
Reprinted: New York: Associated Music Publishers, 1980. New York: Southern Music, 1986. Also reprinted in *American Art Songs: a Collection of 20th-Century Songs by American Composers from Charles Ives to Elliott Carter. For medium voice and piano. Compiled by Barry O'Neal*. New York: Associated Music Publishers, 1980. See also next entry.

Walker, George. Emily Dickinson Songs. New York: Southern Music, 1986.
Commissioned: Fisk University, Nashville, TN, 1982.
Composed: 1986.
Setting: high voice, piano.
Johnson: 277, 374, 1398, 1587.
Recording: (Johnson 374, 1398) *Music by Lockwood and Walker*. Phyllis

Bryn-Julson, soprano; George Walker, piano. Composers Recordings CRI SD 488, 1986. (American Academy and Institute of Arts and Letters Composers Awards.)

The texts are taken from World Publishing Company's 1948 edition, which reproduces the poems as they originally appeared in the Roberts Brothers' edition of Emily Dickinson's poems, 1890.

Wallach, Joelle. Of Honey and Vinegar. New York: American Composers Edition, 1983.

Composed: 1982.

Setting: mezzo-soprano, two pianos.

Johnson: 861, 1334, 1540, 1548.

Recording: Isabelle Ganz, mezzo-soprano; David Levi and Christopher Vassiliades, pianos. Greenville, ME: Opus One 127, 1988.

"'Of Honey and Vinegar' is a setting of four poems by Emily Dickinson, all related to the sweetness and bitterness of persuasion and seduction (without evident sexual context). The composer's challenge to the performers is an unusual tripartite chamber relationship. Duo pianists are accustomed to accommodating one another in one way, and a single pianist and singer in another. Here both types of personal dynamics must be simultaneous. There are thus four permutations of musical interrelationship rather than one: the two pianists to one another, each pianist to the singer, and the chamber ensemble as a whole."—letter of April 29, 1989.

Ward, Robert. Vanished. New York: Peer International, 1951.

Composed: 1941.

Setting: soprano or tenor, piano.

Johnson: 150.

Ward, Robert. Sacred Songs for Pantheists. [N.p.]: Highgate Press; New York: Galaxy, sole agent, 1966 [piano version].

Commissioned: Quincy Society of Fine Arts of Quincy, IL; George Irwin, conductor.

Composed: 1951.

Setting: high lyric soprano, orchestra or piano.

Duration: 15:50.

Johnson: 214.

First performance: Carolyn Blakeslee, soprano; Quincy Little Symphony, George Irwin, conductor; April 26, 1951.

Recordings: Sylvia Stahlman, soprano; Polish National Radio Orchestra, conducted by William Strickland. Composers Recordings CRI 206, 1966. Also Bay Cities CD 1010.

"With one sharp image E.D. could communicate a deep universal emotional experience. The rhythmic flow of her lines seems to cry out for music and dictate a clear structure."—letter of January, 1991.

Bibliography: Kreitner, Kenneth. *Robert Ward, a Bio-Bibliography*. New York: Greenwood, 1988.

Warren, Betsy Frost. Six Poems of Emily Dickinson.

Cambridge, MA: Wiscasset Music Publishing, 1984.

Composed: 1983-84.

Setting: SSATBB chorus a cappella.

Johnson: 318, 436, 599, 687, 946, 1765.

Waters, James L. Goal [manuscript].
Composed: 1982.
Setting: mezzo-soprano solo, percussion
(4 timpani, marimba, orchestral bells
[chimes], 2 tom-toms [low and high],
2 wood blocks), piano, viola, violoncello.
Duration: 12:00.
Johnson: 280, 670, 680, 937.
Location: composer; American Music
Center.
First performance: Mary Sue Hyatt,
mezzo-soprano. Kent State University New Music Ensemble, Frank
Wiley, conductor. November 11,
1982.
"My intention in 'Goal' was to portray
three different psychological states
which might be termed problemati-
cal (at least), followed by a song which
expresses a goal (the word appears in
the poems) or a resolution of the difficult situations just encountered.
"Following the performance of this
work, a friend remarked that my music was dark and depressing. So I wrote
'Songs of Life' to demonstrate that
both Emily Dickinson and I were capable of expressing more positive feelings."—letter of October, 1990.

Waters, James L. Songs of Life [piano
version; manuscript].
Commissioned: Ohio Arts Council, 1983.
Composed: 1983.
Setting: soprano, B-flat clarinet, piano.
Duration: 10:00.
Johnson: 214, 442, 1021, 1532.
Location: composer.
First performance: Janice Harsanyi, sop-
rano. Florida State University, January
22, 1984.
See also next entry.

Waters, James L. Songs of Life [cham-
ber ensemble version; manuscript].
Composed: 1986.
Setting: soprano, solo B-flat clarinet,
chamber ensemble (flute, oboe,
bassoon, harp, violin, viola, cello,
contrabass).
Duration: 10:00.
Johnson: 214, 442, 1021, 1532.
Location: composer.
First performance: Daune Mahy, sopra-
no; Cleveland Chamber Symphony,
Edwin London, director, 1986.

**Weber, Ben. A Bird Came Down the
Walk.** New York: American Com-
posers Edition, 1963.
Commissioned: Alice Esty, "In memory
of Francis Poulenc."
Composed: 1963.
Setting: voice, piano.
Johnson: 328.

Weber, Marc. Ample Make This Bed
[manuscript].
Composed: 1987.
Setting: voice, piano.
Johnson: 829.
Location: composer.
In speaking of Marc Weber's setting, his
teacher Andrew White said: "He wrote
it as a project for a class in 19th-century
music with the intention of modeling
it after Wolf. He failed. Wolf's harmonic language was never so free."

Weigl, Vally. Two Songs. New York:
American Composers Alliance, [n.d.].
Setting: TTBB chorus, piano.
Johnson: 1065.

Weigl, Vally. From Time & Eternity. New York: American Composers Edition, 1952.
Setting: soprano, mezzo-soprano, and contralto soloists, piano.
Johnson: 4.

Weigl, Vally. Five Songs of Remembrance. New York: American Composers Edition, 1953.
Setting: mezzo-soprano, flute, clarinet, piano. Or mezzo-soprano, clarinet, piano, violin.
Duration: 11:45.
Johnson: 47.
Recording: American Chamber Ensemble. New York: Leonarda LE 329, 1989.

Weigl, Vally. Let Down the Bars, Oh Death. New York: American Composers Edition, 1958.
Setting: TTBB chorus, piano.
Johnson: 1065.

Weigl, Vally. Oh Lord of Mysteries. New York: American Composers Edition, 1967.
Setting: medium voice, piano, viola, violoncello.
Johnson: 1732.
"Vally Weigl's record as composer, teacher, music therapist, researcher and writer is long and impressive—to say unique would not be an exaggeration. [ACA's] brochure would be of great interest to Dickinson literary and music scholars."—letter of June 20, 1989, from Rosalie Calabrese, American Composers Alliance.

Weiss, Adolf. Seven Songs for Soprano and String Quartet. New York: Composers Facsimile Edition, 1952.
Composed: 1928.

Setting: soprano, string quartet [2 violins, viola, cello].
Johnson: 155, 214, 569, 585, 813, 1052, 1760.
First performance: Mary Bell, soprano; New World String Quartet. New School for Social Research, New York City, November 13, 1933.
Recording: (three songs) New World String Quartet. New Music Quarterly Recordings, 1011A-B, 1934.

Weld, Arthur. Seven Songs. New York: T.B. Harms, [n.d.].
Setting: voice, piano.
Johnson: 91.

Wertsch, Nancy. Three Songs on Poems of Emily Dickinson. New York: Gene Garbriel Publications, 1985.
Composed: 1981-85.
Setting: high or low voice, piano.
Johnson: 89, 249, 288.
Recording: Nancy Wertsch, mezzo-soprano; Gary Norden, piano. Gene Gabriel Publications, New York, 1988.

Wesley, Samuel Sebastian. See "Miscellany" Section. Gould, John A., arr. The Red Blaze Is The Morning.

Wiemann, Beth. Simple Songs [manuscript].
Commissioned: Karol Bennett, soprano.
Composed: 1990.
Setting: soprano, piano.
Johnson: 320, 572.
Location: composer.
First performance: Karol Bennett, soprano; John MacDonald, piano. Cambridge, Massachusetts, November 3, 1990.

"This cycle includes two Dickinson settings [320 and 572], along with settings of poems by Marianne Moore, T.E. Holme, W.C. Williams, and others."—letter of March, 1991.

Wilder, Alec. Emily Dickinson Songs [manuscript].
Composed: [before 1964].
Setting: voice, piano.
Johnson: 26, 47, 92, 136, 280, 850.

Wilder, Alec. I Hide Myself. New York: Tro-Ludlow Music, 1964.
Composed: 1964.
Setting: voice, piano.
Johnson: 903.
"Wilder was almost as prolific a reader of poetry and fiction as he was a composer. This must have been a poem he particularly liked. I think the words apply to Wilder's own feelings about himself."—Note from Judy Bell, The Richmond Organization, 11 W. 19th Street, New York, NY 10011.
Bibliography: Bell, Judith, et al. *Alec Wilder: An Introduction to the Man and His Music.* Newton Centre, MA: Margun Music, 1991. (A short biography, list of works, discography, letters, and bibliography of articles by and about Wilder.)

Willeby, Charles. Little Pilgrim. (A Child's Fancy.) Cincinnati: The John Church Company, 1907.
Composed: 1907.
Setting: high or low voice, piano.
Johnson: 101.

Williams, Francis. Emily Dickinson. I Shall Not Live in Vain. New York: Harold Flammer, 1945.
Setting: voice, piano.
Johnson: 919.

Wood, Margaret. See to See. Ipswich, MA: Margaret Wood, 1983.
Composed: 1983.
Setting: voice, piano.
Johnson: 465.

Wood, Margaret. Harmony. Opus 8. Ipswich, MA: Margaret Wood, 1984.
Composed: 1984.
Setting: solo voice, piano; or mixed chorus, piano.
Johnson: 126, 162, 254, 318, 321, 322, 324, 429, 451, 463, 466, 657, 790, 794, 919, 1052.
"The music is for voice and piano, although some of the songs would lend themselves to be interpreted with other instruments such as the harp, guitar, harpsichord, or clarinet. Each piece is accompanied by passages from the Scriptures, from Shakespeare, Wordsworth and other poets, and by symbolic designs which help to interpret and synchronize Emily Dickinson's poetic ideas.

"The music is written in a simple manner so that it can be sung and played and enjoyed by many people. The songs may be sung singly, or combined in cycles; they lend themselves as solos or for choral groups singing in churches and schools. Or they may be orchestrated for larger effects. Whatever the performing method is, the intent of the music is to highlight the text, never to overwhelm it. It seems that the simplicity and sensitivity of the pieces is the way in which Emily Dickinson would have enjoyed having her poems played and sung."—letter of June 5, 1989.

Woollen, Russell. Songs. Opus 2. An Amethyst Remembrance. There Came a Day [manuscript].
Composed: 1961.
Setting: high voice, piano.
Johnson: 322.
Location: composer; NYPL.

Ziffrin, Marilyn J. Symphony for Voice and Orchestra. Epilogue: Letters [manuscript].
Composed: 1988-89.
Setting: soprano, orchestra (2.2.2.2, 4.2.3.1, percussion,strings).
Johnson: 441.
Location: composer.

First performance: Neva Pilgrim, soprano. New Hampshire Music Festival, Tom Nee, Director, August 9, August 10, 1990.

"The work was written for Neva Pilgrim. The Dickinson poem 'This Is My Letter to the World' sums up the work as a whole. The instrumental background allows the text of the poem to remain always in the foreground. The subtitle 'Letters' refers to the use of sentences and sections from a variety of letters by other writers used in the three movements of the symphony."—letter of December 21, 1989.

Miscellany

Listed here are miscellaneous types of works and performances involving Emily Dickinson and music: musical arrangements and contrafacta, concerts and recitals, incidental music for plays, pedagogic materials, lectures and lecture-recitals, and readings with musical accompaniment.

Arrangements and contrafacta

Gould, John A., arr. Abraham To Kill Him. Music by Arthur S. Sullivan [manuscript].
Arranged: 1989.
Setting: SATB.
Johnson: 1317.
Location: arranger.
Arranged from the hymn "St. Gertrude," music by Arthur S. Sullivan, 1871.
"In 1984, I collected three colleagues from the Phillips Andover English department for an experiment. We took four popular hymns—'Onward Christian Soldiers,' 'A Mighty Fortress,' 'The Church's One Foundation,' and 'Oh God, Our Help in Ages Past'— and sang poems by Emily Dickinson to them. We performed these songs a cappella in front of our English classes to show them the properties of meter, the relationship between her poems and hymns, and the nature of sung poetry. We also set 'I like to see it lap the Miles' to the popular 'I'd Like to Teach the World to Sing.' The response—especially given the instruments we had to work with—was gratifying."—letter of August 15, 1989.

Gould, John A., arr. I Heard A Fly Buzz When I Died. Music by Martin Luther [manuscript].
Arranged: 1989.
Setting: SATB.
Johnson: 465.
Location: arranger.
Arranged from the Hymn "Ein' feste Burg ist unser Gott," music by Martin Luther, 1529. For the history of this hymn see John Julian, *A Dictionary of Hymnology*, pages 322-324.

Gould, John A., arr. I Like to See It Lap the Miles. With added words by John A. Gould. Music by Bill Backer, Billy Davis, Roger Cook, and Roger Greenaway [manuscript].
Arranged: 1989.
Setting: SAB, piano.
Johnson: 585.
Location: arranger.
Arranged from the song "I'd Like to Teach the World to Sing," music by Bill Backer, Billy Davis, Roger Cook, Roger Greenaway. Original copyright, 1971 by the Coca-Cola Company.

Gould, John A., arr. I Took My Power In My Hand. Music by William Croft [manuscript].
Arranged: 1989.
Setting: SATB.
Johnson: 540.
Location: arranger.
Arranged from the hymn "St. Anne," music by William Croft, 1706.

Gould, John A., arr. The Red Blaze Is The Morning. Music by Samuel Sebastian Wesley [manuscript].
Arranged: 1989.

Setting: SATB.
Johnson: 469.
Location: arranger.
Arranged from the hymn "Aurelia," music by Samuel Sebastian Wesley, 1864.

GOULD: BIBLIOGRAPHY

Gould, John A. "Dickinsinging and the Art Thereof." Andover/Phillips Academy Alumni Magazine, 1989.
An interesting description of Gould's setting ED's poetry to the music of popular hymns and songs.

Joseph Jones, arranger

"The poetry of Emily Dickinson abundantly manifests her adaptations of, and variations upon, the metres of the humble church-hymn. She had no conscious intention of creating songs; yet her verse responds musically to the kind of hymn-tunes she knew and sang. This small assemblage serves to suggest how her poems may be explored, and enjoyed, through song as well as through the spoken word. The two divisions made here are not exhaustive but they do indicate the poet's keen interest in the external world as well as spiritual pathology, often interblended. That she was mistress in both domains we need not argue; reading and listening carry their own conviction.

"Tune settings (chiefly in 'common metre' or 'long metre') for these songs range in origin from the 16th century to Emily Dickinson's own lifetime. She must have been familiar with a fair share of the tunes used here, though most probably not all. Unlike her contemporary, Walt Whitman, she was never tempted into the operatic—a limitation that was in fact for her a source of strength. In singing or listening to such combinations as these, we make ourselves doubly aware of how closely related, in certain personalities, music and poetry have been and continue to be."—letter of September 6, 1991, and preface to *A Garland for Emily.*

Jones, Joseph, arr. Emily Dickinson Recalled in Song. Guilford, CT: Jeffrey Norton Publishers, 1986.
Arranged: 1986.
Setting: soprano solo (unaccompanied).

Johnson: 67, 249, 288, 441, 465, 585, 632, 1068, 1129, 1333, 1540, 1672.
First performance: Cina Crisara, soprano; Radio KUT-FM, University of Texas at Austin, 1986.
Recording: monaural cassette, Jeffrey Norton Publishers, 1987.

Jones, Joseph, arr. A Garland for Emily. Twenty Songs by Emily Dickinson. Poems set to period hymn-tunes by Joseph Jones [manuscript].

Arranged: 1981-84.

Setting: voice, piano or organ.

I. "A Courteous Yet Harrowing Grace": Johnson 89 (Louis Bourgeois, "Nunc Dimittis," 16th c.; arr. 1984); 258 (William Henry Havergal, "Evan," 19th c.; arr. 1981); 290 (William Croft, *St. Matthew*, 18th c.; arr. 1984); 328 ("Heath," Lowell Mason and George Webb, *Cantica Laudis*, 1850; arr. 1984); 441 ("Ballerma," Spanish air, orig. 10th c.; arr. 1984); 585 (C. G. Glazer, "Azmon," early 19th c.; arr. 1981); 1068 ("Southwell," Damon's *Psalmes*, 1579; arr. 1984); 1232 (J. Klug, "Erhalt uns, Herr," 1543; arr. 1981); 1275 ("McKee," American black spiritual, undated; arr. 1981); 1540 (Early American, "Distress," 1835; arr. 1981).

II. "Internal Difference, Where the Meanings Are": Johnson 98 (set to L. Schröter, "Freut euch des Lebens," 16th c.; arr. 1981); 305 (A. R. Reinagle, "St. Peter," 19th c.; arr. 1981); 401 (Early American, "Hiding Place," 1831; arr. 1981); 465 (Thomas Tallis, "Third Mode Melody," 16th c; arr. 1984); 474 ("Manoah," attrib. F. J. Haydn; arr. 1984); 632 (William Gardiner, "Dedham," 19th c.; arr. 1984); 829 ("Gorton," from Beethoven; arr. 1984); 987 (Johannes Crüger, "Nun danket All," 17th c.; arr. 1981); 1078 (A. Williams, "Durham," 18th c.; arr. 1984); 1129 (Jessie S. Irvine [1836-87], "Crimond"; arr. 1984).

Location: arranger.

Jones, Joseph, arr. Poems and Hymn-Tunes as Songs: Metrical Partners. Guilford, CT: Jeffrey Norton Publishers, 1984.

Arranged: 1983.

Setting: SSSAAATTTBBB chorus, organ.

Johnson: 401.

Location: arranger.

First performance: Paul Rutz, organist, First English Lutheran Church, Austin, Texas, February 1983.

Eighty-four page manual and two cassettes that include Dickinson's "The Brain is wider than the Sky," set to the music of "Staff of Faith," Tyrolese origin.

Jones, Joseph, arr. Shormies [manuscript].

Arranged: 1991.

Setting: narrator, electronic keyboard.

"The coinage 'shormie' is a contraction of Short Meter (a quatrain of 6-6-8-6 syllable, riming ABCB, used with some frequency by E.D.). Shormies may be sung and discussed by young students to explore the kinship of music and verse; and with a bit of guidance such students would be capable of setting shormies and perhaps inventing new tunes."—letter of September 18, 1991.

Jones, Joseph, arr. Twenty Songs by Emily Dickinson, Set to Tunes by Thomas Commuck (1845) [manuscript].

Originally composed: 1886-90. Arranged 1991.

Setting: Voice, electric keyboard.

Johnson: 305 ("Yamassee"); 401 ("Ottawa"); 449 ("Caddoe"); 465 ("Pocasset"); 479 ("Cherokee"); 536 ("Yamassee"); 585 ("Annawon"); 632

("Pokanoket"); 829 ("Cummanche"); 986 ("Missouri"); 987 ("Commuck"); 1052 ("Montauk"); 1068 ("Quapaw"); 1078 (2 versions: "Oshkosh," "Quinnebaug"); 1129 ("Mohegan"); 1227 ("Wyandot"); 1232 ("Fox"); 1463 ("Teton"); 1540 ("Pequot").

Location: arranger.

"Thomas Commuck (1804-55) was a remarkable Native American about whom not much seems to be known as yet. The tunes will give you a fair idea of *Indian Melodies*, which was published by a Methodist Church in Brook-lyn in 1845, with harmonization supplied by Thomas Hastings. [*Indian Melodies, By Thomas Commuck, a Narragansett Indian. Harmonized by Thomas Hastings.* New York: Published by G. Lane & C. B. Tippett for the Methodist Episcopal Church, 200 Mulberry St.] As applied to E.D.'s poems the tunes are somewhat uneven, but some are melodious enough."—letter of September 17, 1991.

Morath, Max. See "Musical Settings" section.

Noel Tipton, arranger

"I am interested in the psychological implications of 'right brain' functioning in the creative process as it may related to Emily Dickinson's use of tunes as a springboard for some of her verses. My primary object is to find her verses that have connections with hymns, then to set these verses to old hymn tunes with piano accompaniment. After I have finished with all 1,775 verses, I expect to have a collection of songs from which theories may emerge regarding music, poetry, religion, and the creative process."—letter of December 2, 1991.

Tipton, Noel, arr. A Dying Tiger [manuscript].

Arranged: 1991.

Setting: voice, piano.

Johnson: 566.

Location: arranger.

Set to the tune of "Martyrdom" and fits the theme and meter of Isaac Watts's "Alas! And Did My Savior Bleed."

Tipton, Noel, arr. Adrift, a Little Boat Adrift [manuscript].

Arranged: 1991.

Setting: voice, piano.

Johnson: 30.

Set to the meter of John Newton's "Amazing Grace," No. 41, book 1 of the *Olney Hymns*, and to the Southern Tune now commonly used with this hymn.

Tipton, Noel, arr. Rearrange a Wife's Affection [manuscript].

Arranged: 1991.

Setting: voice, piano.

Johnson: 1737.

Location: arranger.

Set to the tune of "Nettleton" and the verse of Robert Robinson, "Come Thou Fount of Every Blessing." (Hymn from the *Repository of Sacred Music*, Part II, 1813, called "Nettleton." By Asahel Nettleton, compiler of *Village Hymns*, 1824.

Concerts and recitals

Airplay. Maine Public Broadcasting Network, October 6, 1989. "The Library of Congress Concerts." Dawn Upshaw, soprano; Margo Garrett, piano.
A recital featuring musical settings, by various American composers, of the poems of Emily Dickinson.

"A Demonstration of the Musical Settings of the Poems of Emily Dickinson."

Maryann Sewell, soprano. George Peachey, piano. Mostly Music Series. Round House Theatre, Silver Spring, Maryland, April 17, 1988.
Settings by Aaron Copland, Clarence Dickinson, John Duke, Gordon Getty, Ernst Gold, and Vincent Persichetti.
Johnson: 35, 47, 79, 101, 136, 198, 208, 214, 248, 288, 425, 712, 1035, 1593, 1732.

Incidental music

"Colonel Thomas Wentworth Higginson." Michigan Academy of Science, Arts and Letters, Wayne State University, April 20, 1968.
Unpublished play by Esther Broner, with segments on Higginson and Dickinson. Morton Zieve composed the incidental music.

One Bird, One Cage, One Flight. Homage to Emily Dickinson. Poems by Roger White. Music by Jean J. South. Happy Camp, CA.: Naturegraph Publishers, Inc., [1988].
Composed: 1988.
"White's newest collection of poems arrives at a time when interest is keen in unravelling Dickinson's solitary life. Through central themes resembling her own—immortality, loss, renunciation—White narrates Miss Dickinson's life from age fourteen to her death in 1886. In more than 100 poems, he successfully gains close access to her lasting and impressionable spirit, wit, and personage as 'poet' and 'mystic,' 'belle' and 'enigma' of Amherst."
—letter of May 13, 1989.

[Playbill] "Nancy Stern Presents 'Eastward in Eden, The Story of Emily Dickinson,' by Dorothy Gardner. New York: Playbill Inc., [1947]. With Onslow Stevens (and) Beatrice Straight. Original Music by André Singer. Settings and Costumes designed by Donald Oenslager. Directed by Ellen Van Volkenburg. Plymouth Theatre, Week Beginning Tuesday, November 4, 1947." [Another playbill: "... Royale Theatre, Beginning Tuesday, November 18, 1947."]
Location: Yale University Library.

[Playbill] Nassau Community College. "The Committee on the Emily Dickinson Festival in Association with the Department of Theatre Presents the First Performance Production of 'Come Slowly, Eden, a Portrait of Emily Dickinson by Norman Rosten.' Songs by Ernst Bacon and Philip Springer. May 3 through May 15, 1966."
Location: Yale University Library.

Wickwire, Nancy (reader). "The Poems of Emily Dickinson." New Rochelle, New York: Spoken Arts, [1959].

Thirty-nine love and nature poems with original music composed and played by Don Feldman.

Lectures and presentations

Leich, Roland. "Setting Emily Dickinson's Poetry to Music. Notes for a talk at the College Club," Pittsburgh, April 26, 1985, edited 1990. (Privately printed.)

An historical introduction is followed by two useful segments: "Conditions for setting a text," and "Remarks on ED songs presented as examples." Analyses of Johnson 322, 342, 374, 792, 1521.

"Program of Poetry and Letters of Emily Dickinson with Music by Robert Schumann." Mildred Dunnock and George Henry. Williamstown Theatre: August 16, 1970. Amherst: *Amherst Record*, August 12, 1970.

Part of script can be found in *Higginson Journal of Poetry* III, 6 (First Half 1973): 35-50.

A Concordance of Musical Terms in the Poems and Letters

This index, which is arranged alphabetically, cites in part Emily Dickinson's use of terms involving music and sound, referring the user to the location of these terms in the Johnson editions of her poems (P) and letters (L) and giving the relevant text. The "(v)" following the Johnson poem number refers to a variant reading found only in the three-volume edition.

Because of the subtleties of Emily Dickinson's writing, identifying all references to music—or rather to sounds, stated and implied—is difficult. We have found 114 categories in the poems, and 119 categories in the letters. Bird references—singing, maybe singing, maybe not—add up to 150. She wrote: "The Bluebirds are singing cherubically," and "I am studying music now with the jays." And then there are the unidentified quotes from hymns without any reference to musical words.

Accent: P. 373: Take other accents. L. 46: Her native accent.

Accompany: L. 13: Accompanied them with his voice.

Aeolian Harp: L. 115: Aeolian Harp.

Air: L. 36: Humming a little air. L. 42: Humming a pensive air. L. 134: I send you a little air.

Amateur: L. 13: As this amateur was performing.

Anthem: L. 184: To listen to the anthems.

Ballad/Ballads: P. 23: Their ballads were the same. P. 83: A careless snatch—a ballad. P. 746: Than could Border Ballad. P. 1059: Bear with the Ballad. P. 1466: Of Ballads and of Bards. P. 1524: Remanded to a Ballad's Barn. L. 184: As a ballad hummed.

Band/Bands: P. 157: Nor "Band"—in brass and scarlet. P. 321: Winds go round and round in Bands. P. 783: And yet the Band was gone. L. 344: I feel as the band does.

Banjo: P. 620: No Black bird bates his Banjo.

Bar: L. 22: Followed by the first bar.

Bard: P. 1389: Because a Bard too soon. P. 1466: Of Ballads and of Bards.

Bass: P. 630: Whose short, sepulchral Bass. P. 928: In mighty, unremitting Bass.

Basso: L. 392: The only Basso remaining.

Baton: P. 1574: Nor any leader's grim baton. L. 824: Grim baton.

Bell/Bells: POEMS, 24: I wait thy far, fantastic bells. 29: The bells of Ghent would ring. 93: Amid no bells nor bravoes. 98: Bells, also, in the village. 103: And Bells keep saying "Victory." 112: Where bells no more affright the morn. Not father's bells, nor Factories. 172: Bells, that in the Steeples be! 280: All the Heavens were a Bell. 286: Without a Moment's Bell. 324: And instead of tolling the Bell. 386: Show me the Bells. 498: And Bells that boldly ring. 503: Redemption strikes her Bells. 510: Not Night, for all the Bells. 542:

'Twas Sabbath, with the Bells. 604: And it is Bells within. 633: When Bells stop ringing, Church begins. The Positive of Bells. 639: Less Paeans, fewer Bells. 702: When the Bells rejoice. 735: The mixing Bells and Palls. 766: No Bells have Paradise. 891: The Bushes, they were Bells. 912: The Bells a Winter Night. 947: Of Tolling Bell I ask the cause? That Bells should ring till all should know. 981: As Sleigh Bells seem in summer. 1008: How still the Bells in Steeples. 1159: The Bells at Distance called. 1226: Bells for an Auxiliary. 1593: The Bell within. LETTERS, 77, The bells are ringing. Your own village bell. Where the bells are always ringing. 82: And sleighbells. 133: Sets the bells to ringing. 190: Jingling bells. 230: These small bells. 265: Drop the Bells. 269: Where bells toll. 282: A Moment's Bell. 331: Sleigh-bell gown. 339: The Bells at Distance called. 362: We have a chime of bells. 610: The ticking of the bells. The bells tick. 643: The Northampton Bell. 653: Sweeter than a Bell. 691: The fire-bells are oftener. Than the church-bells. 792: Memory is a strange Bell. 888: The Bells are bowing. 934: A Tone from the old Bell. 963: Northampton Bells. 973: Rings her Bell. 976: Sleigh Bells and Jays. 988: To be a Bell.

Bertini, Henri: L. 7: I have the same Instruction book you have, Bertini.

Bow: P. 410: Her Bow, to Atoms blown.

Bugle: P. 83: Ah Bugle! By my window. P. 1593: There came a Wind like a Bugle. L. 868: Like the Bugle. L. 945: Like Bugles at a Grave. L. 976: A reverse of Bugles. L. 1020: Bugle obliterates the Birds.

Buzz: P. 187: Buzz the dull flies. P. 465: I heard a Fly buzz when I died. With Blue, uncertain stumbling Buzz. P. 869: Or Petals, or a Dower of Buzz. P. 1405: Buccaneers of Buzz. L. 502: Buccaneers of Buzz.

Cadence: P. 216: In ignorant cadence. P. 367: Cadences too grand. P. 503: Its smallest cadence. P. 1068(v): Of cadence or of pause. L. 238: In ignorant cadence.

Call: P. 398: And far I heard his silver Call. P. 1159: The Bells at Distance called. L. 339: The Bells at Distance called.

Canticle: P. 1068: Arise this spectral Canticle.

Canto: L. 190: Bear the canto on.

Carol: P. 83: Carolled, and paused, and carolled. P. 167: Ascend in ceaseless Carol. P. 238: "Carol for Him, when I am gone!" L. 242: Birds do not all carol. L. 1004: "Sweet Land of Liberty" is a superfluous Carol.

Castanet: P. 1635: The Jay his Castanet has struck.

Caw: L. 981: Accept a loving Caw.

Chant: P. 22: Let us chant it softly. P. 230: We chant for cheer. P. 295: Or in Dungeons chanted. P. 321: Never heard that fleshless Chant. P. 491: Scooping up the Dust and chanting. P. 616: I sang firm, even Chants. P. 916: His Labor is a Chant. P. 1005: Chanting to Paradise.

Chime: P. 297: Chime, Noon! L. 362: We have a chime of bells.

Chirp/Chirrup: P. 83: It was as if a chirping brook. P. 956: When the Skies a' chirrup. L: 65: And chirps more merrily. L. 146: A little cricket to chirp. L. 380: By my chirrup more.

Choir: P. 276: Like old Caspian Choirs. L. 88: The rest of the choir. L. 190: A simple choir. L. 255: Choirs sang to him. L. 951: "Choir invisible."

Choral: P. 1059: Wait your Chorals.

Chorister: P. 324: With a Bobolink for a Chorister.

Clef: P. 364: To fit some Crucifixal Clef.

Composer: P. 503: But the Composer—perfect Mozart.

Concert: L. 7: I don't know about this Mr Eastcott giving you concert tickets. L. 13: I have attended 2 concerts. L. 46: The concert commenced at eight. L. 118: Gave a concert here. The concert was over.

Cornet: P. 367: Cornets of Paradise. P. 505: I would not talk, like Cornets.

Croon: P. 503: Legend, dimly told (crooned).

Cry: P. 1395(v): Her joyful cry exalts us.

Dirge: P. 1522: Unto itself a Dirge.

Discord: P. 5: Each little discord here.

Ditty: P. 23: And when this mournful ditty. P. 83: A ditty of the street. P. 1373: The Ditty is that Nature Sings. P. 1483: By Ditties to the Enemy.

Drum/Drums: POEMS, l: And beat upon the drum. 103: It is as if a hundred drums. 259: Lit the Drummer from the Camp. 280: A Service, like a Drum. 295: Firm to the Drum. 348: Of their unthinking Drums. 367: Drums off the Phantom Battlements. 582: Are Drums too near. 590: As cool as Satyr's Drums. 639: The drums don't follow Me. 888: The Earth has seemed to me a Drum. 1221: Adequate as Drums. 1226: Subsequent to a Drum. 1227: My Triumph lasted till the Drums. LETTERS, 36: Where you hear the rolling drum. 297: The Drums keep on. 318: Though the drums are out. 950: I love the Drums.

Duet[t]: L. 65: Learn my part of the Duett. L. 71: You sent us the Duett, Austin.

Echo: P. 216(v): But the Echoes stiffen. P. 289: And Echoes, Trains away. P. 1076(v): His Heaven echoed faint. P. 1538(v): Echo has no Magistrate. L. 868: His Elegy and echo.

Elegy: P. 294: Has ought but Elegy! P. 1395: Elegy of Integrity. P. 1775: Of elegy to me. L. 868: His Elegy and echo. L. 945: The element of Elegy.

Fife: P. l: And bring the fife. P. 706: Or a Fife's Fame.

Flute: P. 81: So silver steal a hundred flutes. P. 312: Flute, or Woman. P. 366: Or skip to Flutes.

Germanians: L. 118: The Germanians gave a concert. L. 201: Love for the Germanians.

Glee: P. 364: They'd modify the Glee. P. 774: It is a lonesome Glee. P. 934: Or a Glee among the Garret.

Guitar: P. 1389: Nature's sweet Guitar.

Hallelujah: P. 7: The lips at Hallelujah. P. 501: Strong Hallelujahs roll. L. 88: Singing Hallelujahs.

Harmonious: L. 52: Harmonious stanzas.

Harmony: P. 668: Nay, Nature is Harmony.

Harp: L. 10: Tuned their golden harps.

Hum/Hums: POEMS, l: Doth walk the seashore humming. 142: Humming the quaintest lullaby. 230: By a humming Coroner. 334: Play it were a Humming Bird. 380: The Humming Bird aspire. 436: Of numerous Humming Birds at once. 503: Humming, for promise, when alone. Humming, until my faint Rehearsal. LETTERS, 36: Humming a little air. 42: Humming a pensive air. 58: I hear the bright bee hum. 102: The bee hums. And hums more. 122: Yet the bee hums. There is a humming bee. 133: Whether hum or sing. 184: Will have hummed. As a ballad hummed. 197: And still her hum. 206: And hums and thrums.

Hymn/Hymns: POEMS, 157: It is not Hymn from pulpit read. 196: Tim reads a little Hymn. 260: Clear strains of Hymn. 616: I helped his Film, with Hymn. And so with Thews of Hymn. 746: Or Biscayan Hymn. 944: How awkward at the Hymn. 1177: Bold as a Bailiff's Hymn.

LETTERS, 29: The whole hymn is too familiar. 73: To read a gentle hymn. 110: Village Hymns. 182: His exquisite hymn. 217: As we trust, hymns. 269: Her unnoticed hymn? 418: Your beautiful Hymn. 521: Was in a Hymn. 622: Lowell's "Sweet Despair" in the Slipper Hymn. 790: Have we not a Hymn. 801: In the same Hymn.

Instrument: L. 42: Vinnie is at the instrument.

Intonations: P. 1302: Mediterranean intonations.

Jingle: L. 190: Jingling bells. L. 265: The Bells whose jingling.

Jubilee: L. 792: Bell, Jubilee, and Knell.

Key: P. 315: As Players at the Keys. P. 503: That Keyless Rhyme!

Knell: P. 1505: The mother that has not a knell. P. 1635(v): He is the knell. L. 792: Bell, Jubilee, and Knell.

Lind, Jenny: L. 44: Your discreet opinion concerning Swedish Jenny. We have all been piqued at Jennie's singing so well. L. 46: The night of Jenny Lind. How Jennie came out like a child. We dont care a fig for the museum, the stillness, or Jennie Lind.

Listen: L. 11: I listened to her syren voice. L. 182: I stop the birds to listen. L. 184: To listen to the anthems. L. 269: Themselves ... listened.

Litany: P. 364: Like Litanies of Lead.

Liturgy: P. 1059: Pause in your Liturgies.

Loud: L. 57: There the birds sing loudest.

Low: L. 562: The Low of a Bird.

Lullaby: P. 142: Humming the quaintest lullaby. P. 588: Our only Lullaby.

Lute: P. 261: Put up my lute! P. 366: On Lute the least, the latest. P. 794: Breezes brought dejected Lutes. P. 861: Ear when Lutes be old. L. 29: Sound of the lute.

Major: L. 370: There is a Major and a Minor.

Mandolin: P. 1005: Banish my mandolin.

Mass: P. 1068: Its unobtrusive Mass.

Matins: P. 250: Vespers are sweeter than Matins.

Measure: P. 321: That old measure in the Boughs. P. 1048: Reportless Measures. L. 182: Gentle measures.

Melodious: L. 969: Those melodious moments.

Melody: POEMS, 5: Melody new for me. Bright melody. 297: A dateless Melody. 321: That phraseless Melody. 503: Bubbled a better Melody. 505: With Bolts of Melody. 785: Is metre, nay, 'tis melody. 797: The Definition of Melody. 1008: In frantic Melody! 1072: Stroking the Melody. 1084: Of cautious melody. 1420: With Dirks of Melody. 1578: But Memory like Melody. 1750: Are paltry melody. 1775: Where melody is not. LETTERS, 52: Stanzas become one melody. 86: The air with such melody. 173: Melody new for me. Bright melody for me. 175: Melody new for me. 250: Stroking the Melody. 261: Like Melody. 920: The delightful Melody. 968: Abstinence from Melody.

Metre: P. 593: The Days to Mighty Metres stept. P. 785: Is metre, nay, 'tis melody. P. 1115: The lower metres of the Year.

Minor: L. 370: There is a Major and a Minor.

Minuet: P. 83: Set bleeding feet to minuets.

Moan: L. 888: The Organ is moaning.

Mozart: P. 503: But the Composer—perfect Mozart.

Murmur: P. 64: In murmuring platoon! P. 155: The Murmur of a Bee. P. 161: Of mellow, murmuring thread. P. 276: Murmuring, like old Caspian Choirs. P. 416: A Murmur in the Trees. P. 593: That Nature murmured to herself. P. 1115: The murmuring of Bees. But murmuring of some. L. 222: The murmuring leaves.

Music: POEMS, 14: Herself to her a Music. 31: Thy music still, when Whippoorwill. 261: What of my Music! 294: Because its Music stirs the Axe. 315: Before they drop full Music on. 436: Let go a music, as of tunes. 500: Whose spokes a dizzy Music make. 501: Invisible, as Music. 503: Better than Music! 514(v): While the Music crashed. 582: Music's triumphant. 653: Except a Wake of Music. 673: 'Tis this in Music hints. 755: Whose Music be His. 783: A Music numerous as space. 861: Split the Lark, and you'll find the Music. 956: When the Eggs fly off in Music. 1003: Dying at my music! 1480: Chill that music leaves. 1576: The Music in the Violin. 1585: Her punctual music brings. LETTERS, 8: Getting along with your music? 9: Getting along finely in music. 13: To give us some of his native music. Attending to music. 23: Do you attend to music? 30: Music, conversation. 35: Sing, sing sad music. What music in such quiet ticking. 36: Faintest music. 39: Gentle music. 46: Herself, and not her music. 60: Strange, sad music. With little snatches of music. 65: Thank you for the music, Austin. 76: Vinnie's music. Thanks you very much for her music. 87: Attending French and music. 129: And make sweet music. 134: The "Music of the Spheres." 182: One of the mortal musics. 190: Imbibed this music. 197: Herself to her a music. 242: The cost of Music. 248: But made gay music. 364: Like suspending Music. 370: In adequate Music. 381: Almost like Music. 405: Vanishing in Music. 622: Your relentless Music. 665: I am studying music. 761: The strange Music. 872: The Music in the Violin. 950: Life's portentous Music. 968: Only with Music.

Music Instruction: L. 7: I have the same Instruction book.

Music Lesson: L. 7: I have taken Music lessons. How do you like taking music lessons. I am taking lessons this term. I am taking lessons and am getting along very well. L. 9: Then I take music lessons. L. 13: I am not now taking lessons.

Music Professor: L. 13: A Professor of music.

Music, Sheet: L. 9: A sheet of music. L. 65: For the sake of "Auld Lang Syne." Much pleased with "Charity." L. 491: "Douglass, Douglass, tender and true." L. 509: "My country,'tis of thee, Sweet Land of Liberty."

Music Teacher: L 7: These Music teachers are always such high souled beings.

Musical: L. 113: The girls "Musical."

Musician: P. 157: Musicians wrestle everywhere. L. 13: The Musician played.

Noise: P. 529: From all the noise of Fields. P. 1764: The saddest noise, the sweetest noise, the maddest noise. L. 271: A noiseless noise.

Note: P. 128: Write me how many notes there be. P. 486: How noteless I could die. P. 1009: Little note that others dropt. P. 1395: Her panting note exalts us. P. 1600: And squandered such a Note. P. 1761: Then adjusted his little notes. L. 46: Take some notes from her "Echo." L. 937: Squandered such a Note. PF-97 (page 926): One note from one Bird.

Octave: P. 1003: Hold me till the Octave's run!

Opera: P. 161: Whose Opera the Springs. P. 326: It's full as Opera. P. 593: Titanic Opera.

Oratorio: P. 1466: Betimes an Oratorio.

Orchestra: P. 302: When Orchestra is dumb. L. 60: The orchestra of winds.

Organ: P. 183: I've heard an Organ talk. L. 888: The Organ is moaning. L. 118: Undertow of the Organ.

Paeans: P. 639: Less Paeans, fewer Bells.

Parepa, Rose: L. 643: Memoir of Parepa.

Part: L. 65: My part of the Duett.

Perform: L. 13: As this amateur was performing. L. 60: The orchestra of winds perform.

Performance: L. 13: Edified with his

Perform: L. 13: As this amateur was performing. L. 60: The orchestra of winds perform.

Performance: L. 13: Edified with his performances.

Phrase: P. 321: That phraseless Melody.

Piano: P. 348: Not all Pianos in the Woods. L. 6: Father intends to have a piano. L. 7: I have had a piano of my own. L. 8: And now I have a piano. L. 11: Sabra says you have a new Piano. L. 14: Practising upon the piano. L. 18: I practise upon the Piano. L. 20: Father wishing to hear the Piano. L. 206: Sort of speck piano.

Piano Player: P. 315: As Players at the Keys. L. 9: As fine a piano player.

Piece: L. 7: I have been learning several beautiful pieces lately. "The Grave of Bonaparte," "Lancer's Quick Step," "Wood up," "Maiden Weep no more." L. 12: I have been learning a beautiful thing [piece]. L. 71: There is a piece for two hands.

Pipe: P. 216: Pipe the Sweet Birds. L. 85: Pipes the shrillest roundelay. L. 88. One little voice piping. L. 238: Pipe the Sweet Birds.

Plaintive: L. 824: A plaintive distinction.

Play: P. 366: Or played his chosen tune. P. 503: No one could play it. L. 7: I want very much to hear you play. I wish much to see you and hear you play. L. 20: An obedient daughter, played. L. 44: Vinnie

played pretty well! L. 184: I played the old, odd tunes. L. 255: We will play his tunes.

Practise/Practice: L. 7: You can come and practice on my piano. Are you practising now you are home. L. 9: And practise two hours in a day. L. 12: I have two hours to practise. L. 14: Practising upon the piano. L. 18: I practise upon the Piano. L. 23: I practice only one hour a day. L. 29: By close, and assiduous practise.

Psalm: P. 261: As well as psalm! P. 513: A too presumptuous Psalm.

Psaltery: P. 606: Far Psalteries of Summer.

Refrain: P. 238: Catch her last Refrain. P. 337: And she pours soft Refrains. P. 699: His favorite Refrain.

Requiem: L. 868: His Requiem ecstasy.

Resonance: P. 1175(v): Its Resonance divine. P. 1463: A Resonance of Emerald.

Reverberation: P. 1581: How Life's reverberation.

Ring/Rings: **Poems**, 29: The bells of Ghent would ring. 365: Whose Anvil's even ring. 619: Ring for the Scant Salvation. 633: When Bells stop ringing. 947: That Bells should ring. 1126: And when about to ring. 1761: Till all the churchyard rang. **Letters**, 77: The bells are ringing. The bells are always ringing. 133: Set the bells to ringing. 230: Small bells have rung so long. 973: When Memory rings.

Ritardando: P. 1003. Ritardando!

Roll: P. 103: Did round my pillow roll. P. 295: As Trumpets rolled. P. 501: Strong Hallelujahs roll. P. 861: Bulb after Bulb, in Silver rolled. L. 36: Hear the rolling drum.

Roundelay: L. 85: Pipes the shrillest roundelay. L. 184: 'Tis us a roundelay.

Rubinstein, Anton: L. 390: Glad you heard Rubinstein.

Rumbles: P. 1581: And rumbles still.

Shout: L. 344: Makes it first shout.

Shrill: P. 140: An axe shrill singing. P. 1561: With shrill felicity. L. 43: By their shrill singing. L. 85: Pipes the shrillest roundelay.

Sigh: L. 459: The long sigh of the Frog.

Signals: L. 807: Those enthralling Signals.

Silence: L. 339: Great Streets of Silence. L. 397: Silence. L. 458: Silence's oblation.

Sing/Sings: **Poems**, l: Sing me a strain divine. 5: Which for myself doth sing. 7: Walked singing on the shore. 14: She did not sing as we did. 20: I will singing go. 23: Who sang full many a day. 24: Like thee to sing. 37: That which sings so, speaks so. 131: Besides the Autumn poets sing. 140: An axe shrill singing. 161: That everlasting, sings! 221: Before the Blackbirds sing! 248: Did I sing too loud? 250: I shall keep singing! 254: And sings the tune. 269: Sing at its pain. 324: Our little Sexton sings. 373: On Twigs of singing, rather high. 410: I told my Soul to sing. 495: Sing clear as Plover. 514: Did hoist herself, to sing. 526: To hear an Oriole sing. Who sings the same, unheard. 616: I sang firm, even Chants. 630: But when He singeth. 755: No Bobolink reverse His Singing. 760: 'Twas as Space sat singing. 794: The Birds jocoser sung. 850: I sing to use the Waiting. And tell each other how We sung. 880: The Bird must sing. 1005: Bind me, I still can sing. 1059: Sang from the Heart, Sire. 1061: Text and Village Singing. 1104: The Crickets sang. 1265: And sang for nothing scrutable. 1304: Singing unto the Stone. 1373: The Ditty is that Nature Sings. 1530: In contrast with the things that sing. When what they sung for is undone. 1574: Arraigns it as it sings. 1724: How dare the robins sing. 1761: A bird broke forth and sang. Bowed again and sang. 1764:

Would go and sing no more. **Letters**, 13: Refrain from singing Auld Lang Syne. 18: I sing in Seminary Hall. 20: Sang a few tunes. 29: Sang old snatches of song. You are fond of singing. 30: And bad ones sing songs. 35: Sing, sing sad music. 39: Singing-birds in the spring. 42: If she dont abate her singing. 43: By their shrill singing. 44: We have all been rather piqued at Jennie's singing so well. 45: Oh Youth, come back again, they sing. 46: And sang and sang again. To her manner of singing. "Give me my thatched cottage" as she sang. 50: Ever soaring and singing. Our friends are glorified and singing there. 54: One bird that singeth. 56: And laugh as often and sing. 57: The crickets sing. A belated bird is singing. There the birds sing loudest. 58: And pussy is here a singing. 60: The stove is singing. 62: The people singing songs. 73: She sings and is so merry. 82: To hear birds singing. 85: The birds dont sing. 86: How the Robins sing. Sang so deliciously. Can't sing half so well. 88: When they sang. Kept singing. The choir were singing Hallelujahs. I sang so small. Singing of you. Cause her bird to sing! 92: Every bird that sings. Send him singing. Sing his little songs. I shall keep everything singing. 115: Sing the whole day long! 116: The birds sing beautifully. 123: The birds sing. 128: Everything is singing now. 133: Whether hum or sing. 152: Singing as they came. 154: The singing reminded me. 161: And the crickets begin to sing. 170: And the crickets sing? 173: Then pass on singing Sue. Which for myself doth sing. 178: Each linnet sing. 184: That strain may chance to sing. 189: Brooks that sang. 190: Causes birds to sing. Who it is that sings. 197: She did not sing. 199: You know some cannot sing. 212: Only the pines sing tunes. 215: When you and Vinnie sing. 217: The birds keep singing. Tuneful little aunt, singing. 255: Choirs sang to him. 259: Until the Engine sang. 261: And so I sing. 262: The Frogs sing sweet. 263: The robins' singing. 269: And wherefore sing. "My business is to sing." 293: The whippowil that sang. 298: Sang off charnel steps. 370: I hear him singing now. 379: And sing of it. 388: And sang for nothing. 391: And sang for nothing. 401: Buff sings. 405: He saw it and sung. 410: Tabby is singing "Old Hundred." 444a: Will not sing aloud. 542: Austin's Baby sings. Heard the Students sing. 644: Descendants are singing. 685: A Bird that would sing. 820: Sing without a Crumb. 824: As it sings. 860: The students were singing. 936: Sings in the morning. 942: Bluebirds are singing. 950: They still sing. 951: Your Son's singing. 968: He "sang" to you. Sing in his presence.

Singing School: L. 4: I attend singing-school. L. 5: I go to singing-school.

Siren: P. 1764: Wish those siren throats.

Song/Songs: **Poems**, 1: Wailing instead of Song? 179: Only to break in wilder song. 512: And staples, in the Song. 1465: With specimens of Song. 1575: And not a song pervade his Lips. 1630: Defrauded of its song. 1763: It has a song. **Letters**, 7: Sweet little song. 10: Tuned their golden harps to the song. 29: Sang old snatches of song. 30: And bad ones sing songs. 46: She seemed half lost in song. 60: The merry song of the wood. 62: The people singing songs. 92: Sing his little songs. 122: Whose song is not so merry. 184: And the song "here lies." 227: His songs are

concomitant. 317: And other Songsters. 533: The last song.

Sound/Sounds: **Poems**, 321: The Sounds despatched abroad. Caravan of Sound. 326: I was out of sight, in sound. 430: I clutched at sounds. 501: But positive, as Sound. 652: So miserable a sound. 733: For other Services, as Sound. 912: Bearing the Neighbor out of Sound. 937: Sequence ravelled out of Sound. 1235: Like Rain it sounded. 1302: It would not sound so deep. 1397: It sounded as if the Streets. 1581: A Crash without a Sound. 1636: Makes not as much of sound. **Letters**, 46: The Bird sounds from the "Bird Song." 118: I never heard such sounds. 302: Are better than "sounds." 458: Supersedes sound.

Soundless: P. 216: Soundless as dots. P. 274: His Gait, soundless. P. 365: That soundless tugs. P. 1448: Its soundless travels. L. 333: Be a soundless thing.

Speak: P. 37: That which sings so, speaks so. P. 533: If spoken by the distant Bird. P. 1540(v): The Cricket spoke so clear.

Stanza: P. 167(v): Whose stanza, hushed, below. P. 503: Like other stanza. P. 585: In horrid, hooting stanza. L. 52: Or when harmonious stanzas. L. 110: Favorite stanza of your's.

Strain: P. 1: Sing me a strain. P. 260: Clear strains of Hymn. P. 261: Teach me the strain. P. 302: Her Memories like Strains. P. 503: Not such a strain. L. 184: That strain may chance to sing.

Strife: P. 157: I hear the silver strife.

Strings: P. 410: She said her Strings were snapt. P. 1059: Death twists the strings.

Talk: P. 183: I've heard an Organ talk. P. 505: I would not talk, like Cornets. P. 1723: I gathered from his talk.

Tamborin: P. 157: Nor Tamborin, nor Man. P. 179: My Tamborin were soonest heard.

Tell: P. 498: To tell Him it is Noon, abroad. P. 503: I was telling a tune. P. 639: The Trumpets tell it to the Air. P. 1593: The flying tidings told.

Threnody: P. 634(v): Such Threnodies of Pearl.

Thrum: P. 321: And thrum upon the door. L. 206: Hums and thrums.

Thunder: P. 276: Loud as the Thunder's Tongue. Thundering its Prospective.

Tick: L. 610: The ticking of the bells. The bells tick.

Timbrel: P. 304: Happy Winds their Timbrels took. L. 233: A timbrel is it.

Toll: P. 280: Then Space began to toll. P. 324: And instead of tolling the Bell. P. 619: Toll for the bonnie Souls. P. 947: Of Tolling Bell I ask the Cause? L. 269: Where bells toll.

Tone: P. 283: As tone of Realm. P. 634: At first, a doubtful Tone. P. 947: I'm answered in a lonesome tone. P. 1323: In any Tone commensurate. P. 1722: More tender than the tune. L. 934: A Tone from the old Bells.

Tongue: P. 180: And birds, of foreign tongue!

Treble: P. 157: "Morning Stars" the Treble led.

Trill: P. 1761: And trilled, and quivered. L. 46: Some of her curious trills.

Troubadour: P. 23: Still, for my missing Troubadour. P. 96: And the Troubadour. P. 99: A Troubadour upon the Elm. P. 1483: The Robin is Gabriel. P. 1545: David, the Troubadour. L. 184: If a troubadour.

Trumpet: P. 1: And bring the fife, and trumpet. P. 3: The trumpet, sir, shall wake them. P. 295: As Trumpets rolled. P. 639: The Trumpets tell it to the Air.

P. 1648(v): There is no Trumpet. L. 662: Knock with a Trumpet.

Tune/Tunes: **Poems,** l: Humming a mournful tune. 14: It was a different tune: 64: Of last year's sundered tune! 83: Whistled itself a tune. 188: The orchards stop their tune. 208: To the immortal tune. 250: But I shall bring a fuller tune. 254: And sings the tune. 258: Of Cathedral Tunes. 285: The Robin's my Criterion for Tune. 312: Robin uttered Half the Tune. 321: With tufts of Tune. 333: And stir all day to pretty Tunes. 342: Will not despise the tune. 364: The Birds declaim their Tunes. 366: Or played his chosen tune. 367: Over and over, like a Tune. 380: In sovereign, Swerveless Tune. 436: Let go a music, as of tunes. 503: Of all tunes I knew--and more. 526: The "Tune is in the Tree." 592: And knew One Bird a Tune. 593: And just the meanest Tunes. 606: There seemed to rise a Tune. 639: Don't follow Me with tunes. 653: As did the Down emit a Tune. 699: I only ask a Tune. 735: Makes Lacerating Tune. 824: With threatening Tunes and low. 880: What merit have the Tune. 916: His Idleness, a Tune. 944: A Ruffle or a Tune. 956: Drop a Tune on me. 1046: And chiselled all my tune. 1059: If the Tune drip too much. 1102: Their Miracles of Tune. 1389: Unless thou know'st the Tune. 1418: Stepping to incorporeal Tunes. 1530: A Blue Bird's Tune. 1568: To hear her is a Tune. 1576: Alone is not a Tune. 1722: More tender than the tune. **Letters,** 7: Aunt Selby says she shant let me have many tunes. 10: Tuned their golden harps to the song. 184: Play the old, odd tunes. 197: It was a different tune. 212: Only the pines sing tunes. 217: Tuneful little aunt. 233: Itself to it a tune? 255: We will play his tunes.

259: Sang a pleasant tune. 370: To the Tune of a Nut. 414: The last tune. 802: To hear her is a Tune. 872: Alone is not a Tune.

Twitter: L. 85: Birds dont sing, but twitter.

Vespers: P. 250: Vespers are sweeter than Matins.

Viol, Bass: L. 154: Allowing the Bass Viol.

Violin: P. 302: The Violin in Baize replaced. P. 635: Take up my little Violin. P. 1576: The Music in the Violin. L. 872: The Music in the Violin.

Vocal: L. 614: Vocal is but one form.

Voice: P. 167: Whose voices, trained, below. P. 283: A Voice that Alters, Low. P. 634: You'll know Her by Her Voice. L. 5: To improve my voice. L. 11: I listen to her syren voice. L. 88: One little voice, piping. L. 337: To hear Loo's voice. L. 845: I hear your voices.

Waltz: P. 533: And waltzed upon a Farm.

Warble: P. 1235: It warbled in the Road. 1545: The Tale a warbling Teller. L. 318: A low wind warbled. L. 690: Maggie's hens are warbling.

Wassail: L. 190: Before the wassail's done.

Whirr: P. 64: Lethargic pools resume the whir.

Whistle: P. 83: Whistled itself a tune. P. 198: And whistled in the air. P. 617: When the Birds began to whistle. P. 1449: How slow the whistle sang. P. 1524: The Boys that whistled. L. 43: I find I 'gin to whistle. L. 58: Little boys... are whistling. L. 562: The whistle of a Boy.

Appendix One

Contents of Emily Dickinson's
Personal Album of Sheet Music

"Music": a bound volume of miscellaneous sheet music, without title page, with Emily Dickinson's autograph [?] on flyleaf. Houghton #49-1469. Archive Negative, 49-1469F. The citations below are in the order they appear in the album.

Kreutzer, [Rodolphe]. The Celebrated Overture to Lodoiska. Composed by Kreutzer. Arranged for Two Performers on the Piano Forte, by Charles [Karl] Czerny. New-York: Firth Hall & Pond, [n.d.].

Valentine, T. Aria Alla Scozzese with Variations. Composed for the Piano Forte by T. Valentine. Boston: Keith's Music Publishing House, [n.d.].

Valentine, Thomas. Believe Me If All Those Endearing Young Charms, or My Lodging Is On the Cold Ground. Variations for the Piano Forte. By Thos. Valentine. Baltimore: F.D. Benteen, [n.d.].

Dutton, George. Hope Again. Air with Variations for the Piano Forte. Inscribed by Permission to Rudolph Snyder, Esq. By Geo. Dutton. Utica: Geo. Dutton, [1841].

[Moran, P.K.] Kinlock of Kinlock. Arranged for the Piano Forte with Variations. Boston: C. Bradlee, [n.d.].

[Bellini, Vincenzo.] Take Them, I Implore Thee (Deh Conte). Arranged from the Opera Norma with Variations by F. Hunten. Boston: Oliver Ditson, [n.d.].

[Tancredi. Di Tanti Palpiti.] A Favorite Air from Tancredi. With Variations for the Piano Forte by Edward L. White. Boston: C. Bradlee, 1834.

The Swiss Waltz with Variations, by P.K. Moran. Boston: C.H. Keith, [n.d.].

Auld Lang Syne. With Variations for the Piano Forte or Harp by D. Ross. Boston: C.P. Reed, [n.d.].

The Last Rose of Summer. With Easy Variations by A. Mine. Boston: Geo. P. Reed, [n.d.].

Bonny Doon with Variations. Composed by Wm. Wood, Jnr. New York: Firth & Hall, [n.d.].

A.B.C. A Favorite French Air. With an Introduction and Variations Composed and Arranged as Exercises for the Piano Forte and Respectfully Dedicated to His Pupils by Edward L. White. Boston: Wm. H. Oakes, 1843.

Yankee Doodle. Arranged with Variations for the Piano Forte. Boston: C.H. Keith, [n.d.].

Speed the Plough. A Favorite Dance Arranged with Brilliant Variations for the Piano Forte. New York: William Hall & Son, 1845. Fourth Edition.

[Gung'l, Josef.] The Fest March, or Warrior's Joy. Composed by Josef Gung'l. Boston: Oliver Ditson, [n.d.].

Hesser, J.G. Congress March. By J.Z. Hesser. Boston: Keith's Music Publishing House, [n.d.].

Underhill, H. B. Massachusetts March. Composed for the Piano Forte by H. B. Underhill. Boston: Oliver Ditson, [n.d.].

Russian March. Boston: Keith & Moore, [n.d.].

Louisville March and Quick Step. Composed for and Dedicated to Mrs. A. Bowen by W. C. P. Boston: C. Bradlee, [n.d.]. [Inscribed "Emily Dickinson" on front side.]

[Bellini, Vincenzo.] Grand March in Norma, No. 1. Composed and Arranged for the Piano Forte by Bellini. Boston: Oliver Ditson, [n.d.].

Roderick Dhu's March. Composed and Arranged for the Piano Forte. Boston: Oliver Ditson, [n.d.].

March and Quick Step in the Battle of Prague. New York: Firth & Hall, [n.d.].

Bonaparte's March Crossing the Rhine. Composed and Arranged for the Piano Forte. [N.p.: n.p., n.d.]

Shoulder Arms. Boston: Henry Prentiss, 1842. [Illustrated plate only; no music.]

The Celebrated Spanish Retreat. (Quick Step.) Performed for the First Time by the Brigade Band at the Encampment of the Hancock Light Infantry, July, 1841. Arranged for the Piano Forte by J. De Anguera. Respectfully Dedicated to Mrs. D. B. Stedman. Boston: Henry Prentiss, 1841.

Blockley's Beautiful Melody of Love Not. Arranged as a Quick Step for the Piano Forte by Edward L. White. Boston: Oliver Ditson, 1843.

Wil[l]son, Charles. Camp Barnum Quick Step. As Played by Adams' Band, Composed Arranged & Dedicated to Mason A. Fisher, of the Rochester Grays by Charles Wilson. New York: Firth, Pond, 1847.

Haskell, D. H. Prize Banner Quick Step. Composed & Arranged for the Piano Forte. The Prize Banner Ward, by D. H. Haskell. Boston: Henry Prentiss, 1841.

Glynn, William C. Bayeaux's Quick Step. Composed and Arranged for the Piano Forte. By Wm. C. Glynn. Boston: Keith's Music Publishing House, 1844.

Chadwick, L. Thayer. Locomotive Quick Step. Respectfully Dedicated to C. C. Dennis Esq, of Auburn. N. Y. by the Author, L. Thayer Chadwick. Boston: Keith's Music Publishing House, [n.d.].

Smith, William. Home Quick Step. Composed for the Piano Forte and Respectfully Dedicated to Dr. L. W. Stanton of Ameniaville N. Y. by Wm. Smith. Boston: C. H. Keith, 1842.

Lucy Neal Quick Step. As Performed by the Boston Bands Introducing the Celebrated Airs "Lucy Neal, Dandy Jim and Lovely Fan." Arranged for the Piano Forte by Joseph W. Turner. Boston: Keith's Music Publishing House, 1844.

Comer, T. and Steele, S. S. Favorite Melodies from the Grand Chinese Spectacle of Aladdin or the Wonderful Lamp. Produced at the Boston Museum. Words by S. S. Steele, Esq. The Music Composed by T. Comer. ("Aladdin Quick Step.") Boston: Prentiss & Clark, 1847.

Burditt, B. A. Juniata Quick Step. Played by the Boston Bands. Arranged from the Popular Song of "The Blue Juniata" by B. A. Burditt. Boston: Oliver Ditson, 1847.

Jones, J. G. Coolidge Quickstep. Composed and Arranged for the Piano Forte, and Respectfully Dedicated to Major Chs. Austin Coolidge, The Brigade Staff, by J. G. Jones. Boston: C. H. Keith, 1844.

Bay State Quick Step. As Performed by the Boston Brass Band, Arranged for the Piano Forte by William C. Glynn. Boston: Keith's Music Publishing House, 1844.

Willis, Richard S. The Glenmary Waltzes. Composed by Richard S. Willis and Most Affectionately Dedicated to His Niece Imogen Willis. No. 1. Boston: Oliver Ditson, 1847. (a) Cottage. (b) Lawn. (c) Shade. (d) Meadow. (e) Glade.

Willis, Richard S. The Glenmary Waltzes. Composed by Richard S. Willis and Most Affectionately Dedicated to His Niece Imogen Willis. No. 2. Boston: Oliver Ditson, 1847. (a) Voices of Spring. (b) Voice of the River. (c) Voice of Flowers. (d) Voice of the May-Dance. (e) Voice of the Wood-Nymph. (f) Voice of the Mountain Stream.

Willis, Richard S. The Glenmary Waltzes. Composed by Richard S. Willis and Most Affectionately Dedicated to His Niece Imogen Willis. No. 3 Boston: Oliver Ditson, 1847. Third Set of Glen Mary Waltzes. (a) Imogen's Trip. (b) The Smile. (c) The Joyous Thought. (d) The Pleasant Voice. (e) The Responsive Carol. (f) The Waving Tress. (g) Quick Step.

[Misattributed to Beethoven.] Clara Waltz. Beethoven's Last. Composed and Arranged for the Piano Forte. Boston: Keith's Music Publishing House, [n.d.].

[Misattributed to Beethoven.] La Doleur Waltz. Composed by L. V. Beethoven. Boston: Oliver Ditson, [n.d.].

[Misattributed to Beethoven.] Grand Landler Waltz. Composed by L. V. Beethoven. Boston: Oliver Ditson, [n.d.].

[Kinsky Anhang 14, No. 3; composer unknown.]

[Misattributed to Beethoven.] Beethoven's Dream. A Grand Waltz for the Piano Forte. Boston: Geo. P. Reed, [n.d.].

[Misattributed to Beethoven.] Willow Waltz. Composed for the Piano Forte by L. V. Beethoven. Boston: C. Bradlee, [n.d.].

[Misattributed to Beethoven.] Japonica Waltz. Composed for the Piano Forte by L. V. Beethoven. Boston: C.H. Keith, [n.d.].

[Misattributed to Beethoven.] The Much Admired Waltz. Composed by Beethoven. Arranged by Valentine. St. Louis: Balmer & Weber, [n.d.].

[Misattributed to Beethoven.] The Spirit Waltz. By Beethoven. Boston: C.H. Keith, [n.d.].

[Misattributed to Beethoven.] Tulip Waltz by Beethoven. Boston: C. H. Keith, [n.d.].

Weber, Karl Maria Friedrich Ernst von. Von Weber's Last Waltz. Boston: C. Bradlee, [n.d.].

[W.H.F.] Affection Waltz. Composed by W.H.F. Boston: Oliver Ditson, [n.d.].

Labitzky, Joseph. Firth, Pond & Co's. Collection of Celebrated Waltzes. By Joseph Labitzky. ("Elfin Waltzes.") New York: Firth, Pond & Co., [n.d.].

Gung'l, Josef. Sounds from Home. A Set of Waltzes Played by the Steyermarkische Company by Gungl [sic]. Boston: Oliver Ditson, [n.d.].

Flint, James. L' Ariadne Waltz. Composed by James Flint. Boston: Wm. H. Oakes, [n.d.].

Panormo, Francis. The Bird Waltz. For the Harp or Piano Forte. Composed by

Francis Panormo. Philadelphia: J. G. Klemon, [n.d.].

Unger, Ferdinand. Aurora Waltz. Composed for the Piano Forte by Ferdinand Unger. Boston: C. Bradlee, [n.d.].

Labitzky, Joseph. Aurora Waltz. Boston: E. H. Wade, [n.d.].

Peters, [William Cumming]. The Louisville Waltz. Composed for the Piano Forte or Harp and Dedicated to Mrs. Atkinson. By [W. C.] Peters. New York: Firth, Hall & Pond, 1835.

Smith, John. Any Thing. A New Waltz Composed for Every Body and Respectfully Dedicated to Any Body by John Smith. New York: C. Holt, 1847.

The Home That I Love. Arranged as a Waltz by Edward L. White. Boston: Oliver Ditson, 1846.

Home as a Waltz. Boston: C.H. Keith, [n.d.]. [Inscribed "Lavinia N. Dickinson Jan. 15," 184–.]

Olds, M.L. Jessie Waltz. Composed and Respectfully Dedicated to Miss J.M. by M. L. Olds. Boston: J. Prentiss, 1850.

Herz, Henri. The Celebrated Empress Henrietta's Waltz. Composed by H. Herz. Boston: C.H. Keith, [n.d.].

The Much Admired Sliding Waltz. Boston: C.H. Keith, [n.d.].

Burgmüller, Johann Friedrich Franz. Linden Waltz. Arranged for the Piano Forte by F. Burgmüller. Boston: Oliver Ditson, [n.d.].

Taylor, Richard B. Aeolian Waltz. Composed for the Piano Forte with or without Coleman's Attachment and Dedicated to Miss Anne B. Francis by Richard B. Taylor. Boston: Keith's Publishing House, 1845.

Glynn, William C. The Rockaway Waltzes. Composed and Arranged for the Piano Forte and Dedicated to Miss Georgiana Andrews, by William C. Glynn. Boston: Keith's Music Publishing House, 1844.

Lemoine, Henry. Lawrence Waltz. Composed and Arranged for the Piano Forte by Henry Lemoine. Boston: C. H. Keith, [n.d.].

Bayley, A. W. Mary Louisa Waltz. Composed and Inscribed to Miss Mary L. Snell by A. W. Bayley. Boston: Geo. P. Reed, 1844.

Bohlman, Henri. L'Enfer Quadrille Diabolique. Performed at the Public & Private Assemblies. Composed for the Piano Forte by Henri Bohlman. New York: Wm. Dubois, [n.d.]. (a) L'Arrivée du Chevalier Maudit. (b) Sermens d'Amour. (c) Chasse Infernale. (d) Bal au Palais Enchanté. (e) L'Enfer. [Note: Inserted is a printed page describing this story in French.]

Fowler, J. A. Syracuse Polka. Composed & Arranged for the Piano Forte and Very Respectfully Inscribed to Miss R. H. Loomis of Syracuse, N. Y. By J. A. Fowler. New York: Atwill, 1848.

Offenbach, Jacques. The Celebrated Polka Dance. As Performed with Enthusiastic Applause at the Boston Museum. Composed by J. Offenbach. Boston: Keith's Music Publishing House, [n.d.].

The Celebrated Baden-Baden Polka Pas Bohemian. Arranged by Musard. Philadelphia: Lee & Walker's Music Store and Circulating Library, [n.d.].

The Basket Cotillion. Boston: C. H. Keith, [n.d.]. The Girl I Left Behind Me.

Herr Cline's Dance. Boston: C. H. Keith, [n.d.]. a. Spanish Dance; b. Spanish Dance.

Swiss Guards March. Boston: Keith & Moore, [n.d.].

Fisher's Hornpipe. [N.p: n.p., n.d.]

Durang's Hornpipe. Boston: C. H. Keith, [n.d.]. Drops of Brandy.

Caledonian Hunt. Boston: Keith's Music Publishing House, [n.d.]. Drunken Sailor.

Bonaparte's Retreat from Moscow. Arranged by J. Schell. Boston: C. H. Keith. [n.d.].

Panharmonicon March. Boston: Keith & Moore, [n.d.]. (a) College Hornpipe.

Kinloch of Kinloch. Boston: Keith & Moore, [n.d.].

Balfe, Michael William. Gems from The Bohemian Girl. Arranged for the Piano Forte. Philadelphia: E. Ferrett & Co., [n.d.]. (a) No. 1, I Dreamt I dwelt in Marble Halls. (b) No. 2, Then You'll Remember Me. (c) No. 3, The Fair Land of Poland. (d) No. 4, The Heart Bow'd Down. (e) No. 5, Pity for One in Childhood Torn. (f) No. 6, Oh, What Full Delight. (g) No. 7, The Gipsies' Song and Chorus.

Russell, Henry. The Old Arm Chair, A Ballad. The Music Composed and Respectfully Dedicated to Holton Olmsted, Esquire, by Henry Russell. [Words by Eliza Cook.] 23d ed. Boston: Geo. P. Reed, 1840.

Dempster, William R. and Blackwood, Hon. Mrs. Price. The Lament of the Irish Emigrant. Ballad Poetry by The Hon. Mrs. Price Blackwood. The Music Composed and Most Cordially Dedicated to Mrs. Isaac McGaw of New York, by William R. Dempster. Boston: Geo. P. Reed, 1843. [Note: "Portraying the feelings of an Irish peasant previous to his leaving home, calling up the scenes of his youth under the painful reflection of having buried his wife and child, and what his feelings will be in America."]

[The Hutchinson Family.] The Old Granite State. A Song, Composed, Arranged and Sung, by The Hutchinson Family. Boston: Oliver Ditson, 1843.

Russell, Henry. Our Native Song. A National Refrain as Sung with Great Applause by Mr. H. Russell, at His Public Concerts. The Music Composed, Adapted, Arranged & Most Respectfully Dedicated to the People of The United States by Henry Russell. New York: Firth Hall & Pond, 1841.

Bonnie Doon. Favorite Scotch Song for One or Two Voices. Arranged for the Pianoforte. Boston: Chas. H. Keith, [n.d.].

The Bonny Boat. Boston: C. H. Keith, [n.d.].

Home, Sweet Home. Boston: C. H. Keith, [n.d.].

Kiallmark, C. and Moore, Thomas. Araby's Daughter. Sung with Great Applause by Mr. Williamson. Written by Thomas Moore Esq. Composed by C. Kiallmark. Boston: C. H. Keith, [n.d.].

Nelson, S. and Jeffery, Charles. The Rose of Allandale. A Ballad Written by Charles Jeffery. The Music by S. Nelson. Boston: Keith & Moore, [n.d.].

[The Hutchinson Family.] There's a Good Time Coming. Ballad Composed & Sung by the Hutchinson Family. The Symphonies & Accompaniments by E. L. White. Written by Charles Mackay. Boston: Oliver Ditson. 1846.

Moore, Thomas. The Admired Canadian Boat Song and Trio. Written and Composed by T. Moore Esq. Boston: Chas. H. Keith, [n.d.].

Blackwood, Mrs. Price. The Charming Woman. Words and Music by Mrs. Price Blackwood. Boston: Keith & Moore, [n.d.].

Come, Love, Dance the Polka with Me. An Admired Song Adapted for the Piano Forte by F. Romani. Baltimore: F. D. Benteen, 1844.

Sinclair, John. The Bonnie Clay Flag. Music Composed by John Sinclair. Words by John H. Warland, Esq. And Respectfully Dedicated to the Boston Clay Club No. 1. Boston: C. H. Keith, 1844.

Crosby, L. V. H. and Pike, Marshall S. Oh Give Me a Home If in Foreign Land. Song Sung by the Harmoneon Family as a Quartette. Poetry by Marshall S. Pike. Music Composed & Respectfully Dedicated to Mrs. Samuel Farrar of Bangor, Me. by L. V. H. Crosby. Boston: Oliver Ditson, 1845. [Arranged as a quartette by Edward L. White.]

Hutchinson, J. J. The Little Maid. A Little Song for Little Folks. To be sung in Little (or Large) Rooms with Little Exertion. Composed by J. J. Hutchinson and Dedicated to Every One Who Sings It, Especially Little Singers. Boston: Oliver Ditson, 1846.

Moore, Thomas. Believe Me, If All Those Endearing Young Charms. Written by Thomas Moore. New York: E. Ferrett & Co., [n.d.].

Whitlock, William. Who's That Knocking at the Door. As Composed and Sung by Wm. Whitlock. New York: C. C. Christman, 1846. (Whitlock's Collection of Ethiopian Melodies.) [With separate illustrated title-page.]

The Original Old Dan Tucker. As Sung by the Virginia Minstrels. Words by Old Dan D. Emmit. Arranged for the Piano Forte by Rice. Boston: C.H. Keith, 1843. (Old Dan Emmit's Original Banjo Melodies. Emmit, Brower, Whitlock, Pelham.)

The Jolly Raftsman. Words by Andrew Evans as Sung by Him at His Concerts with Great Success. Boston: Keith's Music Publishing House, 1844. (From "Old Dan Emmit's Original Banjo Melodies Never Before Published. Mr. D.D. Emmit. As Sung by Him with Unprecedented Success...both in Europe and America." Second Series.)

Appendix Two

Music and Books on Music
in the Dickinson library

I. Books with substantive references to music that Emily Dickinson may have read and used. Houghton numbers refer to the *Houghton Library Handlist of Books Found in the Home of Emily Dickinson*.

Bertini, Henri. *A Progressive and Complete Method for the Piano-Forte*. Boston: E. H. Wade, n.d.
> Johnson: Letter 7, p. 16. Lowenberg: *Emily Dickinson's Textbooks*, p. 33.

Blair, Hugh. *An Abridgment of Lectures on Rhetoric. Revised and Corrected, to Which is Applied a New Method of Interrogating*. By Samuel Worcester. Boston: Cummings, Hilliard & Co., 1825.
> "Structure of Sentences—Harmony," pp. 84-91. Lowenberg: *Hampshire County Textbooks, 1812-1850*, p. 24.

Cummings, Preston. *A Dictionary of Congregational Usages and Principles*. Boston: S. K. Whipple and Co., 1852.
> Singing, p. 338. Houghton: reject. A.s. "Edw. Dickinson 1855." Lowenberg: *Emily Dickinson's Textbooks*, p. 41.

[Dickinson, Emily. Emily Dickinson's personal album of miscellaneous sheet music; bound volume, without a title page, with her autograph (?) on flyleaf.]
> Houghton: #49-1469. For the complete contents of this album, see Appendix One.

Gilmore, Joseph Henry. *He Leadeth Me. Baptist Hymn Tune Book*. Philadelphia: n.p., 1871.
> Johnson: Letter 533, p. 599. Julian. *A Dictionary of Hymnology*, p. 424.

[Goodrich, S. G.] *Parley's Magazine, for 1838. Illustrated with One Hundred and Fifty Engravings*. New-York and Boston: Charles S. Francis and Joseph H. Francis, January, 1838.
> Contains nine songs by Lowell Mason, January through November. Leyda: *Years and Hours*, I: 44-45. February 16, 1838. Lowenberg: *Hampshire County Textbooks, 1812-1850*, p. 51.

Guild, Caroline Snowden (Whitmarsh). *Hymns for Mothers and Children*. Boston: Walker, Wise and Company, 1861.
> Houghton: #2287. With a.s. of S.H. Dickinson.

Guild, Caroline Snowden (Whitmarsh). *Hymns for Mothers and Children*. Second Series. Boston: Walker, Fuller, and Company, 1866.
> Houghton: #2288. With a.s. of S.H. Dickinson.

Gung'l, Joseph. "Sounds From Home." Boston: Oliver Ditson, n.d.
> Johnson: Letter 302, p. 438.

Heath, Lyman. "The Grave of Bonaparte." Words by Henry S. Washburn. Boston: Oliver Ditson, 1843.
> Johnson: Letter 7, p. 18.

Holloway, John. "Wood Up." Boston: C. Bradlee, 1834.
> Johnson: Letter 7, p. 18.

Jenkins, Jonathan L. "Mendelssohn's Elijah." Pittsfield, MA: n.p., 1884.
> Houghton: #2356. Inscribed: "With affectionate regards, J.L.J." Sewall: *Life*, pp. 67-68, 274, 533n.

Kames, Lord Henry Home. *Elements of Criticism*. New-York: Collins & Hannay, 1830.
> Chapter 18: "Beauty of Language." (Music, passim.) Amherst Academy textbook, 1839-1840. Amherst College textbook, 1835-1849. Houghton: #2360. (1847 edition.) Lowenberg: *Emily Dickinson's Textbooks*, p. 62.

Luther, Martin. "Old Hundred." In Lowell Mason *et al. The Boston Academy's Collection of Church Music*.
> (See full citation under Lowell Mason *et al.*) Johnson: Letter 410, p. 523.

MacLagan, T. "Captain Jinks." Philadelphia: Lee & Walker, 1868.
> Johnson: Letter 364, p. 489; 397, p. 512.

Marvel, Ik [Donald Grant Mitchell]. *Dream Life*. New York: Charles Scribner, 1851.
> Chapter VII, "The Country Church," pp. 96-97. Houghton: #2414. Johnson: Letter 75, p. 178.

Mason, Lowell. *The Boston Handel and Haydn Society Collection of Church Music. Being a Selection of the Most Approved Psalm and Hymn Tunes, Anthems, Sentences, Chants, &c. Together With Many Beautiful Extracts from the Works of Haydn, Mozart, Beethoven, and Other Eminent Composers. Harmonized for Three and Four Voices, With a Figured Base* [sic] *for the Organ and Piano Forte*. Boston: J. H. Wilkins & R. B. Carter, 1835.
> Mount Holyoke Female Seminary textbook, 1847-1848.

Mason, Lowell. *Carmina Sacra: or Boston Collection of Church Music*. Boston: J.H. Wilkins & R.B. Carter, 1841.
> Mount Holyoke Female Seminary textbook, 1847-1848. Lowenberg: *Emily Dickinson's Textbooks*, pp. 71-72.

Mason, Lowell and David Greene, (editors). *Church Psalmody: Psalms and Hymns, Adapted to Public Worship. Selected from Dr. Watts and Other Authors*. Boston: T.R. Marvin, 1831.
> Edward Dickinson's copy in the Amherst College Library. Martha Winburn England: "Hymns Unbidden," pp. 126n, 127. Lowenberg: *Emily Dickinson's Textbooks*, p. 72.

Mason, Lowell and George James Webb. *The Vocalist: Consisting of Short and Easy Glees, or Songs. Arranged for Soprano, Alto, Tenor, and Bass Voices*. Boston: Wilkins, Carter, & Co., 1844.
> Mount Holyoke Female Seminary textbook, 1847-1848. Lowenberg: *Emily Dickinson's Textbooks*, pp. 72-73.

[Mason, Lowell, et al.] *The Boston Academy's Collection of Church Music. Consisting of the Most Popular Psalm and Hymn Tunes, Anthems, Sentences, Chants, &c. Old and New. Together With Many Beautiful Pieces, Tunes and Anthems, Selected From the Masses and Other Works of Haydn, Mozart, Beethoven, Pergolesi, Righini,*

Romberg, Winter, Weber, Nageli, Kubler, and Other Distinguished Composers, Arranged and Adapted to English Words Expressly for This Work. Including, also, Original Compositions by German, English and American Authors. Boston: J. H. Wilkins and R. B. Carter, 1836.

"Elements of Vocal Music," pp. 4–24, prepared by Lowell Mason. Mount Holyoke Female Seminary textbook, 1847–1848.

Mendelssohn-Bartholdy, Felix. *Letters from Italy and Switzerland.* Philadelphia: Frederick Leopold, 1863.

Houghton: #2408. With a.s. of S. H. Dickinson.

Moore, Thomas. "Believe Me If All Those Endearing Young Charms." Arranged by J. A. Stevenson. Philadelphia: George Willig, 1826.

Johnson: Letter 22, p. 64n.

Moore, Thomas. *Irish Melodies.* Philadelphia: E. H. Butler & Co., 1865.

Houghton: #2420.

Nettleton, Asahel. *Village Hymns for Social Worship. Selected and Original. Designed as a Supplement to the Psalms and Hymns of Dr. Watts.* New-York: E. Sands, 1838.

Johnson: Letter 110, p. 235. Mount Holyoke Female Seminary textbook, 1847–1848. Henry Wilder Foote: *Three Centuries of American Hymnody,* pp. 169, 189–191, 194, 203, 264. Julian: *A Dictionary of Hymnology,* p. 794. Lowenberg: *Emily Dickinson's Textbooks,* p. 77.

Olmsted, Denison. *A Compendium of Natural Philosophy. Adapted to the Use of the General Reader, and of Schools and Academies.* New Haven: S. Babcock, 1844.

Chapter 5, "Acoustics" pp. 212, 216. Amherst Academy textbook, 1841, 1847. Mount Holyoke Female Seminary textbook, 1848. Lowenberg: *Emily Dickinson's Textbooks,* p. 82.

Olmsted, Denison. *An Introduction to Natural Philosophy.* New York: Collins, Brother, & Co., 1844.

Chapter 5, "Acoustics" pp. 355–360, 373–379. Mount Holyoke Female Seminary textbook, 1848. Lowenberg: *Emily Dickinson's Textbooks,* p. 82.

Park, Edwards Amasa; Austin Phelps; Lowell Mason. *The Sabbath Hymn Book. For the Service of Song in the House of the Lord.* New York: Mason Brothers, 1858.

Houghton: #2436. With a.s. of Edward Dickinson, 1861. The Dickinson library had five copies, all signed by Edward Dickinson. Henry Wilder Foote: *Three Centuries of American Hymnody,* pp. 207, 213, 216–218, 221, 233, 235, 363. Lowenberg: *Emily Dickinson's Textbooks,* pp. 84–85.

Raymond, F. L. "The Lancer's Quick Step." Boston: H. Prentiss, n.d.

Johnson: Letter 7, p. 18.

Robinson, Charles Seymour. *A Selection of Spiritual Songs.* New York: Scribner & Co., 1878. Houghton: #2466.

Inscribed: Lavinia Dickinson, Amherst. Julian: *A Dictionary of Hymnology,* p. 969.

Ross, John. "Auld Lang Syne. With Variations for the Piano Forte or Harp." Boston: G. Graupner, 1820.

Johnson: Letter 13, p. 38; 184, p. 328.

Scott, Alicia Anne (Spottiswoode). "Annie Laurie." (New York: n.p., (18–). Houghton: #49-1468.

Smith, Samuel Francis. "My Country, 'Tis of Thee [America]." 1832.
Johnson: Letter 509, p. 586. John Tasker Howard: *Our American Music*, pp. 132-133.

Watts, Isaac. *Christian Psalmody in Four Parts.* Boston: n.p., 1817.
Houghton: reject. Inscribed: Edw. Dickinson. Amherst.

Watts, Isaac. *The Psalms, Hymns, and Spiritual Songs, of the Rev. Isaac Watts, D.D. To Which are Added, Select Hymns, from Other Authors; and Directions for Musical Expression by Samuel Worcester, D.D. A New Edition by Samuel M. Worcester, A.M.* Boston: Crocker & Brewster, Brewster, 1834.

Houghton: #2555. Inscribed: Edward Dickinson. Mount Holyoke Female Seminary textbook, 1847-1848. Jack Capps: *Emily Dickinson's Reading,* pp. 73, 102, 145, 187. Martha Winburn England: "Hymns Unbidden," pp. 126, 127. Thomas H. Johnson: *Emily Dickinson,* pp. 84-86. Lowenberg: *Emily Dickinson's Textbooks,* p. 102.

Whitmarsh, Caroline Snowden and Anne E. Guild (compilers). *Hymns of the Ages. Second Series. With an Introduction by Rev. F. D. Huntington.* Boston: Phillips, Sampson, and Company, 1861.
Houghton: #2289. Inscribed to S. H. Dickinson from Bishop Huntington. This is the second of a series of three, in various printings from 1858-1865. Ruth Miller: *The Poetry of Emily Dickinson,* pp. 270- 271, 406-410.

II. Periodicals to which the Dickinsons subscribed

Only those periodicals that published music articles and notices are cited here. The main source of information is Daniel Lombardo's *Tales of Amherst,* pp. 101-102. The 1862-1866 dates are from post office records; subscriptions very likely ran much earlier and later.

The Atlantic Monthly. November 1857-May 1886.

Boston Courier. 1862-1866.

The Boston Transcript. 1862-1866.

The Century Magazine. November 1881-May 1886.

Congregational Quarterly. 1862-1866.

Greenfield Courier. 1862-1866.

Harper's New Monthly Magazine. June 1850-May 1886.

Observer. (New York.) 1862-1866.

The Round Table. 1863-1869.

Scribner's Monthly. November 1870-October 1881.

The Springfield Republican. 1843-1886.

The Youth's Companion. 1862-1866.

Appendix Three

Music Publications of
Emily Dickinson's Uncles

Mark Haskell Newman

Mark Haskell Newman (1806-1852) was Emily Dickinson's uncle by way of his marriage (October 2, 1828) to Mary Dickinson (1809-1852), her father's sister. His father, Mark Newman, was variously Principal of Phillips Andover Academy, a publisher, and a bookseller. A brother, Samuel Phillips, taught Latin and Greek, rhetoric and oratory, and economics at Bowdoin College, where Mark Haskell was in the class of 1825 along with the novelist Nathaniel Hawthorne and the poet Henry Wadsworth Longfellow. Samuel Phillips was author of one of Emily Dickinson's textbooks, *A Practical System of Rhetoric* (Portland: William Hyde, 1827). He was also notable for his work in establishing, with Horace Mann, the second Massachusetts Normal School at Barre in 1839.

Mark Haskell probably met the Dickinsons when, after his graduation from Bowdoin College in 1825, he moved to Amherst to sell books and rent out horses to Amherst students. His bookshop appears to have been the first in Amherst. About 1827 he moved to Andover to join his father's business. Although it has been recorded that he moved to New York "about 1830," to set up his own publishing and bookselling business, the late 1830s is more likely. He is known to have been the first publisher of graded school books.

Both Mark Haskell and Mary Newman died prematurely in 1852. Two of their five children who survived them, Clara and Anna, best known to Emily Dickinson, were raised by Austin and Susan Dickinson. Mark Haskell Newman had a once-removed hand in Emily Dickinson's education in that he published nine of the books used in her schooling (Lowenberg: *Emily Dickinson's Textbooks*, p. 24). Because Newman's music books, especially those of William Bradbury and Thomas Hastings, went through many printings and were widely circulated, the Dickinsons could well have known about them.

Baker, Benjamin Franklin and L.H. Stoddard. *The School Chimes, A Collection of Songs and Pieces Designed Especially for the Use of Schools, Juvenile Classes and School Exhibition.* Boston: Wilkins, Rice & Kandall; New York: M. H. Newman & Co., 1851.

Baker, Benjamin Franklin and L.H. Stoddard. *The Union Glee Book. Consisting of Glees, Quartetts, and Part Songs.* Boston: Henry Tolman; New York: Mark Newman, 1852.

Bradbury, William and Charles W. Sanders. *The Young Choir. Adapted to the Use of Juvenile Singing Schools, Sabbath Schools, Primary Classes.* New York: M. H. Newman, 1841.

Bradbury, William and Charles W. Sanders. *The Young Choir, or School Singing Book.* New York: Mark H. Newman, 1841.

Bradbury, William and Charles W. Sanders. *The School Singer, or Young Choir's Companion. Including Some of the most Popular German Melodies; also a Complete Course of Instruction in the Elementary Vocal Music, Founded on the German System of Kubler.* New York: M. H. Newman & Co., 1842.

Bradbury, William. *Bradbury's Singing School and Glee Book Combined. Being His Method of Singing by Note; Containing a Thorough Course of Progressive Exercises and Solfeggios, Together with Upwards of Fifty Glees, Rounds, Madrigals, Choruses, Etc.* New York: Mark H. Newman, 1844.

Bradbury, William. *Singing School, For Ladies and Gentlemen. Being His Method of Singing by Note, Comprising a Course of Exercises and Solfeggios Interspersed with Pleasing Melodies.* New York: Mark H. Newman, 1844.

Bradbury, William and Charles W. Sanders. *The School Singer; or, Young Choir's Companion. A Choice Collection of Music, for Juvenile Singing Schools, Sabbath Schools, Academies.* New York: Mark H. Newman, 1845.

Bradbury, William and Charles W. Sanders. *The Singing Choir; or, Church Singing Book.* New York: M. H. Newman, 1845.

Bradbury, William. *The Social Singing Book. A Collection of Glees, Rounds, etc., with a Course of Elementary Exercises and Solfeggios, designed for Classes, and Schools of Ladies and Gentlemen.* New York: Mark H. Newman & Co., 1845.

Bradbury, William. *The Young Melodist. A New and Rare Collection of Social, Moral, and Patriotic Songs, Designed for Schools and Academies. Composed and Arranged for One, Two and Three Voices.* Mark H. Newman & Co., 1845.

Bradbury, William. *Flora's Festival. A Musical Recreation, for Schools, Juvenile Singing Classes, Etc. Together with Songs, Duets and Trios, Solfeggios, Scales and Plain Tunes for Singing by Note, in Thirteen Keys.* New York: M. H. Newman & Co., 1847.

Bradbury, William. *Musical Gems for School and Home. A Rich and Full Collection of Music for the Young, Original and Arranged; with Choice Selections from the Schools of Germany and Switzerland, Together with a New, Easy, and Progressive Course of Elementary Instructions and Exercises, Constituting a Complete Musical Manual for Teachers and Students.* New York: Mark H. Newman & Co., 1849.

Bradbury, William. *Bradbury's Sabbath School Melodies and Family Choir. Complete Collection of Hymns and Music for all Sabbath School Occasions.* New York: M. H. Newman & Co., 1850.

Bradbury, William. *Music and Musicians of Europe. A Series of Letters Written from Germany and First Published in the "New*

York Evangelist." New York: Mark H. Newman & Co., 1850.

Bradbury, William. *The Alpine Glee Singer. A Full and Complete Collection of Glees and Choruses, for Musical Improvement and Social Enjoyment.* New York: Mark H. Newman & Co., 1852.

Bradbury, William. *The Metropolitan Glee Book. Or, Alpine Glee Singer.* Volume Second. New York: Mark H. Newman, 1852.

Bradbury, William. The Seasons, A Juvenile Cantata in Four Parts. New York: M. H. Newman, 1852.

Bradbury, William. *The Singing Bird. Or, Progressive Music Reader; Designed to Facilitate the Introduction of Vocal Music in Schools and Academies.* New York: Newman & Ivison, 1852.

Cleveland, C.D. comp. *Hymns for Schools With an Appropriate Selection of Tunes.* New York: Mark H. Newman & Co., 1850.

Dana, Mary S.B. *The Southern Harp. Consisting of Original Sacred and Moral Songs, Adapted to the Most Popular Melodies for the Piano Forte and Guitar.* New York: Dayton & Newman, 1841.

Dana, Mary S. B. *The Temperance Lyre. A Collection of Original Songs Arranged and Adapted to the Most Popular Music of the Day, and Designed for Temperance Meetings.* New York: Mark H. Newman, 1842.

Dana, Mary S.B. *The Northern Harp. Consisting of Original Sacred and Moral Songs, Adapted to the Most Popular Melodies for the Piano Forte and Guitar.* New: York: Mark H. Newman, 1843.

Hastings, Thomas and William B. Bradbury. *The Psalmodist. A Choice Collection of Psalms and Hymn Tunes, Chiefly New, for the Use of Choirs, Congregations, Singing Schools and Musical Associations.* New York: Mark H. Newman, 1844.

Hastings, Thomas. *The Crystal Fount. A New Collection of Temperance Songs and Music.* New York: Mark H. Newman & Co., 1847.

Hastings, Thomas and William Bradbury. *The New York Choralist. A New and Copious Collection of Psalm and Hymn Tunes.* New York: Mark H. Newman & Co., 1847.

Hastings, Thomas and William Bradbury. The Mendelssohn Collection. New York: Mark H. Newman & Co., 1849.

Hastings, Thomas and William Bradbury. *Congregational Harmony. Or, Appendix to the Mendelssohn Collection of Church Music.* New York: Mark H. Newman & Co., 1849.

Hastings, Thomas. *Devotional Hymns and Religious Poems.* New York: Mark H. Newman & Co., 1850.

Hastings, Thomas and William Bradbury. *The Psalmista, or Choir Melodies.* New York: Newman & Ivison, 1852.

Leavitt, Joshua. *The Christian Lyre. A Collection of Hymns and Tunes, Adapted for Social Worship, Prayer Meetings, and Revivals of Religion.* New York: Mark H. Newman, 1852.

Presbyterian Publication Committee. *Church Psalmist; Or Psalms and Hymns, Designed for the Public, Social, and Private Use of Evangelical Christians. Containing, also, Directions for Musical Expression.* Philadelphia: Presbyterian Committee, 1847. Copyright by Mark H. Newman & Co., 1847.

Stowe, Baron and S.F. Smith. *The Psalmist. A New Collection of Hymns for the Use of the Baptist Denomination.* New York: Mark H. Newman, 1845.
> Contains about twelve hundred hymns, with words for selected music, and twenty-eight pages of chants at the end.

Reverend Asa Bullard

Asa Bullard (1804-1888) was Emily Dickinson's uncle through his marriage (May 16, 1832) to Lucretia Gunn Dickinson (1806-1885), Emily's father's eldest sister. During his years at Amherst College, from which he graduated in 1828, he conducted a Sabbath School Bible class among African-Americans, in a private dwelling a mile from the college. So much interest was shown in this class that its enrollment soon increased from six persons to thirty. He continued his Sabbath School work during his studies at Andover Theological Seminary (1829-1831). In 1831 he was invited to be general agent for the Maine Sabbath School Union, a position he held for three years. Then in March of 1834, he became the general agent for the Massachusetts Sabbath School Society (MSSS), established on May 30, 1832, known after 1870 as The Congregational Sunday School Publishing Society.

He edited a number of the Society's books and journals and wrote a history of the Society, an autobiography, and three children's books. As general agent he travelled extensively in the United States and Europe to fulfill the Society's objective, "to promote the opening of new Sabbath Schools, and to form depositories for supplying these schools with suitable books." As a successful business, educational, and charitable enterprise, the Society's publications, the music books listed below, were widely distributed.

Albro, John Adams. *The Massachusetts Sabbath School Hymn Book. Compiled for the Massachusetts Sabbath School Society, and Revised by the Committee of Publication.* 2d ed. Boston: MSSS, 1843.

Bullard, Asa, ed. *Isaac Watts, 1674-1748. Questions with Answers. Taken from Dr. Watts's Hymns for Children.* Boston: MSSS, 1842.

Mason, Lowell. *Sabbath School Songs. Or, Hymns and Music Suitable for Sabbath Schools.* Boston: MSSS, 1836.

Mason, Lowell. *Juvenile Music. Originally Published in the Sabbath School Visitor, No. 1.* Boston: MSSS, 1839.

Mason, Lowell. The Sabbath School Harp. Being a Selection of Tunes and Hymns Adapted to the Wants of the Sabbath Schools, Families, and Social Meetings. 3d ed. Boston, MSSS, 1841.

(MSSS.) *Hymns for the Infant School. Selected by a Teacher.* Boston: MSSS, 1858.

(MSSS.) Vestry Songs. *A Collection of Hymns and Tunes for Sabbath Schools, Social Meetings and Private Devotions.* 8th ed, rev. and enl. Boston: MSSS, 1854.

Appendix Four

Mount Holyoke Female Seminary
Music Instruction Manuscript, 1837-1840

Mount Holyoke College Library/Archives.
Music Department Records, Series A, Folder 1:
General Material, 1837-1840.

Ray Palmer and Horatius Bonar had not then struck the lyre, but Rev. Asahel Nettleton, whose name the church will never let die, had collected gems from Isaac Watts, from Mrs. Steele, Montgomery and many others. This Nettleton's Village Hymns (I show one) was the first hymn-book in use here. As I look it over, it seems to me that at one time or another we sung nearly all the hymns it contains. Miss Lyon loved the hymns composed by her personal friends—one by Mrs. Brown of Monson, 'I love to steal awhile away' and 'Say, sinner hath a voice within' by Mrs. Lavius Hyde. When wearied, sick, & overborne with the heavy load she was carrying, she would give out the hymn, 'As when the weary traveller gains.' She greatly regretted that she had not her-self been taught to sing but she was indefatigable in her efforts that all her pupils should learn. The whole school was divided into three classes for the study of vocal music—the poor singers, the better and the best. For secular music we used the Odeon. Every scholar was put into one class or another in vocal music. ('They are gone, all gone, from the mountain home,' 'The last rose of summer' and 'Oft in the stilly night' were some of the new pieces upon which we practiced.) For sacred music, Lowell Mason's Boston Academy was the book. Hebron, Boylston and Ortonville were already beginning to displace Manuscript Windham, Wells and St. Martins. We are sure we voice the feeling of a majority here when we say, that the sacred songs at Holyoke were the sweetest ever remembered on earth. As Christ was made known in breaking of the bread, so has He been made known in holy 'hymn and psalm' at the morning hour and as the glow of sunset streamed through the green lattice after evening meal.

Names and Addresses of
Composers

Adams, John. c/o Associated Music Publishers, Inc., 24 East 22nd St., New York, NY 10010 USA.

Adams, Robert Train. 150 John Rezza Dr., Attleboro Falls, MA 02763 USA.

Adler, Samuel H. Professor of Composition, Eastman School of Music, University of Rochester, 26 Gibbs St., Rochester, NY 14604 USA.

Annicchiarico, Michael. 514 North State St., Concord, NH 03301 USA.

Appleton, Jon. RR# 2, Box 377A, White River Junction, VT 05001 USA.

Bacon, Ernst (deceased). For information: Ellen Bacon, 8 Drovers Lane, De Witt, NY 13214 USA; or, Madi Bacon, 1120 Keith Ave., Berkeley, CA 94708 USA

Baksa, Robert. 625 West End Ave., No. 4B, New York, NY 10024 USA.

Barber, Samuel (deceased).

Barkin, Elaine R. Music/2539, Schoenberg Annex, University of California, Los Angeles, CA 90024 USA.

Bartlett, Floyd Little.

Bartow, Jim. Harlem School of the Arts, 645 St. Nicholas Ave., New York, NY 10030 USA.

Beale, James. The School of Music, DN-10, University of Washington, Seattle, WA 98195 USA.

Beaty, Dan. Department of Music, Stephen F. Austin State University, Nacogdoches, TX 75962 USA.

Beckler, Stanworth. Conservatory of Music, University of The Pacific, Stockton, CA 95211 USA.

Belet, Brian. 73 Winifred Ave., Worcester, MA 01602-2027 USA.

Belkin, Alan. 469 Grosvenor Ave., Westmount, P.Q. H3Y 2S5, Canada.

Benjamin, Thomas E. 6305 Blackburn Ct., Baltimore, MD 21212 USA.

Benoliel, Bernard. 13 Nevern Square, Flat 2, London SW5 9NW, England.

Berger, Jean. 2 Adams St., No. 1606, Denver, CO 80206 USA.

Bergh, Arthur (deceased).

Berkowitz, Leonard.

Bialosky, Marshall. Sanjo Music Co., Box 7000-104, Palos Verdes Peninsula, CA 90274 USA.

Bielawa, Herbert. 81 Denslowe Dr., San Francisco, CA 94132 USA.

Binkerd, Gordon W. R.R. 2, Box 1705, Urbana, IL 61801 USA.

Bird, Hubert C. P.O. Box 393, Keene, NH 03431 USA.

Blank, Allan. 2920 Archdale Rd., Richmond, VA 23235 USA.

Bliss, Milton.

Boatwright, Howard. 7153 W Genesee St., Fayetteville. NY 13066 USA.

Bottenberg, Dr. Wolfgang, Department of Music, Faculty of Fine Arts, Concordia University, Loyola Campus, 7141 Sherbrooke St. West, Montréal, Québec H4B 1R6, Canada.

Bottje, Will Gay. 12871 Lake Shore Dr., Grand Haven, MI 49417 USA.

Bourland, Roger. 1312 North Harper Ave., No. 5, West Hollywood, CA 90046 USA.

Boyle, George F. (deceased).

Brown, Allyson (Applebaum). Western Australian Academy of Performing Arts, Edith Cowan University, 2 Bradford St., Mount Lawley, Western Australia 6050.

Brown, Francis James. 28 Agior Petros, Gavrion, Andros, Cyclades 84501, Greece.

Bruce, Neely. Department of Music, Wesleyan College, Middletown, CT 06457 USA.

Burgon, Geoffrey. c/o J.C.W. Chester, Ltd., Eagle Court, London, EC1M 5QD, England.

Butler, Martin. c/o Oxford University Press, 200 Madison Ave., New York, NY 10016 USA.

Butterworth, David Neil. The White House, Inveresk, Musselburgh, Midlothian, EH21 7TG, Scotland.

Callaway, Ann. 540 West 112th St., New York, NY 10025 USA.

Carlsen, Philip. 23 Middle St., Farmington, ME 04938 USA.

Carter, Elliott. 31 West 12th St., New York, NY 10011 USA.

Castiglioni, Niccolò. Kleine Lauben 8, Brixen (Bozen) Italy.

Chalayev, Shirvani. April-September: c/o Ulitsa Bujnakskogo, D.4m 367025 Makhachkala, Russia. October-March: Moskva, Prospect Mira DM. 116 KV. 30, Russia.

Chauls, Robert. Valley Opera, Inc., P.O. Box 3292, Van Nuys, CA 91407 USA.

Ciarlantini, Paola.

Clarke, Henry Leland. One Wapping Rd., Old Deerfield, MA 01342 USA.

Coates, Gloria. Postfach 0661, 8 Munich 43, Germany; (or) 484 West 43rd St., Apt 17-J, New York, NY 10036 USA.

Convery, Robert. 37-27 Crescent St., Apt. 33, Long Island City, NY 11101 USA.

Copland, Aaron (deceased). For estate information: Whitman & Ransom, 200 Park Ave. New York, NY 10166 USA. For manuscript information: James W. Pruett, Librarian, The Music Division, The Library of Congress, 10 First St. SE, Washington, D.C. 20540 USA.

Coulthard, Dr. Jean. No. 407, 2222 Bellevue Ave., West Vancouver, B.C. V7V 1C7, Canada.

Dal Porto, Mark. 1108 South Jay St. Aberdeen, SD 57401-7132 USA.

Davis, Sharon. 3707 65th Ave., Greeley, CO 80634-9626 USA.

Dawson, Sarah. 757 20th St., No. 5, Boulder, CO 80302, USA.

DeFilippi, Amadeo (deceased).

Diaconoff, Ted. 1324 California Ave., Chickasha, OK 73018 USA.

Dickinson, Clarence (deceased).

Dickinson, Peter. c/o Novello and Co., 8 Lower James St., London W1R 4DN, England.

Diemer, Emma Lou. 2249 Vista del Campo, Santa Barbara, CA 93101-4657 USA.

Dinerstein, Norman (deceased).

Dougherty, Celius (deceased).

Dowd, John Andrew. 17 Ebbett Ave., Quincy, MA 02170 USA.

Duke, John Woods (deceased).

Eckert, Professor Michael. School of Music, The University of Iowa, Iowa City, IA 52242 USA.

Escher, Rudolf. c/o Donemus Publishing, Paulus Potterstr. 14, 1071 CZ, Amsterdam, Netherlands.

Farwell, Arthur (deceased). For information: Brice Farwell, 290 West Nevada, Ashland, OR 97520 USA. (Or) Evelyn Davis Culbertson, 7106 E. 53rd Place, Tulsa, OK 74145 USA.

Names and Addresses of Composers

Faulconer, Bruce L. 4128 Shadow Gables, Dallas, TX 75287 USA.

Ferris, William. 750 North Rush St., Chicago, IL 60611 USA.

Fine, Vivian. R.D. 2, P.O. Box 630, Hoosick Falls, NY 12090 USA.

Foreman, Burton V. 2-31-18 Wakabayashi, Setagaya-ku, Tokyo, Japan 154.

Fornuto, Donato. 26 Duncan St., Waldwick, NJ 07463 USA.

Fortner, Jack. Department of Music, California State University-Fresno, Fresno, CA 93740-0077 USA.

Franchetti, Arnold. 20 Eastlake Place, Middletown, CT 06457 USA.

Freed, Isadore (deceased).

Fuchs, Kenneth. 17 Seaman Ave.-IJ, New York, NY 10034 USA.

Galante, Carlo. Via Falzolgher, Trento, Italy.

Gettel, William.

Getty, Gordon P. 2880 Broadway, San Francisco, CA 94115 USA.

Gibas, Barbara. 2616 Harriet Ave. S., No. 312, Minneapolis, MN 55408 USA.

Gibson, Paul F. 20914 Annrita Ave., Torrance, CA 90503 USA.

Ginsburg, Gerald. One Sheridan Square, Apt. 7C, New York, NY 10014 USA.

Glickman, Sylvia. 1210 West Wynnewood Rd., Wynnewood, PA 19096 USA.

Gokita, Taoehiko. Dept. of Music, Harvard University, Cambridge, MA 02138 USA.

Gold, Ernest. 269 North Bellino Dr., Pacific Palisades, CA 90272 USA.

Golub, Peter. 71 Barrow St., New York, NY 10014 USA.

Gould, John A. Andover/Phillips Academy, Andover, MA 01810 USA.

Grantham, Donald. Department of Music, The University of Texas at Austin, Austin, TX 78712 USA.

Green, Ray.

Grier, Lita. 1550 North Lake Shore Dr., Apt. 23A, Chicago, IL 60610 USA.

Guzman i Antich, José Luis.

Hageman, Richard (deceased).

Hall, Juliana. 71 William St., Apt., 3, New Haven, CT 06511 USA.

Hammond, Harold E.

Harbison, John. 449 Franklin St., Cambridge, MA 02139 USA.

Harman, David A. 2-91 Hallam St., Toronto, Ontario M6H 1W7, Canada.

Harris, Roy (deceased). For information: Dan Stehman, 2915 Tennyson Place, Hermosa Beach, CA 90254 USA.

Haxton, Kenneth. 410 Wetherbee St., Greenville, MS 38701 USA.

Heilner, Irwin (deceased).

Heiss, John. Department of Chamber Music, New England Conservatory of Music, 290 Huntington Ave., Boston, MA 02115 USA.

Hemberg, Eskil. Floravagen 3, S-131 41 Nacka, Sweden. (or) Kungl. Teatern AB, Box 16094, 103 22 Stockholm, Sweden.

Hennagin, Michael. School of Music, The University of Oklahoma, Norman, OK 73019-0301 USA.

Herberich, Elizabeth. 17 Sheffield West, Winchester, MA 01890 USA.

Herman, Carol. 357 W. 10th St., Claremont, CA 91711. Or c/o PRB Productions, 963 Peralta Av., Albany, CA 94706-2144 USA.

Hess, Robert E. 115 West 73rd St., New York, NY 10023 USA.

Hewitt, Harry. 345 South 19th St., Philadelphia, PA 19103 USA.

Hilse, Walter. 328 West 43rd St., New York, NY 10036 USA.

Hinkle, Roy B. 5004 Farming Ridge Blvd., Reading, PA 19606 USA.

Hodges, Samuel. 320 So. Bayly Ave. Lexington, KY 40206 USA.

Hoiby, Lee. 71 Rock Valley, Long Eddy, NY 12760 USA.

Højsgaard, Erik. Tordenskjoldsgade 29, 4. 1055 Copenhagen K, Denmark. (or) c/o Dansk Komponist-Forening, Valkendorfsgade 3, DK-1151, Copenhagen K, Denmark.

Holab, William J. 804 West 180th St., No. 43, New York, NY 10033 USA.

Holman, Dr. Derek. 75 George Henry Blvd., Willowdale, Ontario M2J 1E8, Canada.

Holmes, Markwood.

Horvit, Michael. School of Music, University of Houston, Houston, TX 77204-4893 USA.

Howe, Mary (deceased). For information: Dorothy Indenbaum, 315 East 65th St., New York, NY 10021 USA.

Hoyt, Richard. 160 West 73rd St. Apt. 9-F, New York, NY 10023 USA.

Hundley, Richard. 463 West St. D208. New York, NY 10014 USA.

Hunkins, Arthur B.

Iannaccone, Anthony. 521 Kewanee, Ypsilanti, MI 48197 USA.

Irving, David. 100 W. 67th St. Apt 5NW, New York, NY 10023 USA.

Johns, Clayton.

Johnson, Hunter. Rt. 3, Box 439, Benson, NC 27504 USA.

Johnson, Lochrem (deceased).

Johnston, David A.

Jones, Joseph. Department of English, University of Texas at Austin, Austin, TX 78712 USA.

Jordahl, Robert. Department of Music, McNeese State University, Lake Charles, LA 70609 USA.

Jordan, William. 5427 Amherst No. 122, Dallas, TX 75209 USA.

Kaderavek, Milan. Department of Music, 260 Fine Arts Center, Drake University, Des Moines, IA 50311 USA.

Kagen, Sergius.

Kalmonoff, Martin. 392 Central Park West 14P, New York, NY 10025 USA.

Kavasch, Deborah. Department of Music, California State University-Stanislaus, 801 West Monte Vista Ave., Turlock, CA 95380 USA.

Kay, Ulysses. 1271 Alicia Ave., Teaneck, NJ 07666 USA.

Kelly, Kevin. 432 University Drive, Athens, GA 30605 USA.

Kennedy, John B.

Kent, Frederick James. Fleisher Collection, Free Library of Philadelphia, Philadelphia, PA 19103 USA.

Kent, Richard.

Kesselman, Lee R. 44 Travers Ave., Wheaton, IL 60187 USA.

Kettering, Eunice L.

Kirchner, Leon. Department of Music, Harvard University, Cambridge, MA 02138 USA.

Kitzke, Jerome P. 33 Riverside Dr. 7FA, New York, NY 10023 USA.

Klein, Lothar. 44 Wallingford Rd., Don Mills, Ontario M3A 2T9, Canada.

Knowlton, F. S. (deceased).

Kunz, Alfred. P.O. Box 2412, Station B, Duke St., Kitchener, Ontario N2H 6M3, Canada.

Laderman, Ezra. c/o Oxford University Press, 200 Madison Avenue, New York, NY 10016 USA.

Langer, Ken. Department of Music, Waycross College, Waycross, GA 31501 USA.

Langert, Jules. 6504 Raymond, Oakland, CA 94609 USA.

Lardner, Borje. Lovhegevagen 18, 175 38 Jarfalla, Sweden.

Leavitt, Helen S. (deceased).

Leich, Roland. 208 Le Moyne Ave., Pittsburgh, PA 15228 USA.

Leichtling, Alan R. 58 Itendale St. Springfield, MA 01108 USA.

Leisner, David. 900 West End Ave., Apt. 12A, New York, NY 10025 USA.

Lenel, Ludwig. 5176 Huckleberry Rd., Orefield, PA 18069 USA.

Lenk, Thomas T. 1074 Sunshine Canyon, Boulder, CO 80302 USA.

Lerdahl, Fred. Department of Music, 703 Dodge Hall, Columbia University, new York, NY 10027 USA.

Levy, Frank. 19 Virginia St., Tenafly, NJ 07670 USA.

Lidov, David. Music Department, Room 238 BSD, Faculty of Fine Arts, York University, 4700 Keele St., Downsview, Ontario M3J 1P3, Canada.

Lighty, Alan K. 340 Haven Ave., No. 6M, New York, NY 10033 USA.

Lindenfeld, Harris. 30 Albany St., Cazenovia, NY 13035 USA.

Locklair, Dan. 827 Roslyn Rd., Winston-Salem, NC 27101 USA.

Lockwood, Normand. c/o Normand Lockwood Archive, Music Library, University of Colorado, Boulder, CO 80302 USA.

Lorenz, Ellen Jane (Porter). 6369 Pebble Court, Dayton, OH 45459 USA.

Luening, Otto. 460 Riverside Drive, New York, NY 10027 USA.

Lutkin, Peter C.

Macaulay, Janice. 470 Laurel Valley Court, Arnold, MD 21012 USA.

MacDermid, James G. (deceased).

Manzoni, Giacomo. c/o G. Ricordi, 2 via Berchet, 20121 Milan, Italy.

Marcello, Joseph. 85 Columbus Ave., Greenfield, MA 01301.

Marzo, Eduardo.

Matsunaga, Michiharu. Japanese Federation of Composers, Tokyo, Japan.

Mayer, Stephen. 126 E. 57th St. New York, NY 10022 USA.

McAfee, Don.

McKay, George F. (deceased).

McNeil, Jan Pfischner.

Meachem, Margaret R. Swampacres Wildlife Sanctuary, West Rd., P.O. Box 491, Dorset, VT 05251 USA.

Medley, Marsha Marie. 8300 Wooster Pike, No. 4, Cincinnati, OH 45227 USA.

Mennin, Peter (deceased).

Meyerowitz, Jan. 666 Les Evaux, F 68910 Labaroche, France.

Mollicone, Henry. 18709 McFarland Ave., Saratoga, CA 95070 USA.

Moore, Dorothy Rudd. 33 Riverside Dr. 16A, New York, NY 10023 USA.

Morath, Max. 100 Glen Rd., Woodcliff Lake, NJ 06765 USA.

Muczynski, Robert. 2760 N. Wentworth, Tucson, AZ 85749 USA.

Mueter, John. 5000 Oak St., 1020 N, Kansas City, MO 64112 USA.

Murray, Bain. Music Department, Cleveland State University, Euclid Ave. at East 24th St., Cleveland, OH 44115 USA.

Niles, John D. Department of English, University of California, Los Angeles, 405 Hilgard Ave., Los Angeles, CA 90024-1530 USA.

Nixon, Roger. 2090 New Brunswick Dr., San Mateo, CA 94402 USA.

Nowak, Lionel. North Bennington, VT 05257 USA.

Obrecht, Eldon. School of Music, The University of Iowa, Iowa City, IA 52242 USA.

Olan, David. Department of Music, Baruch College, 17 Lexington Ave., New York, NY 10010 USA.

Olin, Esther M. 108 Trading Block Lane, Forest, VA 24551 USA.

O'Meara, Mollie. 242 E. Beaumont, Columbus, OH 43214 USA.

Parker, Alice. 801 West End Ave. 9-D, New York, NY 10025 USA.

Parker, Etta (deceased).

Pasatieri, Thomas.

Patterson, Jamie Alexander.

Pender, Scott. 2441 40th St. Apt. 2, Washington, D.C. 20007 USA.

Pengilly, Sylvia. 254 Orchard Rd., River Ridge, LA 70123 USA.

Perera, Ronald. Dept. of Music, Smith College, Northampton, MA 01063 USA.

Perle, George. c/o American Music Center, 250 West 54th St. Suite 300, New York, NY 10019 USA.

Perry, Julia.

Persichetti, Vincent (deceased).

Pierce, Brent. c/o Walton Music Corporation, Hinshaw Music, Inc., P.O. Box 470, Chapel Hill, NC 27514.

Pilz, Gerhard. Gmundmühle Nr. 1, A-6914, Howenweiler, Austria.

Pinkham, Daniel. 150 Chilton St., Cambridge, MA 02138-1227 USA.

Pisk, Paul A. 2724 Westshire Dr., Los Angeles, CA 90068 USA.

Potter, Virginia.

Rasely, Charles W. Music Program, Saint Bonaventure University, Saint Bonaventure, NY 14778 USA.

Raum, Elizabth. 88 Angus Crescent, Regina, Saskatchewan S4T 6N2, Canada.

Raymond-Ward, Adeline.

Rericha, Robert J. 210 Greencroft, Bedford, OH 44146 USA.

Richter, Marga. 3 Bayview Lane, Huntington, NY 11743 USA.

Riegger, Wallingford (deceased).

Riley, Dennis. 615 W. 164th St., New York, NY 10032 USA.

Rizzetto, Jay. 5600 Snake Rd., Oakland, CA 94611 USA.

Rogers, William K.

Rorem, Ned.

Roy, William.

Ruggiero, Charles H. School of Music, Michigan State University, East Lansing, MI 48824-1043 USA.

Ruiter, Wim de. Donemus Publishing, Paulus Potterstr. 14, 1071 CZ, Amsterdam, Netherlands.

Sacco, John (deceased).

Samuel, Gerhard. 412 Libery Hill, No. 2-C, Cincinnati, OH 45210 USA.

Saya, Mark. 7547 W. Manchester Ave., No. 307, Los Angeles, CA 90045 USA.

Schevill, James E.

Schudel, Dr. Thomas. Department of Music, University of Regina, Regina, Saskatchewan, S4S OA2 Canada. Home address: 149 Shannon Rd., Regina, Saskatchewan, S4S 6H6, Canada.

Schwartz, Paul. Box 115, Brockport, NY 14420 USA.

Sclater, James S. 709 East Leake St., Clinton, MS 39056 USA.

Seeboth, Max.

Shearer, C. M. School of Music, Kent State University, Kent, OH 44242 USA.

Shore, Clare. 12329 Cliveden St., Herndon, VA 22070 USA.

Silsbee, Ann. 915 Coddington Rd., Ithaca, NY 14850 USA.

Silverman, Faye-Ellen. 330 W. 28th St., No. 7G, New York, NY 10001 USA.

Sims, Jo Ann. Department of Music, The University of Mississippi, University, MS 38677 USA.

Siskind, Paul A. Sweet Child Music, 2550 S. Bryant Ave., No. 205, Minneapolis, MN 55405 USA.

Smit, Leo. 39 Dorchester Rd., Buffalo, NY 14222 USA.

Smith, Russell. Unertlstrasse 2, D-8000, Munich 40, Germany.

Snyder, Randall. School of Music, University of Nebraska, Lincoln, NE 68588-0100 USA.

Sørensen, Bent. c/o Dansk Musik Informations Center, Vimmelskaftet 48, DK 1161 Copenhagen K, Denmark.

Soule, Edmund F. 85897 Bailey Hill Rd., Eugene, OR 97405 USA.

Speaks, Oley (deceased).

Sprenkle, Elam Ray. c/o Peabody Conservatory of Music, 1 E. Mt. Vernon Place, Baltimore, MD 21212 USA.

Springer, Philip. Box 1174, Pacific Palisades, CA 90272 USA.

Starer, Robert. P.O. Box, 946, Woodstock, NY 12498 USA.

Steiner, Gitta (deceased).

Stolba, K Marie. 5621 Joyce Ave. (RR 12), Fort Wayne, IN 46818 USA.

Strongin, Theodore.

Stucky, Steven. 303 Estwood Ave., Ithaca, NY 14850 USA.

Surette, Thomas W.

Sydeman, William.

Taggard, Genevieve (deceased).

Talma, Louise. 410 Central Park West, No. 3B, New York, NY 10025 USA.

Taxman, Barry. 2334 Cedar St., Berkeley, CA 94708 USA.

Thygerson, Robert.

Tipton, Noel. P.O. Box 1266, Eastham, MA 02642 USA.

Towner, Earl.

Vehar, Persis (Ms). 65 Hyledge Dr., Buffalo, NY 14226 USA.

Vernon, Sean. P.O. Box 207, Williamsburg, MA 01096 USA.

Vries Robbe, Willem de.

Walker, George. 323 Grove St., Montclair, NJ 07042 USA.

Wallach, Joelle. 866 West End Ave. 2B, New York, NY 10025 USA.

Ward, Robert. 308 Monticello Ave., Durham, NC 27707 USA.

Warren-Davis, Betsy Frost. c/o Wiscasset Music Publishing Company, Box 810, Cambridge, MA 02138 USA.

Waters, James L. School of Music, Kent State University, Kent, OH 44242 USA.

Weber, Ben (deceased).

Weber, Marc. 20068 Avenue of the Oaks, Newhall, CA 91321 USA.

Weigl, Vally (deceased). For information: The Vally Weigl Fund, c/o Dr. David Manes, The College of Charleston, Charleston, SC 29401 USA.

Weiss, Adolf (deceased).

Weld, Arthur.

Wertsch, Nancy. c/o Gene Gabriel Publications, Ltd., P.O. Box 1959, Cathedral Station, New York, NY 10025 USA.

Wiemann, Beth. 2 Shore Drive, Spencer, MA 01562 USA.

Wilder, Alec (deceased). For information: Tro-Ludlow Music Inc., 11 W. 19th St., New York, NY 10011 USA.

Willeby, Charles.

Williams, Francis.

Wood, Margaret. 76 Clark Rd., Ipswich, MA 01938 USA.

Woollen, Russell.

Ziffrin, Marilyn J. P.O. Box 179, Bradford, NH 03221 USA.

Bibliography

For bibliographical information on specific composers, see under the composer's name in the "Musical Settings" section.

EDITIONS OF EMILY DICKINSON'S POEMS AND LETTERS

Dickinson, Emily. *The Poems of Emily Dickinson*. Edited by Thomas H. Johnson. Cambridge, MA: Harvard University Press, 1955. 3 vols.
  The definitve edition. Contains an "Index of First Lines" with Johnson numbers, pp. 1229-1266.

Dickinson, Emily. *The Letters of Emily Dickinson*. Edited by Thomas H. Johnson. Associate Editor, Theodora Ward. Cambridge, MA: Harvard University Press, 1958. 3 vols.
  The definitive edition. Contains an index of Poems that appear in the Letters.

Dickinson, Emily. *The Complete Poems of Emily Dickinson*. Edited by Thomas H. Johnson. Boston: Little, Brown and Company, 1960.
  Single-volume edition of the 3-vol. ed., with the same numbering for the poems but different pagination. Also contains a Subject Index, pp. 723-735, and Index of First Lines, pp. 737-770.

PERIODICALS

Dickinson Studies. See *Emily Dickinson Bulletin*.

Emily Dickinson Bulletin, January 1968-1978. Continued by *Dickinson Studies*, 1978-1990.
  Periodical devoted to Emily Dickinson. Detailed music entries passim throughout. Special essays on music: Nancy Cluck, "Aaron Copland/Emily Dickinson," Second Half, 1977, pp. 141-153; Inez Wager, "Emily Dickinson's Poems in Musical Settings," June, 1984, pp. 32-37.

EXPLICATIONS OF THE POEMS

Buckingham, Willis J. *Emily Dickinson: An Annotated Bibliography*. Bloomington: Indiana University Press, 1970.
  Explication Index, pp. 255-283.

Duchac, Joseph. *The Poems of Emily Dickinson: An Annotated Guide to Commentary Published in English, 1890-1977*. Boston: G. K. Hall & Co., 1979.
  Guide to Commentary, pp. 1-621. Indexed alphabetically by first lines of poems.

The Explicator. 1942-, University of South Carolina; 1975-, Virginia Commonwealth University. Indexes: 1942-1962, vols. 1-20; 1962-1972, vols. 21-30; 1972-1984, vols. 31-42.

Contains some illuminating explanations, especially of the more difficult of Emily Dickinson's images and ideas.

Johnson, Thomas H. *Emily Dickinson: An Interpretive Biography.* Cambridge: Harvard University Press, 1955.

Emily Dickinson's use of hymn meters in her poetry, pp. 84-95. "Poems Analyzed," pp. 270-271, is an index to an explication of many of the poems.

Rosenbaum, Stanford Patrick, ed. *A Concordance to the Poems of Emily Dickinson.* Ithaca, N.Y.: Cornell University Press, 1964.

Unique and essential reference for close study of the poems. Particularly useful in tracking down Johnson numbers wherever titles do not match first lines. Gives direct access to frequency of words used, and ideas and images suggested by words such as musical terms.

Ruppert, James. *Guide to American Explication.* Boston: G. K. Hall, 1989. "Emily Dickinson," I:16-108.

EMILY DICKINSON'S LIFE; THE DICKINSON FAMILY

Bingham, Millicent Todd. *Emily Dickinson's Home: Letters of Edward Dickinson and His Family with Documentation and Comment.* New York: Harper & Brothers, 1955.

Austin's impression of the singing of Watts's hymns, Chapter 4, pp. 35-36.

"Jenny Lind and the Summer of 1851," Chapter 13, pp. 143-159.

Johnson, Thomas H. *Emily Dickinson: An Interpretive Biography.* Cambridge, MA: The Belknap Press of Harvard University Press, 1955.

Sewall, Richard B. *The Life of Emily Dickinson.* New York: Farrar, Straus and Giroux, 1974. 2 vols. Reprinted 1980.

Whicher, George Frisbie. *This Was a Poet: A Critical Bio-Bibliography of Emily Dickinson.* New York: Charles Scribner's Sons, 1939.

EMILY DICKINSON'S READING

American Journal of Education (Russell's). *American Annals of Education.* January, 1826-December 1839.

See Frank Luther Mott: *A History of American Magazines*, I: 1741-1850, pp. 541-543. These journals were sold in the Amherst bookstores of Mark Haskell Newman and J.S. and C. Adams. The journal had, during its thirteen-year run, many articles about music education, reviews of music books, and in later issues, songs with music furnished mainly by Lowell Mason.

Capps, Jack L. *Emily Dickinson's Reading, 1836-1886.* Cambridge, MA: Harvard University Press, 1966.

Carefully prepared survey and annotated bibliography. Appendix A, pp. 151-152, contains Dickinson's quotes from the Psalms in her letters and poems.

Gilmore, Barbara. *A Puritan Town and Its Imprints: Northampton 1786-1845.* Northampton, MA: The Hampshire Bookshop, 1942.

Early Northampton music imprints. Pages and item numbers: 11-55; 29-162; 31-172; 33-190; 41-235.

The Holy Bible, Containing the Old and New Testaments. Philadelphia: J. B. Lippincott & Co., 1843.

> Emily Dickinson's personal Bible. Lowenberg, *Emily Dickinson's Textbooks*, pp. 60-61.

Houghton Library. *Handlist of Books Found in the Home of Emily Dickinson at Amherst, MA. Spring, 1950*. Cambridge, MA: Houghton Library, 1951.

> Lists titles kept by Harvard's Houghton Library, as well as those returned to Amherst as not suitable. Includes music books in the Dickinsons' library.

Lombardo, Daniel. *Tales of Amherst: A Look Back*. Amherst, MA: The Jones Library, Inc., 1986.

> "What the Dickinsons Read," pp. 100-102. Lists newspapers and magazines, many of which contained articles about music.

Lowenberg, Carlton. *Emily Dickinson's Textbooks*. Lafayette, California: Carlton Lowenberg, 1986.

> Cites: H. J. Bertini, Method of Pianoforte; L. Mason, Carmina Sacra, The Vocalist, Church Psalmody; A. Nettleton, Village Hymns; E. A. Park, Sabbath Hymn Book; Isaac Watts, Psalms, Hymns and Spiritual Songs; G. J. Webb, Odeon.

Lowenberg, Carlton. "Hampshire County Textbooks 1812-1850." Unpublished manuscript, 1988.

> Cites music textbooks used in Hampshire County schools, 1812-1850: pp. 23, 51 (*Parley's Magazine*), 63, 69, 70, 74, 99, 100.

EMILY DICKINSON'S EXPERIENCES WITH MUSIC

Bingham, Millicent Todd. *Ancestors' Brocades*. New York: Harper & Bros., 1945. p. 12.

Crowell, Edward Payson. ALS. Amherst, July 4, 1851. To "My dear cousin David." "Jenny Lind and Conic Sections in 1851." *Amherst Graduates' Quarterly* (1851).

Dickinson, William Austin. "Representative Men of the Parish, Church Buildings and Finances." In *An Historical Review. One Hundred and Fiftieth Anniversary of the First Church in Amherst, Massachusetts. November 7, 1889*. Amherst, MA: Press of the Amherst Record, 1890.

> Mentions musical instruments, the singing of Watts's hymns, and a second-hand organ, pp. 56-57.

Goodrich, Samuel Griswold, ed. *Parley's Magazine*, [January-December] 1838. New York: Charles S. Francis, 1838.

> Edward Dickinson gave Emily and Lavinia a copy of this children's magazine. The songs by Lowell Mason may have been their first introduction to song writing.

Hughes, Ted, ed. *A Choice of Emily Dickinson's Verse*. London: Faber & Faber, 1968. Introduction, p. 14.

Jordon, Philip D. *Singin' Yankees*. Minneapolis: The University of Minnesota Press, 1946.

> The Hutchinson Family Singers, passim.

Leyda, Jay. *The Years and Hours of Emily Dickinson*. New Haven: Yale University Press, 1960. 2 vols. Reprinted Hamden, CT: Archon Books, 1970.

> Emily Dickinson's childhood music, I:21, May 9, 1833. Aunt Selby teaches piano, I:94, August 3, 1845. Boston

concerts, I:112, August 27 and September 3, 1846. Jenny Lind, I:203-206, July 3 and 6, 1851.

Massachusetts Sabbath-School Society [MSSS]. *Descriptive Catalogue of the Publications of the ... Society.* Depository No. 10, Cornhill. Boston: C. C. Dean, 1850.
Lists music books published under the direction of Rev. Asa Bullard, Emily Dickinson's uncle.

Mellers, Wilfred. *Music in a New Found Land.* New York: Oxford University Press, 1987.
Emily Dickinson: pp. 22, 24, 37, 94, 221.

Miller, Ruth. *The Poetry of Emily Dickinson.* Middletown, CT: Wesleyan University Press, 1968.
Chapter 10, pp. 270-271; Appendix 3, pp. 406-410.

Sewall, Richard B. *The Life of Emily Dickinson.* New York: Farrar, Straus and Giroux, 1974. 2 vols. Reprinted 1980.
Jenny Lind: pp. 64, 407, 430, 436, 439. Music: pp. 154, 172, 217-218, 272-273, 324, 326, 406-409, 596.

Taggard, Genevieve. *The Life and Mind of Emily Dickinson.* New York: Alfred A. Knopf, 1930. Pages 5, 47-48, and passim.

Ware, W. Porter and Thaddeus C. Lockard, Jr. *P.T. Barnum Presents Jenny Lind: The American Tour of the Swedish Nightingale.* Baton Rouge, Lousiana: Louisiana State University Press 1980.
Jenny Lind in Northampton: pp. 104, 106, 120-121, 126, 129.

Whicher, George Frisbie. *This Was a Poet.* New York: Charles Scribner's Sons, 1939. Pages 56, 167, and passim.

FORMAL EDUCATION:
MT. HOLYOKE, AMHERST

Brown, Bartholomew. *Templi Carmina. Songs of the Temple, or Bridgewater Collection of Sacred Music.* 9th ed., improved and enl. Boston: Richardson & Lord, 1821.
Early textbook at Mount Holyoke Female Seminary.

Cole, Arthur C. *A Hundred Years of Mount Holyoke College: The Evolution of an Educational Ideal.* New Haven: Yale University Press, 1940.
Music at Mount Holyoke Female Seminary: pp. 57, 143-144.

Colombo, Stacie A. "Music Education for Women in Female Seminaries of the Nineteenth Century." Paper presented to fulfill the requirements of the History and Philosophy of Music Education course, Washington, D.C.: Catholic University of America, August, 1988.

Green, Elizabeth Alden. *Mary Lyon and Mount Holyoke: Opening the Gates.* Hanover, N.H.: University Press of New England, 1979.
Music at Mount Holyoke Female Seminary, pp. 65-66, 220, 286, 296.

Hammond, William Gardiner. *Remembrance of Amherst: An Undergraduate's Diary, 1846-1848.* Ed. by George F. Whicher. New York: Columbia University Press, 1946.
Music at Mount Holyoke Seminary, p. 162. Music at Amherst Academy, p. 168.

Hitchcock, Edward (compiler). *The Power of Christian Benevolence, Illustrated in the Life and Labors of Mary Lyon.* 12th ed. Northampton: Bridgman and Childs, 1851.
Mary Lyon and music, pp. 81-82.

[Ipswich Female Seminary.] *Catalogue of the Officers and Members of the Ipswich Female Seminary, for the Year Ending April, 1835.* Salem: Palfray and Chapman, 1835.

Cites vocal and instrumental music along with Mary Lyon's and Z. P. Grant's list of "Text Books" that Mary Lyon used at Mount Holyoke Female Seminary.

James, Elias Olan. *The Story of Cyrus and Susan Mills.* Stanford, CA.: Stanford University Press, 1953.

Susan Tolman (Mills) was in charge of the Mount Holyoke Seminary choir class of 1847-1848; see p.52.

Lyon, Mary. Letter, September 19, 1848, to Miss Susannah Fitch, Hamilton, Ohio. In Mary Lyon. *Letters and Documents.* II: 305-308. Mount Holyoke College Library/Archives.

Discusses the teaching of music.

Lyon, Mary. *Mary Lyon Through Her Letters, as Edited by Marion Lansing.* Boston: Books, Inc., 1937.

Letter to Zilpah Grant, Ipswich, January 29, 1832, p. 83. Discusses the importance of vocal music in education.

Lyon, Mary. "Mount Holyoke Female Seminary." In *Old South Leaflets. Volume VI (Leaflets 126-150).* Boston: Directors of the Old South Work, Old South Meeting House [n.d.], pp. 425-435.

Originally written in South Hadley, September, 1835. Cites vocal music.

Mason, Lowell. *Carmina Sacra: or Boston Collection of Church Music, Comprising the Most Popular Psalm and Hymn Tunes in General Use.* Boston: Wilkins, Carter, & Co., 1841.

Mount Holyoke Female Seminary textbook, 1847-1848. See Lowenberg: *Emily Dickinson's Textbooks,* pp. 71-72. One of the most widely used music textbooks of the time, compiled by Mary Lyon's friend and colleague. This edition contains a thirty-page guide, "Elements of Vocal Music," a one-page guide to "Chanting," and a two-page "Explanation of Musical Terms."

Mount Holyoke Female Seminary. *Eleventh Annual Catalogue of The Mount Holyoke Female Seminary.* South Hadley, MA, 1847-1848. Mount Holyoke College Library/Archives.

Emily Dickinson's class of 1847-1848. Listed under "Books and Stationery": Watts's *Psalms and Hymns,* Nettleton's *Village Hymns,* Lowell Mason's *Carmina Sacra,* Lowell Mason's and George J. Webb's *The Vocalist and The Odeon,* "together with any other musical works they may possess."

Mount Holyoke Female Seminary. *First Annual Catalogue of the Officers and Members of the Mount Holyoke Female Seminary.* South Hadley, MA: 1837-38. Mount Holyoke College Library/Archives.

Under "Text Books required": Asahel Nettleton's Village Hymns, Isaac Watts's Psalms and Hymns, and "some collection of sacred music."

Mount Holyoke Female Seminary. "Mount Holyoke Journal/Letters, 1843-1848." Mount Holyoke College Library Archives: Journal/Letters, 1843-1891.

The Journal/Letters provide significant documentation of the Seminary's early history. A succession of teachers served as writers ("journalists") recounting events at the Seminary, including notes about teachers, students, visitors, gifts and a wide range of miscellany such as musical events and teaching of music.

Bibliography

Mount Holyoke Female Seminary. Unidentified manuscript on music. 2 leaves. Circa
1837-1840. Mount Holyoke College
Library Archives. Music Department Records, Series A, Folder 1: General Materials.
See Appendix 4 for the full text of the
section concerning hymns and hymn
books used at the Seminary, with observations about Mary Lyon and the
teaching of vocal music.

Nettleton, Asahel. *Village Hymns for Social
Worship*. New York: E. Sands, 1840.
Mount Holyoke Female Seminary music textbook, 1847-1848. See Lowenberg: *Emily Dickinson's Textbooks*,
pp. 77-78.

Nietz, John A. *Old Textbooks: Spelling,
Grammar ... Music, As Taught in the
Common Schools from Colonial Days to
1900*. Pittsburgh: University of Pittsburgh
Press, 1961.
Chapter 10, "Penmanship, Art, and
Music," Part III, "Music" pp. 340-
356. Contains the "Beginnings of
Public School Music," "The Aims and
Contents of music books," "Music
textbooks."

Safford, Daniel. ALS, 2 pages, 10 Decem-
ber 1842, Boston [Mass.], to Mary Lyon,
South Hadley, Mass. Mount Holyoke
College Library Archives.
Safford mentions that he is forward-
ing several items to Mount Holyoke
Female Seminary, including two
"piannos."

Steinke, Stacie Colombo. "Music Education
for Women in Female Seminaries of the
Nineteenth Century." Graduate paper for
History and Philosophy of Music Edu-
cation, Catholic University of America,
August, 1988.
Location: Mount Holyoke College
Library/Archives. Discusses the his-
tory and purposes of music education
in the seminaries.

Warner, Frances Lester. *On a New England
Campus*. Boston: Houghton Mifflin Company, 1937.
Chapter 6, Program note for music,
pp. 100-102.

Watts, Isaac. *The Psalms, Hymns, and Spiritual Songs.... To Which Are Added, Select
Hymns From Other Authors; and Directions for Musical Expression, by Samuel
M. Worcester*. Boston: Crocker & Brewster, 1834.
Music textbook used at Mount
Holyoke Female Seminary, 1847-
1848. See Lowenberg: *Emily Dickinson's Textbooks*, p. 102.

Webb, George J. and Lowell Mason. *The
Odeon: a Collection of Secular Melodies,
Arranged and Harmonized for Four Voices*.
5th ed. Boston: J. H. Wilkins and R. B.
Carter, 1844.
Music textbook used at Mount
Holyoke Female Seminary, 1847-
1848. See Lowenberg: *Emily Dickin-
son's Textbooks*, p. 103.

HYMNODY

Brown, Theron and Hezekiah Butterworth.
The Story of the Hymns and Tunes. New
York: American Tract Society, 1906.
Capsule information on a variety of
hymns with portraits of Lowell Mason,
Thomas Hastings, William Bradbury,
George Webb and Isaac Watts. Phoebe
Hinsdale Brown, Mary Lyon's friend,
pp. 229-232. Thomas Hastings, passim.
Lowell Mason, passim.

Duffield, Samuel Willoughby. *English
Hymns: Their Authors and History*. 3d
ed., rev. and corr. New York: Funk &
Wagnalls, 1888.

Contains a "Chronological Table [of] American Hymn-Writers," pp. 635-639. Entries on Phoebe Hinsdale Brown and Abigail Bradley Hyde, as well as on Rev. Asahel Nettleton's *Village Hymns*, textbook used at Mount Holyoke Female Seminary.

England, Martha Winburn and John Sparrow. *Hymns Unbidden: Donne, Herbert, Blake, Emily Dickinson, and the Hymnographers*. New York: The New York Public Library, 1966.
"Emily Dickinson and Isaac Watts," pp. 113-147.

Foote, Henry Wilder. *Three Centuries of American Hymnody*. Cambridge, MA: Harvard University Press, 1940.
Places Lowell Mason, Asahel Nettleton, Phoebe Brown, Abby Hyde, and others in context.

Julian, John, ed. *A Dictionary of Hymnology, Setting Forth the Origin and History of Christian Hymns of all Ages and Nations*. London: John Murray, 1892. Reprints: New York: Dover, 1957; New York: Gordon, 1977.
"American Hymnody," pp. 57-61; "Phoebe Brown," p. 185; "Congregational Hymnody," pp. 258-261; "Thomas Hastings," pp. 494-495; "Abby Hyde," p. 546; "Isaac Watts," pp. 1236-1241.

"Lowell Mason. An Appreciation of His Life and Work." *Papers of the Hymn Society of America* 8 (1941) 12 pp.

MacDougall, Hamilton C. *Early New England Psalmody: An Historical Appreciation, 1620-1820*. Brattleboro, VT: Stephen Daye Press, 1940.
Informative history, serving as a background for the influence of psalmody on Emily Dickinson.

Mason, Henry Lowell, and David Greene. *Church Psalmody: A Collection of Psalms and Hymns, Adapted to Public Worship. Selected from Dr. Watts and Other Authors*. Boston: T. R. Marvin, 1856. [Edward Dickinson's copy was in the Dickinson library.]
Lowell Mason was a friend and early music-advisor to Mary Lyon and a pioneer in introducing music in the schools. Mason and Greene's Preface, which Emily Dickinson may have read, is as much concerned with lyric poetry as with music. Discusses unity, meaning, emotion, completeness of sense, pauses, accents, and uniformity.

Mason, Henry Lowell. *Hymn-Tunes of Lowell Mason: A Bibliography*. Cambridge, MA: Harvard University Press, 1944. Reprint: New York, AMS Press, 1976.
Lists Mason's hymn-tune compositions.

Mason, Lowell. Lowell Mason Papers. Yale University, Music Library Archival Collection, MSS 33. New Haven: Yale University Library, 1982. Compiled by Adrienne Nesnow.
A large archival collection. Constitutes a unique resource for the study of music in 19th-century America.

Miller, Cristanne. *Emily Dickinson: A Poet's Grammar*. Cambridge, MA: Harvard University Press, 1987.
"The Hymns of Isaac Watts," pp. 141-143.

Ryden, Ernest Edwin. *The Story of Christian Hymnody*. Rock Island, IL: Augustana Press, 1959.
Phoebe Hinsdale Brown, pp. 470-473. Thomas Hastings pp. 475-477.

Tipton, Noel. "Hymns and Emily Dickinson. (The Power of Melody)." Unpublished manuscript, 23 p.

Bibliography

Wolonsky, Shira. "Rhetoric or Not: Hymnal Tropes in Emily Dickinson and Isaac Watts." *New England Quarterly* 61 (March 1988), 214-232.

THE MUSIC OF EMILY DICKINSON'S POETRY

Blackmur, R. P. "Emily Dickinson's Notation." In Richard B. Sewall, ed. *Emily Dickinson: A Collection of Critical Essays*. Englewood Cliffs, NJ: Prentice-Hall, 1963, pp. 78-87.
    "The words resemble the notes in music...the notes on the musical score."

Buckingham, Willis J. *Emily Dickinson's Reception in the 1890s. A Documentary History*. Pittsburgh: University of Pittsburgh Press, 1989.
    Many musical terms are used throughout these "Reviews and Notices" (e.g. "music," "song," "melody," "chant"), suggesting a close relationship between her poetry and music.

Dabney, Julia Parker. *The Musical Basis of Verse: A Scientific Study of the Principles of Poetic Composition*. London: Longmans, Green, and Co., 1901. Reprint: New York: Greenwood Press, 1968.
    Early discussion of Emily Dickinson's use of the imperfect cadence, pp. 106-107.

Davidson, James. "Emily Dickinson and Isaac Watts." *Boston Public Library Quarterly* 6 (July 1954): 141-149.
    See Martha Winburn England's fuller discussion of the influence of Watts on Emily Dickinson's writing.

Lindberg-Seyersted, Brita. *The Voice of the Poet: Aspects of Style in the Poetry of Emily Dickinson*. Cambridge, MA: Harvard University Press, 1968.
    "Meter and Speech Rhythm," pp. 127-155.

Porter, David T. *The Art of Emily Dickinson's Early Poetry*. Cambridge, MA: Harvard University Press, 1966.
    Emily Dickinson's use of the hymn form, pp. 55-74.

Stephenson, William E. "Emily Dickinson and Watts's Songs for Children." *English Language Notes* 3 (June 1966): 278-281.

Whicher, George Frisbie. *This Was a Poet: A Critical Bio-Bibliography of Emily Dickinson*. New York: Charles Scribner's Sons, 1939.
    Emily Dickinson and music: 7, 240-242.

INFORMATION ON SETTINGS

Carman, Judith Elaine. *Art-Song in the United States, 1801-1976: An Annotated Bibliography*. By Judith Elaine Carman, William K. Gaeddert, Rita M. Resch. With a Special Section "Art-Song in the United States, 1759-1810" by Gordon Myers. 2d ed., rev. and enl. Jacksonville, FL: The National Association of Teachers of Singing, Inc., 1987.
    A selective list with miscellaneous data. Comments on the character of each work and gives suggestions on performance.

Clendenning, Sheila T. *Emily Dickinson: A Bibliography: 1850-1966*. Kent, OH: The Kent State University Press, 1968.
    Emily Dickinson settings: Nos. 1, 7, 10, 25.

Cullen, Rosemary L. "Musical Settings of Emily Dickinson's Poetry." M.A. Thesis, Brown University, 1983.
    Arranged alphabetically by title of first line. Contains indexes of collections,

first lines, Johnson numbers, and composers, as well as a bibliography.

Friedberg, Ruth C. *American Art Song and American Poetry*. Metuchen, NJ: The Scarecrow Press, Inc., 1981-1987. 3 vols. Volume I, Bacon, Copland, Duke, Farwell, Persichetti; Volume II, Copland, Duke; Volume III, Baksa, Duke, Persichetti.

Hampson, Alfred Leete. *Emily Dickinson: A Bibliography*. Compiled by Alfred Leete Hampson. Northampton: The Hampshire Bookshop, 1930.
Poems set to music, pp. 10-11.

Hovland, Michael. *Musical Settings of American Poetry: A Bibliography*. Westport, CT: Greenwood Press, 1986.
Emily Dickinson, pp. 62-90. Arranged alphabetically by first lines of the poems, with Johnson numbers.

The Jones Library, Inc. *Emily Dickinson, December 10, 1830-May 15, 1886: A Bibliography*. With a Foreword by George F. Whicher. Amherst, MA: The Jones Library, Inc., 1930.
Music citations, pp. 21-22.

The Jones Library, Inc. The Jones Library Special Collections. "Emily Dickinson's Poetry Set to Music." Amherst: The Jones Library, Inc., 1988.

Lubbers, Klaus. *Emily Dickinson: The Critical Revolution*. Ann Arbor: The University of Michigan Press, 1968.
"Sources IV. Poems Set to Music," pp. 275-277.

Pankake, Marcia and Jon. *A Prairie Home Companion Folk Song Book*. New York: Viking Publishers, 1988.
Discusses setting Emily Dickinson's poems to American folk music; e.g., "The Yellow Rose of Texas."

Peabody-Gibson, Martha. "The Mature Singer." M.A. Thesis, Lesley College Graduate School, May, 1991.
Appendix III: "Emily Dickinson. Her Poetry and Letters Through Song and Speech."

Sims, Jo Ann Margaret. "Capturing the Essence of the Poet: A Study and Performance of Selected Musical Settings for Solo Voice and Piano of the Poetry of Emily Dickinson." DMA Thesis, Graduate College of the University of Illinois at Urbana-Champaign, 1987.
Technical analyses of works by a variety of composers who set Emily Dickinson's poems. "Examines the poetry of Dickinson in order to identify its characteristics and the techniques which the poet employed in creating her verses. Its purpose is to 'distil the essence' of her style, and to enumerate reasons for her popularity among American composers of the twentieth century." Lists "Poems Set to Music," pp. 71-73. Discusses the effect of hymns on the Dickinsons, pp. 154-159.

Wager, Inez. "Emily Dickinson's Poems in Musical Settings." *Dickinson Studies* 49 (June 1984) 32-37.
Interesting personal comments, but the reader is cautioned about the facts presented.

Willison, Ann. "Composer as Interpreter: Musical Settings of the Poems of Emily Dickinson." Seminar Paper, Department of Comparative Literature, Indiana University, 1990.
Focuses on the song cycles of Aaron Copland, Ernst Bacon, George Perle, and Gordon Getty.

Woodley, Priscilla. "Nineteen Settings of Five Emily Dickinson Poems by Thirteen American Composers." Thesis, University of Missouri, Kansas City, 1982.
> Discusses settings by Aaron Copland, John Duke, Edmund Soule, Robert Ward, William Sydeman, Michael Horvit, Ernst Bacon, Sergius Kagen, Vincent Persichetti, Robert Baksa, T. Timothy Lenk, Norman Dinerstein, and Marshall Bialosky.

Yale University Library. *Emily Dickinson. December Tenth MCMXXX. 1830-1930. An Exhibition Commemorating the Centenary of the Birth of Emily Dickinson.* [Catalogue compiled by Wm. H. McCarthy, Jr.] New Haven: Yale University, 1930.
> Musical settings: pp. 9, 11, 13, 14.

BIBLIOGRAPHIES AND CATALOGS —GENERAL

Blanck, Jacob, ed. *Bibliography of American Literature.* Vol. 2. New Haven: Yale University Press, 1957.
> Emily Dickinson settings: Nos. 4662, 4663, 4665, 4667, 4668, 4676, 4677, 4678, 4680, 4681, 4682, 4686, 4692, 4693, 4694, 4696, 4697.

Boston Public Library. *Dictionary Catalog of the Music Collection.* Boston: G. K. Hall, 1972-. 20 vols. 1st supplement, 1977-. 4 vols.

Library of Congress. *The National Union Catalog: Music and Phonorecords.* Ann Arbor, Michigan: J. W. Edwards, 1958-73. Continued by *Music, Books on Music, and Sound Recordings.* Totowa, NJ: Rowman and Littlefield, 1978-.

New York Public Library. Reference Department. *Dictionary Catalog of the Music Collection.* Boston: G. K. Hall, 1964-1976.
> With two cumulative supplements, 1973, 1974.

BIBLIOGRAPHIES AND CATALOGS —ON EMILY DICKINSON

Buckingham, Willis J. *Emily Dickinson: An Annotated Bibliography. Writings, Scholarship, Criticism, and Analyses, 1850-1968.* Bloomington: Indiana University Press, 1970.
> Emily Dickinson settings: Nos. 17.1, 17.4, 17.12, 17.31, 17.36, 19.1-19.7, 19.9-19.11, 19.18, 19.20, 19.22, 20.2.

Clendenning, Sheila T. *Emily Dickinson: A Bibliography: 1850-1966.* Kent, OH: The Kent State University Press, 1968.
> Emily Dickinson settings: Nos. 1, 7, 10, 25.

Hampson, Alfred Leete. *Emily Dickinson: A Bibliography.* Northampton, MA: The Hampshire Bookshop, 1930.
> Poems set to Music, pp. 10-11.

The Jones Library, Inc. *Emily Dickinson, December 10, 1830-May 15, 1886: A Bibliography.* With a Foreword by George F. Whicher. Amherst, MA: The Jones Library, Inc., 1930.
> Music citations, pp. 21-22.

Whicher, George Frisbie. *This Was a Poet: A Critical Bio-Bibliography of Emily Dickinson.* New York: Charles Scribner's Sons, 1939.
> Emily Dickinson and music: 7, 240-242.

Sources of Information
Libraries, Institutions, and Individuals

Alfred Whitehead Memorial Music Library, Mount Allison University, Sackville, New Brunswick, Canada E0A 3C0. Peter Higham, Librarian.

Mary Mellish Archibald Collection of Music.

American Composers Alliance, 170 W. 74th St., New York, NY 10023, USA. Rosalie Calabrese, Executive Director.

Membership organization devoted to the promotion of concert music. Serves as a databank for information concerning members' works.

American Composers Edition, Inc. 170 West 74th St., New York, NY 10023, USA.

Sales and rental division of the American Composers Alliance.

American Music Center (AMC). 250 West 54th St., Suite 300, New York, NY 10019, USA.

Depository of 22,000 scores and 3,000 tapes.

American Music Research Center, College of Music, University of Colorado at Boulder, Campus Box 301, Boulder, CO 80309-0301, USA. Williams Kearns, Director.

Research fellowship center with large collection of American music.

American Society of Composers, Authors, & Publishers (ASCAP). One Lincoln Plaza, New York, NY 10023, USA.

Performing rights organization.

Amherst College Library. Amherst, MA 01002, USA. John Lancaster, Curator, Special Collections.

Large holdings of Emily Dickinson materials.

Mrs. Ellen Bacon, 8 Drovers Lane, De Witt, NY 13214, USA.

Widow of Ernst Bacon; Bacon archivist.

Ms. Madi Bacon, 1120 Keith Ave., Berkeley, CA 94708, USA.

Sister of Ernst Bacon; Bacon archivist.

Broadcast Music, Inc. (BMI). 320 West 57th Street, New York, NY 10019, USA.

Performing rights organization.

Brown University Library. The Harris Collection. Rosemary Cullen, Curator. Providence, RI 02912, USA.

Important resource for Emily Dickinson and music.

Canadian Music Centre. Chalmers House, 20 St. Joseph St., Toronto, Ontario M4Y 1J9, Canada. Mark Hand, National Librarian.

The library has an in-house database that indexes its collection of 11,000 works, mainly unpublished.

Ms. Evelyn Davis Culbertson, 7106 East 53rd Place, Tulsa, OK 74145

Owner of the Davis-Farwell collection, which fills eight large file boxes and contains personal correspondence with over seventy-five notable persons; two diaries written by Arthur Farwell and five by his mother; many essays, lecture notes, music manuscripts, photographs, Farwell drawings, and memorabilia. See also the entry under Brice Farwell.

Sources of Information

Dansk Musik Informations Center (MIC), Vimmelskaftet 48, DK 1161 Copenhagen K, Denmark. Bodil Hogh, Director.
> Maintains an MIC information base (regularly updated), with about 8,000 works by contemporary Danish composers.

Emily Dickinson Center, c/o Niels Kjaer, Lyo Bygade 6, Lyo 5600 Faaborg, Denmark.
> Danish Chapter of the Emily Dickinson International Society.

Emily Dickinson International Society, 1300 Greenleaf Canyon Rd., Topanga, CA 90290, USA. Margaret Freeman, President.
> Membership organization with 300 members from 34 states and 17 countries. Encourages the study of Emily Dickinson; sponsors the Society's *Bulletin*.

Emily Dickinson Music Society, 737 St. Mary's Rd., Lafayette, CA 94549, USA. Carlton Lowenberg, Corresponding Secretary.
> Membership organization for musicians and scholars. Collection contains some unique musical settings of Emily Dickinson's poems and letters.

The Emily Dickinson Society of Japan, c/o Professor Takao Furukawa, School of Letters, Okayama University, 3-1-1 Tsusima-naka, Okayama City 700, Japan.
> Membership organization for Japanese scholars. Publishes occasional bulletins.

Mr. Brice Farwell, 290 West Nevada, Ashland, OR 97520, USA.
> Son of Arthur Farwell; Farwell archivist. See also the entry under Evelyn Davis Culbertson.

Houghton Library. Harvard University. Cambridge, MA 02138 USA.
> Emily Dickinson collection.

The Jones Library, Inc. 43 Amity Street, Amherst, MA 01002, USA. Daniel Lombardo, Curator of Special Collections.
> Source for materials on Emily Dickinson and music in Hampshire County.

Library of Congress. Music Division. Washington, D.C. 20540.

Mount Holyoke College, Williston Memorial Library, South Hadley, MA 01075-1493, USA. Elaine D. Trehub, Archives Librarian.

OCLC, Inc. [Online Computer Library Consortium]. Dublin: Ohio.
> Large online database of many libraries' holdings.

RLIN [Research Libraries Information Network]. Research Libraries Group [RLG], Sunnyvale, California.
> Online database of research libraries' holdings.

The Swedish National Radio Co. [Sveriges Riksradio AB], Music Library, S-105 10 Stockholm, Sweden. Lisbeth Holm, Librarian.
> Friendly resource for information about Scandinavian and East European music.

Yale University Library, New Haven, CT 06520-1729 USA.
> Important collection of papers of Millicent Todd Bingham (Todd family). Music Library: Large collection of papers by and materials about Lowell Mason.

Index of First Lines of the Poems
& Key Lines of the Letters

The numbers following the first lines are those used in Thomas H. Johnson's editions (*The Poems of Emily Dickinson* [1955]; *The Letters of Emily Dickinson* [1958]), where full texts can be found. Dates of composition are given for composers with numerous settings. Entries are alphabetical by initial word, including articles. The original punctuation and capitalization have not been retained.

The Poems:

A Bee his burnished carriage, 1339. Bialosky, Kesselman, Leisner. Sel: Klein.

A bird came down the walk, 328. Beckler, Jones [Miscellany], Leichtling, Pinkham, Ben Weber.

A burdock clawed my Gown, 229. Meachem.

A clock stopped, 287. Fine.

A curious cloud surprised the sky, 1710. Pinkham.

A day! help! help! Another day, 42. Fine.

A death blow is a life blow to some, 816. Snyder.

A door just opened on a street, 953. Annicchiarico.

A drop fell on the apple tree, 794. Bacon (1944), C. Dickinson, Farwell (1926), Richard Kent, Shore, Taxman, Wood.

A dying tiger moaned for drink, 566. Tipton [Miscellany].

A face devoid of love or grace, 1711. Harman.

A lady red amid the hill, 74. Taxman.

A light exists in spring, 812. Richard Kent, Niles, Smit, Snyder.

A little dog that wags his tail, 1185. DeFilippi.

A little madness in the spring, 1333. F. Brown, Irving, Jones [Miscellany], O'Meara.

A little road not made of man, 647. Taxman.

A long, long sleep, a famous sleep, 654. Harman.

A loss of something ever felt I, 959. Smit, Steiner.

A narrow fellow in the grass, 986. Bielawa, Jones [Miscellany].

A night there lay the days between, 471. Barkin.

A precious mouldering pleasure 'tis, 371. Hoyt (1980-85).

A route of evanescence, 1463. Bottje, Jones [Miscellany], Taxman.

A sepal, petal, and a thorn, 19. Castiglioni, Convery, Farwell (1944), Hammond.

A shade upon the mind there passes, 882. Harbison.

A shady friend for torrid days, 278. Baksa.

A single clover plank, 1343. Convery.

A slash of blue, 204. Barkin, Bourland, Pinkham.

The Letters:

Index to Musical Settings
by Johnson Numbers

Arranged numerically by Johnson numbers (first for the poems, then the letters), this index lists the names of the composers who have set each work, giving dates of composition for composers with voluminous settings. Johnson numbers refer to Thomas H. Johnson's edition of *The Poems of Emily Dickinson* (1955) and *The Letters of Emily Dickinson* (1958), both published by The Belknap Press.

The Poems

1: Klein

2: McFarland

4: Bacon (1926-28), Boatwright, Farwell (1941-44), Kalmanoff, Leich, Pinkham, Taxman, Vehar, Weigl

6: Riley

9: Smit

10: Gibas

12: Baksa, A. Brown, Clarke, Hewitt, Kalmanoff, R. Kent, Marzo, Riley, Steiner

13: Copland, Taxman

18: Ginsburg, McFarland

19: Castiglioni, Convery, Farwell (1944), Hammond

23: Getty

24: Bacon (1931), Diemer[2], Getty, Irving

26: Bacon (1930s-40s, 1936-44), Boatwright, Convery, Ginsburg, Kennedy, Langer, Leich, A. Parker, Taxman, Wilder

30: Benoliel, Steiner, Taxman, Tipton [Miscellany]

31: Callaway, McFarland, Steiner, Taxman

32: Bacon (1944), Taxman

33: Convery, Taxman

35: Duke, Kalmanoff, Leich, Roy

36: Kaderavek

41: Baksa, Gibas, Taxman

42: Fine

44: Getty

47: Bartow, Beaty, Convery, Copland, Duke, Escher, Farwell (1944), Hennagin, Meyerowitz, Riley, Smith, Soule, Steiner, Taxman, Weigl

50: Fine, Fuchs

52: Kennedy, Taxman

54: Barkin

57: Bacon (1930s-40s)

61: Farwell (1944), Hall, Smit

63: H. Johnson

64: Farwell (1938-41)

67: Bird, Jones [Miscellany], F. Kent, Leichtling

70: Sprenkle

74: Taxman

76: Eckert, Fine, H. Johnson, Leisner, A. Parker, Snyder

77: Taxman

79: Copland, Hennagin

81: Farwell (1944), McFarland

83: Carter, Klein, Leich, Smit

86: Perera, Taxman

89: Bialosky, Jones [Miscellany], A. Parker, Taxman, Wertsch

90: Taxman

91: Bacon (1936-44), Weld

92: H. Johnson, Taxman, Wilder

The Letters

56: Hall	298: Bottje	520: Bottje
78: Hall	330: Bottje	524: Bottje
105: Hall	342a: Bottje	555: Bottje
216: Pender	354: Bottje	586: Bottje
225: Pender	364: Bottje	735: Bottje
234: Pender	381: Bottje	781: Bottje
260: Hall	388: Pender	785: Jordan
261: Bottje, Hoiby	389: Bottje	835: Glickman
265: Bottje	454: Hall	835a: Glickman
268: Bottje	471: Bottje	860: Bottje
270: Hall	498: Bottje	1014: Hall
271: Bottje	519: Bottje	

THE
YOUNG CHOIR.

ADAPTED TO THE USE OF

JUVENILE SINGING SCHOOLS, SABBATH SCHOOLS, PRIMARY CLASSES, &c.

BY
WILLIAM B. BRADBURY
AND
CHARLES W. SANDERS.

NEW YORK:
MARK H. NEWMAN.
199 Broadway.
1842.

The Young Choir ... by William B. Bradbury and Charles W. Sanders. New York: Mark H. Newman, 1842. (Mark Newman was Emily Dickinson's uncle.)

General Index

Amherst Academy, xviii, xix, 144-146
Amherst College, xviii, xix, xxii, 132
Amherst, MA, ix, xviii, 7, 62, 78, 94, 129, 143, and passim
Andover, MA, 129
Andover Theological Seminary, 132
Anthon, Kate Scott, xxiv
Ballets. See *Letter to the World. Rowing in Eden.*
The Belle of Amherst (William Luce), xvii, 38
Bianchi, Martha Dickinson (niece), xviii, xxiv
Bingham, Millicent Todd, xxiv
Bowdoin College, 129
Bradbury, William, 129-131
Broner, Esther. *Colonel Thomas Wentworth Higginson*, 107
Brown, Phoebe Hinsdale, xx-xxi
Bullard, Asa (uncle), xv, 132
Colonel Thomas Wentworth Higginson (Esther Broner), 107
Come Slowly, Eden (Norman Rosten), 8, 93, 106
Common meter, x, xi, 78, 104, and passim
Consider the Lilies (Robert Hupton), 57
Culbertson, Evelyn Davis, xxiii
A Day in the Life of Emily Dickinson, 14
Dickinson, Edward (father), xviii, 142
Dickinson, Emily
  As pianist, xxiii-xxiv
  Conferences devoted to
    Emily Dickinson: A Celebration for Readers, 49
    Emily Dickinson International Society Conference, 19
  Experiences with music, xviii ff., 143-144 (sources)
  Family and home life, xviii ff., 142 (sources)
  Music lessons, xviii, xix
  Musical taste, xxii, 119-124
  Musicality, xxiv

Dickinson, Emily
  Poetry
    Appropriateness for musical setting, xxv, 46, 47, 49, 61, 62, 69, 74, 84, 93, 98, 101, 104, 148 (sources), and passim
    "Flood subjects," xxvi. *See also* Dickinson, Emily. Poetry, themes
    Imagery, 11, 14, 32, 40, 42, 47, 49, 62, 63, 65, 69, 73, 74, 84, 93, 97, 98, and passim
    References to music, 89, 109-118, 148 (sources)
    Rhythm and meter, x, 10, 17, 34, 98, 103, 104. *See also* Common Meter
    Style, 26, 49, 61, 67, 68, 73, 74, 75-76, 93, and passim
    Themes, xxvi, 107, and passim
      Death, xi, xxvi, 9, 19, 40, 46, 53, 63, 80, 83, 89, 96, and passim
      Immortality and eternity, xxvi, 2, 80, 83, 107, and passim
      Life, xxvi, 77, 99, and passim
      Love, 44, 70, 78, and passim
      Nature, xxvi, 12, 13, 17, 21, 39, 40, 56, 62, 73, 78, 83, 89, and passim
      Solitude, 68, 74, 107, and passim
      Time and space, 63, and passim
    Universality of, 15, 44, 49, 98
  Reading, xv, xviii, 125-128, 142-143
  Education, ix, x, xviii-xix ff., 144-146 (sources)
  Sheet music, 119-124
  Textbooks, x, xviii-xix, 129
Dickinson, Lavinia (sister), xvii, xviii, 80
Dickinson, Lucretia Gunn (aunt), 132
Dickinson, Martha (niece). *See* Bianchi, Martha Dickinson
Dickinson, Mary (aunt). *See* Newman, Mary Dickinson

General Index

Dickinson, Samuel Fowler (grandfather), xviii
Dickinson, Susan (sister-in-law), 129
Dickinson, William Austin (brother), xviii, xxi, xxiv, 129, 142
Eastward in Eden (Dorothy Gardner), 72, 107
Feldman, Don, 108
Gale, Nahum, xix
Gardner, Dorothy. *Eastward in Eden*, 72, 107
Germania Serenade Band, xxii
Gorham, William O., xix
Graham, Martha. *Letter to the World*, xxvi, 57
Grant, Zilpah Polly, xix
Hammond, William Gardiner, xix-xx
Harris, Julie, xvii
Hastings, Thomas, xx, 129, 131
Higginson, Thomas Wentworth, xvii, 59, 64, 106, and passim
Horgan, Paul, 3
Hupton, Robert. *Consider the Lilies*, 57
Hutchinson Family Singers, xx, 143
Hyde, Abby (Mrs. Lavius), xx, 133
Hymns, hymnals, and hymnody, x, xx, 43, 78, 103-106, 125 ff., 132, 133, 142, 146-148, and passim
Ipswich Female Seminary, xix, 145
Johnson, Thomas H., xiii, xviii, 141, and passim
Letter to the World (Martha Graham ballet), xxv, 57
Lind, Jenny, xxii-xxiii, 142, 143, 144
Longfellow, Henry Wadsworth, 129. *Kavanagh,* xxi
Luce, William. *The Belle of Amherst*, xvii, 38
Lyon, Mary, xix, xxi, 133, 144
MacLeish, Archibald, 64
Mann, Horace, 129
Marvell, Ik (pseud. of Donald G. Mitchell). *Dream Life,* xxi-xxii
Mason, Lowell, xviii, xix-xx, xxii, xxvii, 126-127, 132, 133, 145, 147, and passim

Massachusetts Sabbath School Society (MSSS), 132
Mills, Susan Tolman, 145
Mitchell, Donald G. *See* Marvell, Ik
Mount Holyoke Female Seminary, xv, xviii, xix-xx, 144-146
Music Instruction Manuscript, 133
Nettleton, Asahel, xxi, 78, 106, 133, 146
Newman, Anna (cousin), 129
Newman, Clara (cousin). *See* Turner, Clara Newman
Newman, Mary Dickinson (aunt), xxiii, 129
Newman, Mark Haskell (uncle), xv, xx, xxiii, 129-131, 142
Norcross, Lavinia (aunt), xviii
Northampton, MA, xxii, xxiii, 142, 143
One Bird, One Cage, (Roger White), 197
Parley's Magazine, xviii, xxvii
Perkinson, Grace, xxiii
Philipps Andover Academy, 103, 129
Phillips, Samuel, 129
Plays. See *The Belle of Amherst. Colonel Thomas Wentworth Higginson. Come Slowly, Eden. Consider the Lilies. A Day in the Life of Emily Dickinson. Eastward in Eden.*
Ragtime, 73-74
Rock music, 82
Root, Abiah, xix
Rosten, Norman. *Come Slowly, Eden*, 8, 93, 107
Rowing in Eden (ballet), 1
Sacred Harp tradition, 15
Shostakovich, Dimitry, 19
Singer, André, 107
The Single Hound, xviii
South Hadley, MA, xviii, xx
South, Jean J., 107
Springer, Philip, 8, 107
Todd, Mabel Loomis, xvii, xxiii
Turner, Clara Newman (cousin), xxiii, 129
Watts, Isaac, 133, 142, 146, and passim
White, Roger. *One Bird, One Cage*, 107
Zieve, Morton, 107

Index of Composers and Titles

This index refers to the "Musical Settings" and "Miscellany" sections. Entries are alphabetical by composer, with titles subarranged alphabetically under each composer. Because works are arranged chronologically under individual composers in the "Musical Settings" section, dates of composition are given here for clarification.

Index by Performance Medium

Entries in this index are arranged alphabetically. Individual entries begin with the indexed instrument or voice, after which instruments are listed in score order (see below), and voices are listed from highest to lowest. Thus, entries beginning with the word CLARINET precede entries beginning with the word OBOE, but within an individual entry, oboe precedes clarinet. Similarly, entries for SOLO VOICE: BARITONE file before entries for SOLO VOICE: SOPRANO, but within an individual entry, soprano precedes baritone. In entries under individual instruments, chamber ensembles, or orchestra, voices are listed last.

Score order is as follows: WOODWINDS (flute, oboe, clarinet, bassoon); BRASS (horn, trumpet, trombone, tuba), PERCUSSION, KEYBOARD, PLUCKED STRINGS, BOWED STRINGS (violin, viola, violoncello, contrabass).

- Works for a single solo voice are entered under SOLO VOICE, subdivided by voice type.

- Works for multiple solo voices are listed under VOCAL ENSEMBLES. Works for chorus are listed under CHORUS, subdivided by type. The following abbreviations are used for choral voices and solo voices in combination: A = alto; B = bass; Bar = baritone; CT = countertenor; Mez = mezzo-soprano; S = soprano; T = tenor.

- Works for a single instrument plus voice(s) or chorus are listed under the name of the instrument as well as under the type of voice or chorus. Thus, works for guitar and voice will be found both under GUITAR and under SOLO VOICE. If piano or organ is the accompanying instrument, however, the work is listed only under voice or chorus.

- Works for two or more instruments and voice(s) or chorus are listed under voice type as well as under CHAMBER ENSEMBLE. The individual instrumentation of these works will be found under CHAMBER ENSEMBLE. In selected cases, works for more than one instrument are also listed under the individual names of the instruments.

- Works for orchestra and solo voice(s) or chorus are listed both under voice type or choral type and under ORCHESTRA.

- Works without voice are listed under INSTRUMENTAL WORKS.

- Dramatic works are listed by genre (e.g., BALLET, OPERA) as well as by performance medium.

All entries refer to the MUSICAL SETTINGS section, except those marked "Misc," which refer to the MISCELLANY section.

Ballet

Hemberg, Three Love Songs

Johnson, H., Letter To the World

Baritone. See Solo voice: baritone

Bass [instrument]. See Contrabass

Bass voice. See Solo voice: bass

Bassoon

BASSOON, FLUTE[2], HARP, CHORUS: WO-MEN'S SSAA

Parker, A., Three Seas

BASSOON, FLUTE, HORN[2], CHORUS: WO-MEN'S

Riegger, Eternity

BASSOON, FLUTE, PIANO, VIOLIN, VOICE: TENOR

Beckler, Five Poems

BASSOON, OBOE, MARIMBA, VOICE: SOPRA-NO

Boziwick, Beyond the Last Thought

BASSOON, SOLO VOICES: CT[2]TBAR[2]B

Dickinson, P., Winter Afternoons

Chamber chorus. See Chorus: chamber

Chamber ensembles (with voice; for pure-ly instrumental chamber ensembles, see INSTRUMENTAL WORKS)

[UNSPECIFIED], CHORUS: MIXED

Schevill, Emily Dickinson

[UNSPECIFIED], VOICE

Bottje, Five Songs

Ruggiero, Songs from ED

[UNSPECIFIED], VOICE: MEZZO-SOPRANO

Eckert, Sea-Changes

[UNSPECIFIED], VOICE: SOPRANO

Eckert, Three Poems

Ruggiero, Songs from Emily

BASSOON, STRINGS, VOICE: BARITONE

Hemberg, Love Fancies

BRASS QUINTET, VOICE: MEZZO-SOPRANO

Sprenkle, Six Songs

CLARINET, GUITAR, VOICE: SOPRANO

Silverman, In Shadow

Chamber ensembles (with voice)

CLARINET, PIANO, VIOLIN, VIOLONCELLO, VOICE: SOPRANO

Pasatieri, Far from Love

CLARINET, PIANO, VIOLIN, VOICE: MEZZO-SOPRANO

Weigl, Five Songs

CLARINET, PIANO, VOICE

Obrecht, Three Dickinson Songs

CLARINET, PIANO, VOICE: SOPRANO

Butler, Three ED Songs

Lindenfeld, Three Dickinson Songs

Waters, Songs of Life (1983)

CLARINET[2], TROMBONE, PERCUSSION[2], PIANO, VOICE: SOPRANO

Blank, Coalitions

CLARINET, VIOLA, VOICE: LOW

Kavasch, I Died for Beauty

CLARINET, VIOLONCELLO, VOICE: TENOR

Lenk, Two Songs

ENGLISH HORN, ORGAN, VIOLONCELLO, CHORUS: MIXED

Murray, Safe in Their Alabaster

FLUTE[2], BASSOON, HARP, CHORUS: WO-MEN'S

Parker, A., Three Seas

FLUTE, BASSOON, HORN[2], CHORUS: WO-MEN'S

Riegger, Eternity

FLUTE, BASSOON, PIANO, HARP, VIOLIN, VIOLONCELLO, VOICE: SOPRANO

Lighty, Music From Amherst

FLUTE, BASSOON, PIANO, VIOLIN, VOICE: TENOR

Beckler, Five Poems

FLUTE, CLARINET, BASSOON, HORN, PIANO, VIOLIN[2], VIOLA, VIOLONCELLO, CON-TRABASS, VOICE: MEZZO-SOPRANO

Guzman i Antich, Dos poemas

FLUTE, CLARINET, BASSOON, PERCUS-SION[2], PIANO, VIOLA, VIOLONCELLO, CONTRABASS, VOICE: CONTRALTO (OR MEZZO-SOPRANO OR SOPRANO)

Fine, Women in the Garden

Chamber ensembles (with voice)

FLUTE, CLARINET, BASSOON, PIANO, VIO-
LONCELLO, VOICE: LOW

Nowak, Summer Is Away

FLUTE, CLARINET, HORN, VIOLIN[2], VIOLA,
VIOLONCELLO, VOICE: SOPRANO

Parker, A., Echoes from the Hills

FLUTE, CLARINET, PERCUSSION, PIANO, VIO-
LIN, VIOLONCELLO, VOICE: SOPRANO

Kyr, Maelstrom

FLUTE, CLARINET, PIANO, HARP, VIOLA,
VIOLONCELLO, VOICE: SOPRANO

Marcello, Heir of Heaven

FLUTE, CLARINET, PIANO, VIOLIN[2], VIOLA,
VIOLONCELLO, CONTRABASS, SOLO
VOICES: SMezBar

Johnson, L., Letter to Emily

FLUTE, CLARINET, PIANO, VIOLIN, VIOLON-
CELLO, VOICE

Kagen, Eight Poems

FLUTE, CLARINET, PIANO, VIOLIN, VIOLON-
CELLO, VOICE: MEZZO-SOPRANO

Heiss, Songs of Nature

FLUTE, CLARINET, PIANO, VOICE: MEZZO-
SOPRANO

Weigl, Five Songs

FLUTE, CLARINET, VOICE: SOPRANO

Blank, Four Poems

FLUTE, HARP, VOICE: SOPRANO

Golub, Three Songs

FLUTE, OBOE, CLARINET, BASSOON, HARP,
VIOLIN, VIOLA, VIOLONCELLO, CONTRA-
BASS, VOICE: SOPRANO

Waters, Songs of Life (1986)

FLUTE, OBOE, CLARINET, BASSOON, HORN,
CHORUS: WOMEN'S

Benjamin, Night Songs

FLUTE, OBOE, CLARINET, BASSOON, HORN,
HARP, VOICE: SOPRANO

Bialosky, Birds, Bees (1988)

FLUTE, OBOE, CLARINET, BASSOON, HORN,
PIANO, VIOLIN, VIOLA, VIOLONCELLO,
VOICE: SOPRANO

Ruiter, Four Songs

Chamber ensembles (with voice)

FLUTE, OBOE, CLARINET[3], BASSOON,
HORN[2], TRUMPET, TUBA, PERCUS-
SION, CHORUS: MIXED, VOICE: BARI-
TONE

Snyder, Two Poems

FLUTE, OBOE, CLARINET, BASSOON, PERCUS-
SION, PIANO, HARP, VOICE: SOPRANO

Hennagin, Time of Turning

FLUTE, OBOE, CLARINET, VOICE: MEZZO-
SOPRANO

Bialosky, Far Theatricals (1981-83)

FLUTE, OBOE, PERCUSSION, HARPSICHORD/
PIANO, VIOLONCELLO, VOICE: MEZZO-
SOPRANO

Barkin, Supple Suitor

FLUTE, OBOE, PIANO, VOICE: SOPRANO

Vehar, Emily D

FLUTE, OBOE, VOICE: SOPRANO

Beaty, Four Songs

FLUTE, PERCUSSION, CHORUS: CHAMBER

Lenel, Five Poems

FLUTE, PERCUSSION, HARP, VIOLONCELLO,
VOICE: SOPRANO

Højsgaard, Variations (1980)

FLUTE, PERCUSSION, PIANO, VIOLA, VOICE:
SOPRANO

Belet, Five Songs

FLUTE, PIANO, CHORUS: WOMEN'S

Kesselman, Libera Me

FLUTE, PIANO, VIOLIN, VIOLONCELLO, VOICE

Heiss, Songs of Nature

FLUTE, PIANO, VOICE: SOPRANO

Annicchiarico, Four Dickinson Songs
Callaway, Besides This May

FLUTE, VIBRAPHONE, VOICE

Vries Robbe, Poems

FLUTE, VIOLONCELLO, VOICE: SOPRANO

Højsgaard, Variations (1976)

GUITAR, VIOLIN, VOICE: SOPRANO

Højsgaard, Fragmenter

HARP, CONTRABASS[5], CHORUS: MIXED,
VOICE: SOPRANO

Pinkham, Getting to Heaven

- 191 -

Index by Performance Medium

Chamber ensembles (with voice)
HARP[2], STRINGS[10]
  Manzoni, Dieci versi
HARP, VIOLA, VOICE
  Bourland, Slash of Blue
HORN, HARP, VIOLA, VOICE: SOPRANO
  Smit, Under a Tender Moon
HORN[2], PIANO, CHORUS: WOMEN'S
  Pender, From the Letters
HORN, PIANO, VOICE: SOPRANO
  Irving, Four Songs
OBOE, BASSOON, MARIMBA, VOICE: SOPRANO
  Boziwick, Beyond the Last Thought
OBOE, STRINGS, VOICE
  Rorem, After Long Silence
PERCUSSION[3], CONTRABASS[30], VOICE: SOPRANO
  Samuel, What of My Music
PERCUSSION, GUITAR, VOICE: FEMALE
  Sørensen, Garnet
PERCUSSION, ORGAN, VOICE
  Coates, Formal Feeling (1975); Go the Great Way (1982)
PERCUSSION, PIANO, HARP, CHORUS: WOMEN'S
  Mennin, Reflections of Emily
PERCUSSION, PIANO, VIOLA, VIOLONCELLO, VOICE: MEZZO-SOPRANO
  Waters, Goal
PERCUSSION, PIANO, VOICE
  Coates, Amethyst Remembrance (1979); In Search of Something (1966); It Just Begins To Live (1979); To Be Somebody (1965); Were I with Thee (1971)
PERCUSSION, PIANO, VOICE: SOPRANO
  Olin, Elegy on Three Dickinson Poems
PERCUSSION, PIANO, SOLO VOICES: SMEZT
  Silsbee, Acre for a Bird
PERCUSSION, VIOLIN, VIOLONCELLO, VOICE: MEZZO-SOPRANO
  O'Meara, Songs of Life, Death

Chamber ensembles (with voice)
PERCUSSION, VOICE
  Coates, Tune without (1975)
PIANO, GUITAR, ELECTRONIC TAPE, CHORUS: MIXED VOICE
  Bielawa, Dickinson Album
PIANO, VIOLA, VIOLONCELLO, VOICE: MEDIUM
  Weigl, Oh Lord of Mysteries
PIANO, VIOLIN, VIOLONCELLO, VOICE: SOPRANO
  Davis, S., Three Moods of ED
PIANO, VIOLONCELLO, VOICE: HIGH
  Vehar, Three from Emily
STRING QUARTET. SEE CHAMBER ENSEMBLES: VIOLIN[2], VIOLA, VIOLONCELLO
STRINGS, CHORUS: MIXED
  Riley, Three Little Commentaries
TRUMPET, GUITAR, CONTRABASS, VOICE
  Bartow, American Poet's Songbook
VIOLIN[2], VIOLA, VIOLONCELLO, VOICE: SOPRANO
  Diaconoff, Songs of Transition
  Dinerstein, Four Settings
  Fuchs, And God Cannot Be Found
  McNeil, And When a Soul
  Weiss, Seven Songs
VIOLIN, VIOLA, VOICE: SOPRANO
  Beale, Three Songs for Soprano
WOODWINDS, CHORUS: MIXED
  Snyder, Blue Sea
WOODWINDS, CHORUS: WOMEN'S
  Benjamin, Night Songs
WOODWINDS, VOICE: MEDIUM
  Jordahl, Death and the Maiden
WOODWINDS, VOICE: MEZZO-SOPRANO
  Bialosky, Far theatricals (1981)

Chamber orchestra. See Orchestra: chamber orchestra

Children's chorus. See Chorus: children's

Chorus: chamber
  Smit, Ecstatic Pilgrimage

Chorus: chamber
  CHAMBER CHORUS, FLUTE, PERCUSSION
    Lenel, Five poems
  CHAMBER CHORUS, CHAMBER ORCHESTRA,
    VOICE: SOPRANO
    Bottje, Wayward pilgrim
  CHAMBER CHORUS, SOLO VOICES: SA
    Escher, Songs of Love and Eternity

Chorus: children's
    Ginsburg, To Make a Prairie
  CHILDREN'S CHORUS, PIANO
    Ginsburg, To Make a Prairie

Chorus: men's
  MEN'S CHORUS: TBarB
    Adams, R.T., It Will be Summer
  MEN'S CHORUS: TTBB
    Kent, Spring Songs
    Pinkham, Down an Amherst Path
  MEN'S CHORUS: TTBB, PIANO
    Weigl, Let Down the Bars; Two Songs

Chorus: mixed
  MIXED CHORUS [UNSPECIFIED]
    Smit, Last Hour
  MIXED CHORUS [UNSPECIFIED], CHAMBER
    ENSEMBLE
    Schevill, Emily Dickinson
  MIXED CHORUS [UNSPECIFIED], PIANO
    Wood, Harmony
  MIXED CHORUS [UNSPECIFIED], PIANO, VOICE
    Wood, Harmony
  MIXED CHORUS: ATB
    Holab, Absence Disembodies
  MIXED CHORUS: SAB, CHAMBER ENSEM-
    BLE
    Riley, Three Little Commentaries
  MIXED CHORUS: SAB, PIANO
    Gould, J., arr., I Like to See [Misc.]
  MIXED CHORUS: SAT
    Bourland, Dickinson Madrigals, III
  MIXED CHORUS: SATB
    Adams, R.T., It Will be Summer
    Annicchiarico, I Shall Keep Singing
    Barber, Let Down the Bars

Chorus: mixed
  MIXED CHORUS: SATB
    Barkin, Two ED Choruses
    Benoliel, Eternity-Junctions
    Berkowitz, Four Songs
    Carlsen, I Heard a Fly Buzz; I'm No-
      body!
    Carter, Heart Not So Heavy
    Dal Porto, Five Pieces
    Escher, Songs of Love and Eternity
    Gibas, Five Poems
    Gibson, He Fumbles at Your Spirit
    Gould, J., arranger, Abraham [Misc.];
      I Heard a Fly Buzz [Misc.]; I Took
      My Power [Misc.]; Red Blaze
      [Misc.]
    Grantham, Seven Choral Settings
    Iannaccone, Sky Is Low
    Kaderavek, Once a Child; Talk Not
    Kennedy, I'm Nobody!
    Kesselman, Buzzings
    Kitzke, I Felt a Cleaving
    Lardner, Three American Poems
    Leichtling, Book of Madrigals; Second
      Book of Madrigals
    Levy, This is My Letter
    Lockwood, Three Verses
    McFarland, Dickinson Dialogue
    Muczynski, I Never Saw a Moor
    Pierce, Who Are You?
    Rasely, Hope Is a Thing;
    Rogers, Three Songs
    Shearer, C. M., Of All the Souls
    Starer, Hope Is the Thing; On the
      Nature of Things
    Steiner, Five Poems; Four Choruses;
      Four Settings
    Stucky, Nature, Like Us
  MIXED CHORUS: SATB, CHAMBER ENSEM-
    BLE
    Bielawa, Dickinson Album
    Murray, Safe in Their Alabaster
    Pinkham, Getting to Heaven
    Snyder, Blue Sea

- 193 -

Chorus: Women's

WOMEN'S CHORUS [UNSPECIFIED], OR-
CHESTRA
Parker, A., Commentaries
Pinkham, ED Mosaic

WOMEN'S CHORUS [UNSPECIFIED], PIANO
Pinkham, ED Mosaic

WOMEN'S CHORUS: SA, PIANO
Bergh, Grass
Brown, A., Songs from Emily
Hageman, Charity [arr. Moore]
Hennagin, Three ED Songs

WOMEN'S CHORUS: SSA
Adams, R.T., It Will be Summer
Bliss, There Came a Wind
Bourland, Dickinson Madrigals, I-II
Green, Three Choral Songs
Kennedy, It's All I Have
Kent, R., Spring Songs
Kunz, To Hear an Oriole Sing
Rasely, Hope Is a Thing
Smith, Three Songs
Starer, I'm Nobody!

WOMEN'S CHORUS: SSA, CHAMBER EN-
SEMBLE
Benjamin, Night Songs
Kesselman, Libera Me
Mennin, Reflections of Emily
DeFilippi, Once a Child

WOMEN'S CHORUS: SSA, CHAMBER EN-
SEMBLE
Hess, Our Little Kinsman
Kay, ED Set
Kettering, Sun
McAfee, I'll Tell You

WOMEN'S CHORUS: SSA, PIANO
McKay, Indian Summer
Thygerson, Emily Dickinson

WOMEN'S CHORUS: SSA, WOODWIND QUIN-
TET
Benjamin, Night Songs

WOMEN'S CHORUS: SSAA
Binkerd, Hope is the Thing
Bourland, Dickinson Madrigals, I-II

Chorus: Women's

WOMEN'S CHORUS: SSAA
Kyr, Toward Eternity
Pisk, Sunset

WOMEN'S CHORUS: SSAA, CHAMBER EN-
SEMBLE
Parker, A., Three Seas

WOMEN'S CHORUS: SSAA, HARP
Mollicone, Five Poems of Love

WOMEN'S CHORUS: SSAA, HORN[2], PIANO
Pender, From the Letters

WOMEN'S CHORUS: SSAA, OBOE
Kyr, Toward Eternity

WOMEN'S CHORUS: SSAA, ORCHESTRA:
STRING, HORN, PIANO, SOLO VOICES:
SA
Bacon, From Emily's Diary (1944)

WOMEN'S CHORUS: SSAA, PIANO
Mollicone, Five Poems of Love

Clarinet

CLARINET, FLUTE, OBOE, VOICE: MEZZO-
SOPRANO
Bialosky, Far Theatricals (1981-83)

CLARINET, FLUTE, PIANO, VOICE: MEZZO-
SOPRANO
Weigl, Five Songs

CLARINET, GUITAR, VOICE: SOPRANO
Silverman, In Shadow
Waters, Songs of Life (1983)

CLARINET, PIANO, VIOLIN, VIOLONCELLO,
VOICE: SOPRANO
Pasatieri, Far from Love

CLARINET, PIANO, VIOLIN, VOICE: MEZZO-
SOPRANO
Weigl, Five Songs

CLARINET, PIANO, VOICE
Obrecht, Three Dickinson Songs

CLARINET, PIANO, VOICE: SOPRANO
Lindenfeld, Three Dickinson Songs

CLARINET[2], TROMBONE, PERCUSSION[2],
PIANO, VOICE: SOPRANO
Blank, Coalitions

CLARINET, VIOLA, VOICE: LOW
Kavasch, I Died for Beauty

Clarinet

CLARINET, VOICE: SOPRANO
Boatwright, Three Songs
Sclater, Four Songs

Contrabass

CONTRABASS, DRUMS, KEYBOARDS, GUITARS
Pilz, Brain is Wider
CONTRABASS, FLUTE, CLARINET, BASSOON, HORN, PIANO, VIOLIN[2], VIOLA, VIOLONCELLO, VOICE: MEZZO-SOPRANO
Guzman i Antich, Dos poemas
CONTRABASS, FLUTE, CLARINET, PIANO, VIOLIN[2], VIOLA, VIOLONCELLO, SOLO VOICES: SMEZBAR
Johnson, L., Letter
CONTRABASS[5], HARP, MIXED CHORUS: SATB, VOICE: SOPRANO
Pinkham, Getting to Heaven
CONTRABASS[30], PERCUSSION[3], VOICE: SOPRANO
Samuel, What of My Music
CONTRABASS, TRUMPET, GUITAR, VOICE
Bartow, American Poet's Songbook

Countertenor. See under Vocal ensembles: men's

Double bass. See Contrabass

Electric guitar

ELECTRIC GUITAR, KEYBOARDS, CONTRABASS, DRUMS
Pilz, Brain is Wider than the Sky
ELECTRIC GUITAR, PERCUSSION, VOICE: FEMALE
Sørensen, Garnet to Garnet

Electronic keyboard(s)

ELECTRONIC KEYBOARDS, CONTRABASS, DRUMS, GUITARS
Pilz, Brain is Wider than the Sky
ELECTRONIC KEYBOARD, NARRATOR
Jones, Joseph, arr., Shormies [Misc.]

Electronic tape

ELECTRONIC TAPE, CHORUS: MIXED SATB
Horvit, Two Songs
ELECTRONIC TAPE, PIANO, GUITAR, CHORUS: MIXED SATB, TROUBADOUR
Bielawa, Dickinson Album
ELECTRONIC TAPE, VOICE
Diemer, Three Poems
ELECTRONIC TAPE, VOICE: MEDIUM
Pinkham, Safe in Their Alabaster
ELECTRONIC TAPE, VOICE: SOPRANO
Olan, After Great Pain

English horn

ENGLISH HORN, VOICE: CONTRALTO
Silverman, Echoes of Emily
ENGLISH HORN, VOICE: MEZZO-SOPRANO
Bialosky, Three Mysteries (1978)

Flute

FLUTE[2], BASSOON, HARP, CHORUS: WOMEN'S SSAA
Parker, A., Three Seas
FLUTE, BASSOON, HORN[2], CHORUS: WOMEN'S
Riegger, Eternity
FLUTE, BASSOON, PIANO, VIOLIN, VOICE: TENOR
Beckler, Five Poems of Dickinson
FLUTE, HARP, PERCUSSION, VIOLONCELLO, VOICE: SOPRANO
Højsgaard, Variations
FLUTE, HARP, VOICE: SOPRANO
Golub, Three Songs
FLUTE, OBOE, CLARINET, VOICE: MEZZO-SOPRANO
Bialosky, Far Theatricals (1981-83)
FLUTE, OBOE, PIANO, VOICE: SOPRANO
Vehar, Emily D
FLUTE, OBOE, VOICE: SOPRANO
Beaty, Four Songs
FLUTE, PERCUSSION, CHORUS: CHAMBER
Lenel, Five Poems

Flute

FLUTE, PERCUSSION, PIANO, VIOLA, VOICE: SOPRANO
Belet, Five Songs

FLUTE, PIANO
Fine, Emily's Images

FLUTE, PIANO, CHORUS: WOMEN'S SSA
Kesselman, Libera Me

FLUTE, PIANO, VOICE: SOPRANO
Annicchiarico, Four Dickinson Songs
Callaway, Besides This May

FLUTE, VIBRAPHONE, VOICE
Vries Robbe, Poems

FLUTE, VIOLONCELLO, VOICE: SOPRANO
Højsgaard, Variations

Guitar. See also Electric guitar

GUITAR, CLARINET, VOICE: SOPRANO
Silverman, In Shadow

GUITAR, DRUMS, KEYBOARDS, CONTRABASS
Pilz, Brain is Wider than the Sky

GUITAR, PERCUSSION, VOICE: FEMALE
Sørensen, Garnet to Garnet

GUITAR, PIANO, ELECTRONIC TAPE, CHORUS: MIXED SATB, TROUBADOUR
Bielawa, Dickinson Album

GUITAR, TRUMPET, CONTRABASS, VOICE
Bartow, American Poet's Songbook

GUITAR, VOICE
Niles, Gifts
Rericha, There's a Certain Slant
Vernon, I Felt a Funeral

GUITAR, VOICE: HIGH
Leisner, Confiding

GUITAR, VOICE: MEDIUM
Leisner, Simple Songs

GUITAR, VIOLIN, VOICE: SOPRANO
Højsgaard, Fragmenter

Harp

HARP, CHORUS: WOMEN'S SSAA
Mollicone, Five Poems of Love

HARP, CONTRABASS[5], CHORUS: MIXED SATB, VOICE: SOPRANO
Pinkham, Getting to Heaven

Harp

HARP, FLUTE[2], BASSOON, CHORUS: WOMEN'S SSAA
Parker, A., Three Seas

HARP, FLUTE, BASSOON, PIANO, VIOLIN, VIOLONCELLO, VOICE: SOPRANO
Lighty, Music from Amherst

HARP, FLUTE, CLARINET, PIANO, VIOLA, VIOLONCELLO, VOICE: SOPRANO
Marcello, Heir of Heaven

HARP, FLUTE, OBOE, CLARINET, BASSOON, HORN, VOICE: SOPRANO
Bialosky, Birds (1988)

HARP, FLUTE, OBOE, CLARINET, BASSOON, PERCUSSION, PIANO, VOICE: SOPRANO
Hennagin, Time of Turning

HARP, FLUTE, PERCUSSION, VIOLONCELLO, VOICE: SOPRANO
Højsgaard, Variations

HARP, FLUTE, VOICE: SOPRANO
Golub, Three Songs

HARP, HORN, VIOLA, VOICE: SOPRANO
Smit, Under a Tender Moon

HARP, OBOE, PERCUSSION[3], PIANO FOUR-HANDS
Holman, Laudes Creationis

HARP, PERCUSSION, PIANO
Mennin, Reflections of Emily

HARP, SHAKUHACHI, VIOLONCELLO
Matsunaga, Invisible Cosmos

HARP[2], STRINGS[10]
Manzoni, Dieci versi

HARP, VIOLA, VOICE: MEZZO-SOPRANO
Bourland, Slash of Blue

Harpsichord

HARPSICHORD, FLUTE, OBOE, PIANO, PERCUSSION, VIOLONCELLO, VOICE: MEZZO-SOPRANO
Barkin, The Supple Suitor

HARPSICHORD, PIANO, CHORUS: MIXED SATB
Beckler, Man and Divers

HARPSICHORD, VOICE: SOPRANO
Shore, Four Dickinson Songs

Opera
　　Meyerowitz, Eastward in Eden
CHAMBER OPERA
　　Fine, Women in the Garden
　　Johnson, L., Letter to Emily

Orchestra
　　Johnson, H., Letter to the World: Concert Suite
ORCHESTRA, CHORUS: MIXED SATB
　　Adams, J., Harmonium
　　Diemer, There Is a Morn
　　McFarland, Dickinson Dialogue
ORCHESTRA, CHORUS: MIXED SATB, SOLO VOICES: STB
　　Burgon, Revelations
ORCHESTRA, CHORUS: WOMEN'S
　　Pinkham, ED Mosaic
ORCHESTRA, CHORUS: WOMEN'S [DOUBLE]
　　Parker, A., Commentaries
ORCHESTRA, NARRATOR[2]
　　Laderman, Magic Prison
ORCHESTRA, PERCUSSION[3]
　　Samuel, As Imperceptibly as Grief
ORCHESTRA, VOICE: BASS
　　Rands, Canti dell'eclissi
ORCHESTRA, VOICE: CONTRALTO
　　Franchetti, Aria Variata
ORCHESTRA, VOICE: MEZZO-SOPRANO
　　Belkin, Four ED Songs
ORCHESTRA, VOICE: SOPRANO
　　Meyerowitz, Emily Dickinson
　　Riley, Seven Songs
　　Ward, Sacred Songs
　　Ziffrin, Symphony
ORCHESTRA, VOICE: TENOR
　　Appleton, Three American Songs
ORCHESTRA, SOLO VOICES [4, UNSPECIFIED]
　　Rorem, Swords and Plowshares

Orchestra: Chamber orchestra
CHAMBER ORCHESTRA, CHORUS: CHAMBER, VOICE: SOPRANO
　　Bottje, Wayward Pilgrim
CHAMBER ORCHESTRA, CLARINET, VOICE
　　Kagen, Mob within the Heart

Orchestra: Chamber orchestra
CHAMBER ORCHESTRA, FLUTE/PICCOLO, OBOE, CLARINET[2], BASSOON, HORN, TRUMPET, TROMBONE, HARP, STRINGS, VOICE: HIGH
　　Copland, Eight Poems
CHAMBER ORCHESTRA, HORN, PIANO, CHORUS: WOMEN'S SSAA, SOLO VOICES SA
　　Bacon, From Emily's Diary (1944)
CHAMBER ORCHESTRA, VOICE
　　Brown, F. J., Seven
　　Chalayev, Circumference Between
　　Coates, Amethyst Remembrance (1979); Chanting to Paradise (1979); If I Can Stop One Heart (1978); It Just Begins (1979); Place Called Morning (1982); Sign in the Scarlet Prison (1978); There Breathed a Man (1984); Thy Dust to Keep (1979); To the Civil War Dead (1971); Word is Dead (1979)
CHAMBER ORCHESTRA, VOICE: HIGH
　　Copland, Eight Poems
　　Gold, Songs of Love and Parting
CHAMBER ORCHESTRA, VOICE: MEDIUM
　　Copland, Eight Poems
CHAMBER ORCHESTRA, VOICE: MEZZO-SOPRANO
　　Harbison, Elegiac Songs
CHAMBER ORCHESTRA, VOICE: SOPRANO
　　Castiglioni, Dickinson-Lieder
　　Dawson, Divinity Dwells Under Seal
　　Lerdahl, Beyond the Realm of Bird

Orchestra: String orchestra
STRING ORCHESTRA, CHORUS: MIXED SSATB
　　Carter, Musicians Wrestle
STRING ORCHESTRA, HARP, PERCUSSION, VOICE: BARITONE
　　Bacon, Songs of Eternity (1932)
STRING ORCHESTRA, HORN, CELESTA, PERCUSSION, VOICE: MEDIUM
　　Bacon, My River (1936)

Orchestra: String orchestra

STRING ORCHESTRA, PERCUSSION, PIANO, CHORUS: MIXED SATB
Bacon, Last Invocation (1968-70)

STRING ORCHESTRA, TIMPANI, VOICE: CONTRALTO
Hewitt, Chartless

Organ

ORGAN, PERCUSSION, VOICE
Coates, Formal Feeling (1975); Go the Great Way (1982)

Percussion

PERCUSSION[2], CLARINET[2], TROMBONE, PIANO
Blank, Coalitions

PERCUSSION[3], CONTRABASS[30], VOICE: SOPRANO
Samuel, What of My Music

PERCUSSION (DRUMS), KEYBOARDS, GUITARS, CONTRABASS
Pilz, Brain is Wider than the Sky

PERCUSSION, FLUTE, CHORUS: CHAMBER
Lenel, Five Poems

PERCUSSION, FLUTE, HARP, VIOLONCELLO, VOICE: SOPRANO
Højsgaard, Variations

PERCUSSION, FLUTE, OBOE, PIANO, HARPSICHORD, VIOLONCELLO, VOICE: MEZZO-SOPRANO
Barkin, Supple suitor

PERCUSSION, FLUTE, PIANO, VIOLA, VOICE: SOPRANO
Belet, Five Songs

PERCUSSION, FLUTE, VOICE
Vries Robbe, Poems

PERCUSSION, GUITAR/ELECTRIC GUITAR, VOICE: FEMALE
Sørensen, Garnet to Garnet

PERCUSSION, HARP, FLUTE, OBOE, CLARINET, BASSOON, PIANO, VOICE: SOPRANO
Hennagin, Time of Turning

PERCUSSION, HARP, PIANO
Mennin, Reflections of Emily

Percussion

PERCUSSION (MARIMBA)
Boziwick, Beyond the Last
Carlsen, Evening's Sabres

PERCUSSION[3], OBOE, HARP, PIANO FOUR-HANDS
Holman, Laudes Creationis

PERCUSSION, ORGAN, VOICE
Coates, Formal Feeling (1975); Go the Great Way (1982)

PERCUSSION, PIANO, VOICE
Coates, Amethyst (1979); In Search of Something (1966); It Just Begins To Live (1979); To Be Somebody (1965); Were I with Thee (1971)

PERCUSSION, PIANO, VOICE: SOPRANO
Olin, Elegy

PERCUSSION, PIANO, SOLO VOICES: SMEzT
Silsbee, Acre for a Bird

PERCUSSION, VIOLIN, VIOLONCELLO, VOICE: MEZZO-SOPRANO
O'Meara, Songs of Life

PERCUSSION, VIOLIN, VOICE: SOPRANO
Samuel, Hope Is the Thing

PERCUSSION[3], VIOLONCELLO
Samuel, Put Up My Lute!

PERCUSSION, VOICE
Beaty, Habit of a Laureate
Coates, Tune Without the Words (1975)

Piano

PIANO, CLARINET, VIOLIN, VIOLONCELLO, VOICE: SOPRANO
Pasatieri, Far from Love

PIANO, CLARINET, VIOLIN, VOICE: MEZZO-SOPRANO
Weigl, Five Songs

PIANO, CLARINET, VOICE
Obrecht, Three Dickinson Songs

PIANO, CLARINET, VOICE: SOPRANO
Butler, Three ED Songs
Lindenfeld, Three Dickinson Songs
Waters, Songs of Life (1986)

Solo voice

SOLO VOICE, GUITAR

Niles, Gifts

Rericha, There's a Certain Slant

Vernon, I Felt a Funeral

SOLO VOICE, OBOE, STRINGS

Rorem, After Long Silence

SOLO VOICE, ORCHESTRA: CHAMBER

Brown, F. J., Seven

Chalayev, Circumference Between

Coates, Chanting to Paradise (1979);
If I Can Stop (1978); Place Called
Morning (1982); Sign in the Scarlet
Prison (1978); To the Civil War
Dead (1971); There Breathed a Man
(1984); Thy Dust to Keep (1979);
Tune without the Words (1975);
Word is Dead (1979)

SOLO VOICE, ORCHESTRA: CHAMBER, CLAR-
INET

Kagen, Mob Within the Heart

SOLO VOICE, ORGAN

Jones, Joseph, Garland [Misc.]

SOLO VOICE, PERCUSSION

Beaty, Habit of a Laureate

Coates, Tune Without (1975)

SOLO VOICE, PERCUSSION, PIANO

Coates, Amethyst Remembrance
(1979); In Search of Something
(1966); It Just Begins To Live
(1979); To Be Somebody (1965);
Were I with Thee (1971)

SOLO VOICE, PIANO

Bacon, And This of All (1936); Angels in the Early (1965); Arctic
Flower (1938); As Well as Jesus
(1935); At the Gate (1930s-
40s); Banks of the Yellow (1930s-
40s); Bat (1970-80); Few Get
Enough (1930s-40s); Fifty Songs
(1926-28); Morning Is the Place
(1930s-40s); She Dwelt So Close
(1930s-40s); Snowfall (1930s-40s);
So Set Its Sun in Thee (1935);
Solitude (1940-50); Songs From
ED (1931); Summer's Lapse (1970-
80); Train (1930s-40s); Tributaries
(1930s-40s); We Never Know
(1930s-40s); Word (1930s-40s);
Yellow (1930s-40s)

Bartlett, I Shall Not Live in Vain

Bourgeois, Louis, Nunc Dimittis,
arr. J. Jones [Misc.]

Boyle, Silent Brook

Coates, Bind Me (1979); I Held a
Jewel (1966); I'm Nobody (1965);
I've Seen a Dying Eye (1966); If I
Can Stop One Heart (1978); In
Falling Timbers (1984); Mine by
the Right (1978); Now I Lay
(1979); There Breathed a Man
(1984); They Dropped Like Flakes
(1966); To Be Somebody (1965);
Wild Nights! (1971); Will There
Really Be (1982); Word Is Dead
(1979)

Croft, William, St. Matthew, arr.
J. Jones [Misc.]

Crüger, Johannes, Nun danket All,
arr. J. Jones [Misc.]

Damon's Psalmes, arr. J. Jones
[Misc.]

Farwell, Four ED Songs (1936); Four
ED Songs (1941-44); I Had No
Time (1949); Ten ED Songs (1944);
These Saw Vision (1941); Three
ED Songs (1949); Twelve ED Songs
(1938-41)

Fine, Riddle

Gardiner, William, Dedham, arr.
J. Jones [Misc.]

Glazer, C.G., Azmon, arr. J. Jones
[Misc.]

Hammond, Book, a Rose, a Prairie

Havergal, William Henry, Evan, arr.
J. Jones [Misc.]

Solo voice

SOLO VOICE, PIANO

Haydn, F. J. [attrib. to], Manoah, arr.
J. Jones [Misc.]

Holmes, Birds

Irvine, Crimond, arr. J. Jones [Misc.]
Solo voice

Jones, Joseph, arr. Garland for Emily
[Misc.]; Twenty Songs [Misc.]; ED
Recalled [Misc.]

Klug, J., Erhalt uns, Herr, arr. J. Jones
[Misc.]

Langert, Three ED Songs [second set]

Lutkin, If I Can Stop

MacDermid, Charity

Marzo, Eduardo, Autumn

Mason, Lowell, and George Webb,
Cantica Laudis, arr. J. Jones [Misc.]

Nettleton, Asahel, "Nettleton," arr.
Noel Tipton [Misc.]

Parker, E., Have You Got a Brook

Pasatieri, Reflections

Potter, Heart Asks Pleasure First

Raymond-Ward, Day

Reinagle, A.R., St. Peter, arr. J. Jones
[Misc.]

Roy, W., Spring; This Little Rose

Sacco, Three Songs

Schröter, L., Freut euch des Lebens,
arr. J. Jones [Misc.]

Smit, Light and Landscapes

Stolba, This World Is Not; Word

Tallis, Thomas, Third Mode Melody, arr. J. Jones [Misc.]

Tipton, Noel, arranger, Adrift [Misc.];
Dying Tiger [Misc.]

Vernon, After Great Pain

Walker, C.R.H., Hope Is the Thing

Weber, B., Bird Came Down

Weber, M., Ample Make This Bed

Weld, Seven Songs

Wilder, ED Songs; I Hide Myself

Williams, A., Durham, arr. J. Jones
[Misc.]

Solo voice

SOLO VOICE, PIANO

Williams, F., Emily Dickinson

SOLO VOICE, TRUMPET, GUITAR, CONTRA-
BASS

Bartow, American Poet's Songbook

Solo voice: baritone

SOLO VOICE: BARITONE [UNACCOMPANIED]

Hilse, Nine Dickinson Songs

SOLO VOICE: BARITONE, BASSOON, STRINGS

Hemberg, Love Fancies

SOLO VOICE: BARITONE, ORCHESTRA: STRING

Bacon, Songs of Eternity (1932)

SOLO VOICE: BARITONE, PIANO

Bacon, Six Songs (1942)

Butterworth, Letter to the World

Coulthard, Five Love Songs

Fornuto, Four Songs

Hemberg, Three Love Songs

Hilse, Nine Dickinson Songs

Mayer, S., Six Poems

SOLO VOICE: BARITONE, VIOLONCELLO

Leichtling, Three Songs

Solo voice: bass

SOLO VOICE: BASS [UNACCOMPANIED]

Hilse, Nine Dickinson Songs

SOLO VOICE: BASS, ORCHESTRA

Rands, Canti dell'eclissi

SOLO VOICE: BASS, PIANO

Bacon, No Dew upon the Grass (1935)

Hilse, Nine Dickinson Songs

Langer, Because I Could Not (1986);
Only News (1986); This is My
Letter (1986)

Solo voice: contralto

SOLO VOICE: CONTRALTO [UNACCOMPA-
NIED]

Bird, Distant Trumpet; Gift of Self

SOLO VOICE: CONTRALTO, CHAMBER EN-
SEMBLE

Fine, Women in the Garden

SOLO VOICE: CONTRALTO, ENGLISH HORN

Silverman, Echoes of Emily

Index by Performance Medium

Index by Performance Medium

Violoncello

VIOLONCELLO, PERCUSSION, VIOLIN, VOICE: MEZZO-SOPRANO
O'Meara, Songs of Life

VIOLONCELLO, PIANO, VIOLIN, VOICE: SOPRANO
Davis, S., Three Moods

VIOLONCELLO, PIANO, VIOLA, VOICE: MEDIUM
Weigl, Oh Lord of Mysteries (1967)

VIOLONCELLO, PIANO, VOICE: HIGH
Vehar, Three from Emily

VIOLONCELLO, SHAKUHACHI, HARP
Matsunaga, Invisible Cosmos

VIOLONCELLO, VOICE: BARITONE
Leichtling, Three Songs

VIOLONCELLO, VOICE: MEDIUM
Clarke, ED Canons

VIOLONCELLO, VOICE: SOPRANO
Sydeman, Three Songs

VIOLONCELLO, VOICE: TENOR
Sydeman, Three Songs

VIOLONCELLO, SOLO VOICES: SA
Coulthard, Songs from the Distaff

Vocal ensembles (solo voices)

VOCAL ENSEMBLES [UNSPECIFIED 3 VOICES]
Bourland, Dickinson Madrigals, I

VOCAL ENSEMBLES: MEN'S (COUNTER-TENOR[2], TENOR, BARITONE[2], BASS), BASSOON
Dickinson, P., Winter Afternoons

VOCAL ENSEMBLES: MIXED [UNSPECIFIED], ORCHESTRA
Rorem, Swords and Plowshares

VOCAL ENSEMBLES: MIXED (CONTRALTO, TENOR, BASS)
Holab, Absence Disembodies

VOCAL ENSEMBLES: MIXED (SOPRANO, MEZZO-SOPRANO, BARITONE), CHAMBER ENSEMBLE
Johnson, L., Letter to Emily

Vocal ensembles (solo voices)

VOCAL ENSEMBLES: MIXED (SOPRANO, MEZZO-SOPRANO, TENOR), PIANO, PERCUSSION
Silsbee, Acre for a Bird

VOCAL ENSEMBLES: WOMEN'S (SOPRANO, CONTRALTO), PIANO
Bacon, There Came a Day (1930s-40s)
Hageman, Charity [arr. Moore]
Hennagin, Three Emily
Klein, Of Bells, Birds, and Bees

VOCAL ENSEMBLES: WOMEN'S (SOPRANO, CONTRALTO), VIOLONCELLO
Coulthard, Songs from the Distaff

VOCAL ENSEMBLES: WOMEN'S (SOPRANO, MEZZO-SOPRANO), PIANO
Ginsburg, Colors

VOCAL ENSEMBLES: WOMEN'S (SOPRANO, MEZZO-SOPRANO, CONTRALTO), PIANO
Weigl, From Time and Eternity

VOCAL ENSEMBLES: WOMEN'S (SOPRANO[2], CONTRALTO[2])
Adler, In Nature's Ebb and Flow

Woodwind ensembles

Coates, Fünf Stücke (1967)

WOODWIND ENSEMBLES, CHORUS: MIXED SATB
Snyder, R., Blue Sea

WOODWIND QUARTET, VOICE: MEDIUM
Jordahl, Death and the Maiden

WOODWIND QUINTET, CHORUS: WOMEN'S SSA
Benjamin, Night Songs

—Compiled by Ann Basart